FIFTY DATES
IN
FIFTY STATES

One Woman's Road Trip in Search of
Love & Adventure

by Tiffany Malcom

All rights reserved. Printed in the United States of America. No part of this book may be reproduced, stored in a retrieval system, or transmitted, in any form or by any means, electronic or photocopy or otherwise, without the prior written permission of the author.

Copyright © 2013 Tiffany Malcom

ISBN-10: 1494720809

ISBN-13: 978-1494720803

to Kevin

INTRO

There's something we need to get straight from the very beginning: if you're picturing the typical reality TV dating show contestant driving around the country, you're way off. First, I don't look the part. I do not have the tall, willowy body of a model, nor do I have long, glossy hair. I generally avoid make-up, and my wardrobe consists mostly of t-shirts, so my fashion sense leaves a lot to be desired. In other words, I'd never get past a casting director. Second, and probably more telling, I would rather die alone than have everyone in America watch me make out in a hot tub with a different man every night of the week. So no, clear that stereotype right out of your mind.

Honestly, the dating part of the adventure wasn't even my idea. My original plan was to do a grown-up version of running away from home: set out on the open road and drive, drive, drive. Then my friends Mark and Molly came to visit and pretty much changed my life forever.

"So what are your plans, once your house sells?" Mark asked. They'd moved from Colorado to Seattle a few years before and knew I was now planning to leave Colorado, too.

"I'm going on a road trip," I declared.

"Any place in particular?" he asked.

"I want to go to the Virginias and the Carolinas, and I want to drive around the Pacific Northwest. Ooh, I can come see you guys!"

"Those are two opposite sides of the country," he helpfully pointed out.

"Yeah, I know. But those are the places I most want to see."

"How are you going to pay for it?" he asked.

"I've been saving up. I think I can go for at least six months, especially if I stay with friends. Could I crash on your couch for a couple of nights?"

"We've got a guest room you could sleep in," Molly said. Awesome. Staying with friends was a major part of my plan to keep costs down. The less I spent on hotels, the more I could spend on gas.

"So what are you going to do when you get to each of those states?" Mark pressed.

"Well . . . just relax, I suppose. Enjoy not working, not having to plan anything or keep any appointments. Hang out in the woods. I'm picturing a lot of camping and hiking and catching up with old friends. Oh, and I think I might write a book," I threw in at the end, kind of sheepishly. (I had majored in English back in college, so "publish a book" was on my list of things to do before I died.)

"There are lots of books out there already about road trips," Molly commented, obviously skeptical. "If you want people to pick it up, you'll need a hook."

I couldn't predict that anything excessively compelling would happen as I drove around, other than the strong possibility of breaking down in The Ghettomobile, my crummy car.

"I've got it!" she declared. "You should combine the road trip with a search for a husband!"

"Ummm . . . I don't know about that," I said hesitantly.

"Well, are you dating anyone?" she pushed.

"Um . . . no . . . but that's kind of the beauty of my plan. I'm free to do whatever I want. I purposely haven't dated since I put my house on the market back in June. I don't want to be attached to anyone right now. I just want to be free to travel."

"Maybe you could do fifty dates in fifty states," she suggested. "I bet no one's written a book about that yet."

My eyebrows shot up. It was brilliant. It was daunting. Fifty states instead of the eight I'd originally planned to see? It would take a lot more time and a lot more money. But fifty dates in fifty states? It was definitely catchy. And since I hadn't had any luck finding the right guy during my ten years in Colorado, maybe opening up the dating pool wasn't a bad idea either. At 34, I'd never married or had kids. I'd always thought it would happen eventually, but it hadn't. I had, however, been in a few serious relationships and gone on multitudes of blind dates, so I figured I had enough experience to set up fifty blind dates around the country.

I know several people who met their spouses that way. Some friend, relative, or coworker saw something and took a chance, and that set-up led to romance, wedding bells, a house, kids, and joint IRA's. That's why whenever anyone asked me, "Would you like to meet my [fill in the blank: neighbor, son's soccer coach, third cousin's dog groomer]?" I generally said yes. You just never know where true love awaits.

My first blind date ever should have tipped me off to the fallibility of this theory, but had I sworn off set-ups forever, I wouldn't have such entertaining stories to tell my friends today.

I had been out of college for about a year and my life plan was completely off course. I'd gone to a small, Christian college to get a B.A. and an M-r-s. The glossy brochures, however, had not divulged one important piece of data: women outnumbered men. It was rare to get a date, let alone land a boyfriend . . . which was why I was living in a cheap apartment in a small town in Iowa post-graduation, eating Tuna Helper all by myself night after night.

One morning before I began the daily joy of teaching uninterested middle schoolers, the school nurse cornered me in the office as I was checking my mailbox.

"I was at my husband's company Christmas party this weekend and I found a guy for you," she said. "He's *really* good looking."

It wasn't much to go on, but let's be honest: only going out once a week — to church choir practice — does not constitute an active social life. I gave her my number to pass along.

A few days later, he called. To protect his privacy, let's call him Bobby. The conversation was less than dazzling, but when he asked if I'd be up for dinner and a movie, I said yes. When I asked when, he said Sunday afternoon would be good, because movies are cheaper at matinees. That should have been a red flag.

Sunday afternoon I eagerly opened my door when he knocked and was struck by the realization that *"really* good looking" means different things to different people. I smiled brightly at him, though, reminding myself that appearances aren't everything. Unfortunately, I didn't have time to firm up that happy thought before he directed me to his truck.

Please remember my aging Chevy Prism was nicknamed "The Ghettomobile" by the teens I worked with. I'm not the type of person who finds a man more attractive if he has a nice car. I do, however, like to believe I am not in danger. His truck had seat belts. That's the best I could say about it. I'm not sure how chunks didn't fall off of it with every bump, it was so rusty. I tried to smile politely, but cleared my throat when we missed the turnoff for Main Street.

"Um . . . aren't we going to see a movie?" I asked.

"They don't have anything good playing here in town, so I thought we'd go down to the mall," he replied.

Lord, help us. Going to the mall – in another town about twenty miles away – meant he was about to rev this rusted-out hunk of metal up to fifty-five miles per hour on the open highway. I gave my seatbelt a little tug to make sure it was secure. I could feel him looking at me. I looked over and gave him a nervous grimace.

"Gosh, you're purty," he drawled. I felt pain. Real, physical pain. I wondered how much pain I'd feel if I jumped out of a moving vehicle.

After twenty agonizing minutes of mostly awkward silences, we arrived at the mall for the romantic afternoon he had planned. He parked near the food court and headed straight for Taco Bell; he stepped up to the counter, ordered, and paid for himself. I meekly did the same. Our next stop was the movie box office, where he paid for one ticket to *The Waterboy*. I sighed and bought my own. With half an hour to kill until show-time, he directed me to the NASCAR store where he bought himself a t-shirt. I chose not to play copycat on that one. We got into the theater just before the movie started and filled the last two empty seats.

I've always wished I could find out who the poor guy was who sat on the other side of me for those two hours. I'd really like to apologize to him. Every time Bobby's leg touched mine on the right, I moved closer to the guy on my left. When Bobby put his arm on our shared armrest, I practically nuzzled up to Bachelor Number Two. He must have been confused . . . and probably scooted to his left, too.

As we left the theater, Bobby thrust his NASCAR purchase at me and grunted, "Hold my bag while I go to the can." Wow. I could almost imagine the flowery language with which he would declare his affections. What had the school nurse been thinking? Later on when he pulled up in front of my apartment, I jumped out of the truck before it even stopped.

Flash forward ten years. My social life had improved by leaps and bounds. I'd left my teaching position in rural Iowa and moved to Colorado. I had an incredible job working with youth and families at a Lutheran church, and I'd made tons of friends. I'd traveled to far-off countries and volunteered with inspiring people. My life was awesome. But you know that U2 song, "I Still Haven't Found What I'm Looking For"? That was pretty much my theme song. And what exactly was it that I was looking for? I didn't think it was asking too much to want a smart and funny Christian man. I mean, that's only three qualifiers. It's not like I had a laundry list of must-have qualities, like "deep, brown eyes" and "plays guitar" and "loves *The Notebook*." I was just looking for a great guy to marry and maybe have children with. A guy I could see myself with for the next fifty years.

As I got more serious about Molly's suggestion and started planning a fifty-state dating adventure, I worried about the all-important first impression . . . not so much *my* appearance but The Ghettomobile's. If I met these dates, which would be safer than riding with them, then they would undoubtedly get a good look at my 1998 Chevy Prism. There was very little paint left on the hood and a piece of trim on the passenger side flapped in the wind. That was just the exterior, though. If any man got *inside* my car, there would be no hiding the finer details. The front windows rolled down just fine, but then the motors overheated and they wouldn't go back up. The air conditioner didn't work. The ceiling fabric was unattached and drooping in places. An ear-piercing whistle emitted from the passenger side fan, and the radio volume couldn't go above level 16 unless you wanted to hear more snap, crackle, and pop than a bowl of cereal. There was no interior light, unless you counted moonlight (which could be kind of romantic, I guess), and at speeds of sixty-five miles per hour or higher, the whole car shook like a rocket leaving the atmosphere. Worst of all, the passenger side dashboard had a mystery noise I could only liken to an angry squirrel locked in the glove box.

More worrisome than what guys would think, though, was the bigger question: would this car really get me to all fifty states? I sure hoped so. I didn't want to be stranded on the side of the road. The engine still worked, which I figured was more important than all the cosmetic issues.

And then, being honest with myself, I wondered what kind of first impressions *I'd* make after sleeping in my tent instead of hotels. The bottom line was that my travel fund would be wiped out long before getting to all fifty states if I paid for lodging. I racked my brain, trying to think of places I could get a shower along the way. YMCAs? Truck stops? Yikes! And what was I going to wear, for Pete's sake? When my plan only entailed driving around the country and not also finding the love of my life, I'd planned to take hiking boots, t-shirts, and some comfy old pants. That wasn't going to fly with this new dating plan (unless I could persuade every date to hike with me). I would have to go through my closet and pick out a few easily packable pieces. Probably a flat iron and a razor, too.

This was seriously going to cramp my casual style.

Sadly, a few months into trip preparations and planning, I had to face the hard fact that The Ghettomoblie could not accompany me. As fast as she burned through oil, I had to admit she wasn't likely to get me across the country. I began the car shopping process.

My first thought was to get something economical: good gas mileage, small, & cheap. But then one day, as I fishtailed on an icy Colorado road, I thought maybe getting something with four-wheel drive might be smart. My friends who knew about this kind of thing advised me that this would adversely affect my gas mileage; that didn't sound good with my plan of driving, driving, driving for the next several months.

I did a little online shopping via Craigslist to see what was out there and what I could afford. I came across something fascinating: the conversion van! The bench seat in the back folded down into a BED! How incredible! Too cold to sleep in a tent? Sleep in the van! Too tired to drive another mile? Three steps and I'm in bed! It seemed like one heck of a good idea, and it was only $3500! But would a 1993 conversion van make it across America any better than a 1998 Chevy Prism? I wasn't sure.

My friends found the idea ridiculous.

"You'll never find a man in that," one said.

"Unless, of course, they think the bed in back indicates the kind of girl you are," another chimed in.

Ummm . . . NO!!

I ended up buying a three-year-old red 2007 Toyota Corolla I promptly named Cherry Cherry after the Neil Diamond song (I love Neil!!). It promised good gas mileage but had no bed in the back. Sometimes you have to compromise.

This big ticket purchase, while necessary, wiped out over 2/3rds of my savings account. It left me with about $5000 for the trip, and while math was never my strong subject, I was smart enough to figure out I'd only have $100 per state. That wasn't much.

I told some friends I was thinking about picking up a part-time job to stockpile some cash. I asked if they knew of anything I could do that would make a lot of money in a short amount of time. One friend said she knew someone who made a ton of money stripping. I didn't think that was really for me. I mean, aside from finding it morally wrong, I'd have to invest wads of money in a whole new wardrobe. Who would pay money to see me strip from mom jeans down to white cotton Fruit of the Looms? My friend Julie helpfully pointed out that men would be blinded by my pasty white skin and therefore unable to see my unattractive underwear. Add in the cost of spray tans and it just wasn't lucrative enough.

When people find out you're thirty-four and have never been married, they come up with theories. My mom said I couldn't land a man because I wore Crocs and had no fashion sense. My brother thought I subconsciously feared being tied down and therefore pushed men away. One friend said men were intimidated by my awesomeness (and I swear I didn't pay her to say it). Most people declared I was just too picky; I preferred to think of it as *making wise choices*. I could have gotten married by thirty-four if I'd desperately wanted to. It's not like I'd never been in a serious relationship. I'd even been proposed to several times. (Okay, fine, all those proposals came from men who didn't even know my name while I was living in

Africa and probably had more to do with their desire to go to America than being captivated by my mesmerizing charm and striking beauty, but still). The point is, despite a variety of previous dating experiences, I'd never fallen madly and desperately in love.

I didn't want to get married just to *be* married. I didn't *need* a husband. My life pretty much rocked as it was. I'd traveled the world and had incredible experiences I couldn't have had if I'd been married with children. Climb Mount Kilimanjaro? Not with a Baby Bjorn strapped on me. Hike the Inca Trail to Machu Pichhu? I would have died on Dead Woman's Pass lugging a Pack & Play along. I didn't regret my single years and all the incredible things I'd done, but a part of me still wished for a husband to go home to at the end of the day and kids to tuck into bed at night. As amazing as my life had been, I still wanted more.

I planned to marry only once, so I didn't feel like it was a bad quality, being selective. The older I became, the more I saw the reality of marriage. If I had gotten hitched straight out of high school like I thought I would back in junior high, I would have cried myself to sleep every night. I believed the fairy tale: get married and live happily ever after. But after having years to observe friends' marriages without those Cinderella blinders on, I saw that marriage was work. *Hard* work. And I hadn't yet met anyone I wanted to work that hard with to create more better than worse. That didn't mean he wasn't out there, just that I hadn't met him yet.

I also knew he wasn't going to come knocking on my door while I sat on my couch watching dating shows on TV. It was time for an adventure, and maybe I'd meet the man of my dreams along the way. If nothing else, I'd have one heck of a story to tell by the end of the journey. And so, the whirlwind dating tour of America began . . .

#1 – NEW MEXICO

Land of Enchantment? Not so much. My shoes were ruined. I'm not into shoes, so it wasn't that; it's just that I only had two pairs to choose from: my hiking shoes and my two-inch-heeled "going out" boots. Somewhere deep in the depths of my Corolla closet/trunk, several pairs of flip flops and Crocs lurked, waiting for summer, but as far as easy access goes, I only had two choices.

I had pulled over at the "Welcome to New Mexico" sign. I'd thought that taking a picture of myself at every state welcome sign would be a fun (and cheap) souvenir. At my first stop, I set the timer, ran over to the sign, and smiled for the camera. Walking back to my car, my feet felt really heavy. Looking down, I found them covered in mud. Great. I sat in my car, keeping my feet outside, and carefully removed my shoes, then smacked them together to get the mud off. Little bits flew shrapnel-style onto my seat, my door, and myself, but for the most part, the shoes were still covered in mud. I leaned awkwardly out the door, not wanting to put my socked feet on the ground, and scraped them on a nearby rock. After nearly falling out, I gave up my efforts. I grabbed the plastic sack I was using for a garbage bag and gingerly set my shoes on top of it on the passenger side floor, then drove through New Mexico in my socks.

I'd sold my house just two days before. I'd put it on the market the first week of June 2009, and being the eternal optimist, had planned to be on the road by Labor Day. It was a horrible time to sell, though, right in the midst of the housing crisis. I dropped the price, then dropped the price, then dropped the price again. When I finally got an offer, it was $500 less than what I'd originally paid for it, but after having had it on the market for over seven months (and looking forward to the road trip I'd been planning for over seven months!), I feared I might not get another offer anytime soon. I was ready to go. I accepted. The closing date was set for one month out.

That month was a whirlwind: selling everything I could, taking box after box to Goodwill, and trying to squeeze in one last visit with every friend I'd made in the last ten years. My friend Alicia generously offered me her basement crawl space so I wouldn't have to rent a storage unit. I wasn't sure where I was going to end up after the road trip, so I pared down my possessions as much as I could; if I couldn't lift and carry it myself, it had to go. I kept mostly personal and sentimental items like photo albums, journals, and travel souvenirs. I couldn't part with my kitchenware or my skis, but I let go of books, clothes, and pretty much anything decorative. With the help of Craigslist and Facebook, I sold every stick of furniture I owned to friends and strangers, feeling a mix of sadness and liberation. The last item to go was my TV, carted away by a volunteer who helped resettle refugees. I waved good-bye and headed back inside to scrub and vacuum. It had been a good little home for me and I loved it; I wanted its new owner to feel the same way, so I left it looking as good as I could, although it looked sad, totally empty.

The next day I signed the papers, and the day after that, I put the money in the bank. I hadn't made a lot, but what I did earn from the sale I kept separate from my travel stash. I called it my "resettlement fund," knowing I was going to need something to live on once the fun was over and I was job- and house-hunting again.

I packed Cherry Cherry's trunk to capacity: three under-bed plastic tubs of clothing (mentally labeled "good summer," "good winter," and "not-so-good camping/driving clothes"); four shoebox totes (one each for socks, underwear, bras, and toiletries); a small box of camping gear (cookstove, bug spray, clothesline, backpacking towel); my sleeping bag and tent (both new and very pricy from REI, but as much as I planned to use them, they'd better be warm and dry), and my new-to-me refurbished MacBook Pro (also a very expensive purchase, even though it was an older, used model, but a necessary one if I planned to write a book). In the backseat I put a crate of food, my pillow, jumper cables, and extra jackets. I figured the less that was visible, the less chance someone would break a window to get in for a look.

And then I was off. It was a bit surreal.

Six hours later, I got off the interstate in Albuquerque. I followed the directions of the GPS some friends had given me as a going-away present, but I was doubting it with every turn. I started to worry, wondering if I'd ever find my friend Lanz's house, and if I did finally find it, whether or not I'd have enough time to get in and out and off for my date. I was worried about my appearance, too. I had dark circles under my eyes from the exhausting house selling/moving out process. I hadn't been to the gym in weeks, spending all my time packing or meeting up with friends one last time, so I felt out of shape and blob-like. I had a zit on my chin, which seemed completely unfair, being almost thirty-five. Worst of all, just before I left, I'd gone to a new stylist (bad idea) to get a trim (no big thing, right?). I'd exited forty-five minutes later with a horrible haircut (I said I wanted to GROW IT OUT! Why is it three inches shorter???) that did absolutely nothing to flatter my face. As I hurriedly changed clothes in Lanz's guest room, the new date jeans I'd just bought somehow seemed bigger than they'd been in the mall dressing room last week.

Overall, I wasn't feeling pretty. Not even cute. Nowhere close to confident. I started to believe I was crazy, thinking I could pull this off. I pictured all those women from reality TV dating shows: long hair, perfect skin, breast implants, and fake tans. Would I be disappointing fifty guys across America?

My feelings changed when I saw Mr. New Mexico. He was cute and kind and I relaxed right away. He reminded me of a guy I'd had a crush on ten years earlier; he'd worked in a position similar to mine at another church. I'd met him at a youth worker retreat where he'd played guitar and sang, "I Wanna Grow Old With You" from *The Wedding Singer*, rendering me instantly smitten. I just sat at his feet, dreamily listening, and I knew that he had to be different from other guys because generally feet gross me out, but there I was, inches away from his feet, not minding at all. That had to be a good sign.

I saw the church boy again a few weeks later and flirted shamelessly with him, laughing at every funny thing he said and touching his knee under the table when I talked. He lived in another state, and we sent flirtatious emails back and forth. I gushed over the phone to my friends about how perfect he was. His last name was Ruth, and I secretly dreamed of the day we'd send out baby announcements with little Baby Ruth candy bars attached. How cute would that be? In reality, though, it was going nowhere, so I (desperately) composed a zinger of an email:

"Are you ever going to call me, or are we just going to email for the rest of our lives? I'm not getting any younger." (I was twenty-seven.) He replied that while he thought I was a great girl, he just wasn't interested in dating someone who lived eight hours away. To me, that sounded an awful lot like, "I don't think you're worth an eight hour drive." Reeee-jected!

So standing in the dark Sandia Peak Tramway, gliding to the top of a mountain with Mr. New Mexico, it was easy to slip back into that old dream (although the ride became slightly awkward when I realized we were the only couple *not* sneaking kisses in the dark while gliding through the night sky up to the restaurant). When the tram came to a stop at the top of the mountain, the lights came on and I reminded myself I wasn't with the cute guy I'd had a crush on ten years before, but a stranger I'd just met ten minutes ago. He smiled at me and I smiled back. He may not have been that guy I'd had a crush on, but he was cute enough to make me feel like I'd made a good decision, setting out on this crazy trip.

I followed him out of the little tram car and onto the balcony overlooking the entire city of Albuquerque. It was breathtaking in two ways: the scenic beauty and the bitter chill of the February wind. He pointed out different areas, like where he lived and where he worked and where my friend Lanz lived. I giggled nervously and tried not to shake from the cold, relieved when we headed inside.

We settled into a table at the High Finance Restaurant, up there on top of the mountain, and I was instantly charmed by it. It almost felt a little too romantic, being a first date. The seating areas were terraced so that everyone could look out the windows at the twinkling lights of the city below. It had a fancy ski lodge feel to it . . . and a fancy menu, too.

I grew up in Iowa. We ate meat & potatoes at every meal. I have very bland tastes when it comes to food, so adventurous eating is not one of my specialties. It's pretty easy for me to look at a menu and eliminate anything that's not chicken, pork, or beef. I ordered the bacon-wrapped pork tenderloin, figuring if one kind of pork is good, two kinds in one entree had to be even better.

This was how I pictured dating as a little girl – an attractive man, a romantic setting – and it seemed like all those Barbie & Ken dinner dates I'd played out as a child were coming to life. Our waiter made us feel like celebrities, and I felt like a kid playing dress up (except I wasn't dressed up . . . maybe getting a stylist would be a good thing after all). It was fancy and romantic and a perfect date spot. Date 1 of 50 was starting off amazingly.

The conversation was good, too. Mr. New Mexico and I had both been to Africa and worked with orphans, so we talked about that a lot. We had teaching and skiing in common, too, and I couldn't help but smile at him because he was just plain adorable. We kept talking and talking, then sheepishly collected our things to leave when we realized the restaurant workers were stripping tables of their tablecloths and closing down for the night. We hopped back on the tram and it slowly glided back to the base of the mountain.

He walked me to my car like a perfect gentleman, and I breathed a sigh of relief as I slid behind the wheel. I was impressed by my first date and excited for what was to come over the next few months. If all dates went that well, I'd be the luckiest woman in America.

I drove away feeling hopeful, which was a one-eighty from earlier in the night. I wasn't a supermodel, but I realized most guys knew dating a supermodel was just a fantasy. I guessed most of them would be happy to spend an evening with someone who was decent looking, easy to talk to, and quick to laugh at their jokes. Maybe I couldn't pose for magazines, but I could offer that.

Besides agreeing to keep all my worldly possessions in her basement, my friend Alicia had also volunteered to be my Chief Safety Officer. As my CSO, she'd keep track of who I was going out with and when. I'd email her all the info I had on each guy and tell her where I was meeting him so she'd know where to send the police if I went missing. At the end of each date, I'd call her and let her know I was safe. I rang her up on the way back to Lanz's house and told her all about Mr. New Mexico.

"You're sounding positive," she declared in her Alabaman

drawl.

"I'm feeling optimistic," I responded.

"You're doing this. Girl, you are actually doing this!"

"I know! I mean, how long have I been planning this? It sounded like a fun idea, but it also kind of felt like it was never going to happen, you know?"

"Do you have any idea how many people wish they were in your shoes?"

"Well, lots of people are already happily married and content not to be out on a slightly strange husband-finding scavenger hunt."

"But the traveling part. Who doesn't dream of quitting their job and just taking off on a long road trip?"

"I know," I agreed. "I'm blessed. Let's hope the feeling lasts."

The next morning I reveled in the luxury of my friend Lanz's house. I laid in bed reading, one of my favorite things in the whole world to do, but something I hadn't done in months. I got up, watched *The Price is Right*, went for a long walk, read some more, and took a nap. I was thankful to have such a relaxing day after the stress of packing and moving. My peaceful mood vanished, though, when he came home and said we were going to dinner at a place with a dress code. Perhaps you missed this bit of info before: dressing up is not my thing.

The restaurant was in a local hotel, and as we walked in, it was instantly evident that it was a fancy-pants kind of place way out of my norm. I opened the menu and tried not to let my mouth drop open, too. A twelve-oz steak was $73. Some of the wines were over $300 a bottle. I ordered the $6 soup. The waiter asked with a hint of disdain if I wanted that as my meal.

"Yes, please," I said with a smile, holding back the real comment I wanted to make: "I could never spend $73 on a steak, Mr. Snobby Pants, knowing that amount of money would pay for dinner for the entire orphanage full of kids I love in Ghana. And could I get some more of this free tap water when you've got a sec? Thanks."

I could maybe understand dining at this place on a special evening like your birthday or anniversary or something. I had a feeling, though, that some of the patrons were regulars. I overheard a waiter ask a woman if she'd like her leftovers boxed up.

"Oh, I've got a German Shepherd at home who would just love that," she gushed. I grimaced.

Driving home after dinner, I pointed out a billboard that said MC Hammer would be performing at the local casino next week.

"Oh my gosh, how great of a date would that have been?" I gushed. "I totally know the moves from the 'U Can't Touch This' video."

"I'm sure you do," Lanz said. He'd witnessed my amazing dance moves multiple times when we both lived in Colorado.

"There's a bar on top of that casino with a great view of the city," he said, conveniently changing the subject. "We should go."

We went up and had a drink and enjoyed the view, occasionally eavesdropping on a couple at a table next to ours. It wasn't like we were *trying* to eavesdrop, but they were talking pretty loudly and we couldn't help but overhear and try not to laugh. They'd gotten connected on eHarmony and were meeting for the first time. I couldn't tell if she was into him, but I found him a little odd. Lanz assured me that she'd made some comments while I was in the bathroom that made her seem just his type. Maybe there really was someone for everyone.

We stopped by the casino on the way out. They had a club that gave you $20 in free slot play and $20 in free table play when you joined. You had to put a buck in your slot machine to activate the card, but spending a dollar seemed within my budget.

I was annoyed instantly, though, not being an experienced gambler. I wanted nothing more complicated than a slot machine with three columns, and if you pull the lever and get three cherries, you're a winner! Not so here. Every machine was a jumbled mess in my eyes. I dutifully pushed buttons and watched my free $20 rapidly disappear, never really understanding how the heck you won. All I could figure out was that plenty of flashing and dinging was going on, but no winning.

Then something magical happened: a burning building flashed up on the screen and I was instructed to pick a fire hydrant. I did. It helped put out part of the fire. I repeated the process a few times, and suddenly the screen was blinking and my eyes got wide.

"Did I just win $50?" I asked Lanz. He high-fived me. Looking back at the screen, it was instructing me to choose a multiplier. I pressed one last fire hydrant.

"4x," it flashed.

"Did I just win $200?" I yelled. And then I screamed a little bit. And then I instantly hit "cash out." That would buy me six tanks of gas, all for a dollar. Maybe New Mexico was kind of enchanting after all.

#2 – TEXAS

  I set out the next morning dreading the ten-hour drive ahead of me. I was tired from staying out too late at the casino, but I had $200 in twenties tucked into my wallet, so it seemed like a fair trade-off. I thought about listening to an audiobook, but I feared it would make me even sleepier. I chose the radio instead, figuring I should probably enjoy it while I could; I was going to be driving through places that day where radio stations would be few and far between. It was a good choice; I heard songs I hadn't heard in years. I entertained fellow drivers with my "Push It" seat dancing. I rejoiced when they played "November Rain" the whole way through, silently cursing those radio stations that cut off the great instrumental endings of the best-ending songs: "November Rain," "Layla," & "Hard to Say I'm Sorry." I gave my best impersonation of a heartbroken woman as I sang along with "Nothing Compares 2 U." I started to worry about my sanity when I found myself interpretive dancing to "Wind Beneath My Wings." It was going to be a long drive. I checked the clock. I'd been on the road for half an hour. A long drive indeed.

  Song lyrics are one of my specialties. I've been made fun of quite a bit over the years because I'll often burst into song when someone says something that triggers some lyric in my head. I don't have much that's useful up there, like anything that would help me when I'm (fingers crossed!) a contestant on Jeopardy someday. Presidents? I know the major ones, but not many other than that. The periodic table? Not a clue. But quotes from chick flicks and lyrics to every song ever written? Endless brain space available.

There wasn't much to see between Albuquerque and Amarillo. It's not a drive I would recommend. I freaked out momentarily when something started dinging. My car was still new enough to me that I didn't know where it was coming from. I searched the dashboard lights and sensors as I cruised along, trying to figure out what was going on. The seat belt light was flashing, which confused me since I always buckle up. I reached over to the passenger seat and pushed my laptop bag onto the floor. The dinging kept ringing. I pushed my purse onto the floor, too. The dinging stopped. Seriously? My car thought a laptop and a purse equaled the weight of a person who needed to be strapped in? Maybe it was time to clean out the purse.

The only signs of life along the highway were little gas station/tourist shops, but I didn't stop at any of them. The most intriguing one had a big sign advertising "Road Kill Apparel." I was tempted to go in and see if this meant t-shirts with pictures of road kill on them, or actual items made of road kill, like a coon-skin cap made from a real raccoon they'd recently scraped off the highway. I refrained.

It got a little better after Amarillo, and once I met my Texas date, I quickly decided he was worth the boring drive. I met up with Mystery Man Number Two at a dock in a Dallas suburb where a Venetian-style gondolier was waiting for us. I was a little worried that this date might be miserable, cruising canals on a cold February night, but the gondolier gave us blankets and hot cider to keep us warm. Cuddling under the blankets seemed out of the question, having just met the guy, but believe me when I say I considered it – on a scale of 1 to George Clooney, Mr. Texas was a solid 8 or 9, and if I'd known him a little better, I could've cozied up no prob.

As we drifted along Lake Carolyn and the Mandalay Canals, I realized this would probably be one of the most romantic dates I'd go on during the entire fifty-date adventure: the gentle sway of the boat, the twinkling stars reflecting on the water, the gondolier singing Italian arias. It seemed off-kilter, though, to be in such a romantic setting without the romantic relationship. I was with a handsome man, but instead of getting to know each other in a normal first-date way, we'd jumped into an overly-intimate situation that turned the atmosphere awkward.

"The tradition is to kiss as you pass under each bridge," the gondolier said. Hmmmm. Like the cuddling, I gave it a moment of consideration but then passed. Not that he wasn't attractive enough to kiss. He definitely was. He seemed smart, too. And – get this – he was Lutheran! Not a requirement, but worthy of bonus points. Still, I figured I shouldn't make out with every man I went out with. If one of them ended up being the guy I'd been waiting for, I didn't want to have to confess to lip-locking forty-nine other men around the country. So instead of romantic kisses and cute conversation, we just listened to the gondolier sing.

"So . . . that was great," I told Mr. Texas when we docked, "but I haven't gotten to know you at all."

"I think there's a bar in that hotel," he responded, pointing to a looming structure a little further down the shoreline.

"Works for me."

We played pool once we got there, which felt more casual and first-date appropriate than the swoon-worthy gondola ride. We watched some Olympic coverage on the bar TVs and talked about life. He was so attractive in so many ways. I sat there wanting to kiss him and wondering what the heck had gotten into me. Truthfully, I hadn't kissed all that many guys in my life, partially because I was picky, but also because I wanted my kisses to mean something. That might sound old fashioned, but that was me . . . so why, two dates into a fifty-date adventure, could I think about nothing but how kissable this smart, Lutheran man seemed?

Luckily there was no threat of temptation since he wasn't giving me an interested vibe. I understood. When planning the trip, I'd had to decide whether or not to tell all the guys I'd be dating that they were one of fifty prospects. I thought maybe men would be more interested in a date if they thought it was just a regular date rather than one of fifty blind dates. I weighed some pros and cons for telling them about the fifty-state dating adventure:

Pro: If I should happen to meet the man of my dreams, we'd be laying a foundation of honesty.

Con: If I should happen to meet the man of my dreams, he may want me to stop traveling and dating random men and only date him.

Pro: He might think I was adventurous and be attracted to me.

Con: He might think I was adventurous and spend the entire date asking where I'd been and what I'd done rather than telling me anything about himself.

Pro: If he knew I'd be writing about our date, he might go out of his way to do something fabulously romantic, like meet me at the top of the Empire State Building or take me for a hot air balloon ride.

Con: If he knew I'd be writing about our date, he might go out of his way to do something fabulously romantic . . . and after he'd won my heart, revert to his usual style of dating: sitting on the couch, drinking beer, and watching ultimate cage fights.

Mr. Texas knew he was one of fifty, and I think he went into our date viewing it as a one-time-only deal. He was a nice guy who was willing to help me out with a date in Texas, but he didn't seem interested in anything more than that. I was disappointed, because he seemed to have all the qualities I was looking for in a husband. I know you can't tell that from one date, but I wanted to keep seeing him until I figured out whether or not he really was. I said good-bye wishing I wasn't moving on to Oklahoma quite so quickly.

#3 – OKLAHOMA

As I drove into Oklahoma, I thought, *It's not West Texas, but it's not good either.* I was probably a little jaded, being spoiled by the beauty of Colorado for the previous ten years, but every other state just seemed so blah comparatively. Perhaps I just couldn't appreciate the special beauty of this state because my noggin was jiggling like a bobble head doll. When had these roads been paved? 1950? And who had paved them? Drunken six-year-olds? Yowza. If I'd had an infant along, she'd have had shaken baby syndrome for sure.

I got into Oklahoma City with plenty of time to spare before date number three. Being so early and not having anything else to do, I thought I'd scout out the place where I was supposed to meet Mr. Oklahoma for dinner a few hours later. I figured I'd find a place in the neighborhood, like a coffee shop or library, to sit and blog while I waited.

Bad decision.

Historic Stockyards City may have been full of history, but it also appeared to be full of people I didn't want to leave my car near. In full freak-out mode, I drove to a newer, nicer area and shoved everything I possibly could into my trunk, thinking again that if thieves couldn't see anything worth breaking a window for, then hopefully they'd just leave my car alone. I drove back to Stockyards City, nervously checking my rearview mirror every time I hit a pothole, fearing my overstuffed trunk might pop open at any moment.

Cattlemen's Steakhouse, right by the stockyards, turned out to be a popular place. People were standing in line, waiting to get in, and none of them looked at all like they might go strip Cherry Cherry after they'd polished off their prime rib. Mr. Oklahoma came in a bit after me and might have been the nicest guy in the entire state (and cute – I was totally lucking out, going three for three so far with attractiveness).

He seemed really shy, and I found myself talking more to make up for his lack of talking. I'm gonna guess his first impression of me was "cartoon character-ish." I can do that sometimes.

I was worried my steak might still be mooing when they brought it to the table, being so close to the food source, but it was absolutely delicious. And since my on-the-road and on-a-budget diet consisted mostly of granola bars, I was in heaven. I had a hard time eating, though. I'm a very slow chewer. When I was a teenager, I read in a magazine that if you chew each bite twenty times before swallowing, you feel fuller faster and don't overeat and therefore don't gain weight. It seemed easier to manage than the previous dieting tip I'd read about (eating half a grapefruit before every meal, which is completely inconvenient for an Iowa farm girl), so I tried it. Slow chewing became a habit, and twenty years later I still chewed every bite for a long time before I swallowed. My mom taught me not to talk with my mouth full, so I was having the darnedest time getting my twenty-chew bites down while trying to fill the silence when Mr. Oklahoma wouldn't talk. I sadly looked at my steak and baked potato as they grew colder by the minute.

I tried several questions I thought might get him talking . . . to no avail. After a solid half hour of carrying the conversation, I finally hit on a topic he was interested in: Chevy's. Hallelujah! I gobbled up my dinner while he talked.

"I have something for you in my truck," he said as we were walking out the door. I hesitated. Was this about to become a made-for-TV movie moment where I got clubbed in the head and shoved unconscious into his pick-up?

"Where is it?"

"In the back of this parking lot here," he replied.

Hmmm. It seemed like one of those situations you're warned not to get yourself into, but the parking lot was well lit. And though I'd only spent an hour with him over dinner, he didn't give off a dangerous vibe at all. He was really nice. Way too nice to knock me out and dump my body in the nearby cattle feedlot. So nice, in fact, that when we got to his truck, he reached in and retrieved a card thanking me for choosing him as my Mr. Oklahoma. Tucked inside was a gift card to a local gas station.

I felt horrible for having thought a single skeptical thought about his intentions. I also felt bad that I hadn't felt any chemistry or possibility of a romantic connection, even though he was such a nice guy. I walked away thinking I should start a little side project, matching up the guys I dated with girls in their states. Just because I didn't click with a guy didn't mean someone else wouldn't. He'd be a great catch for some nice girl who wanted to go to the Cattleman's Steakhouse once a week for a quiet, romantic dinner – reeeeally quiet.

I pointed Cherry Cherry toward a residential neighborhood to meet a girl who was going to let me sleep in her guest room. I'd checked into couchsurfing.org on a friend's recommendation to find places to sleep in cities where I didn't know anyone. It seemed a bit sketchy, but I figured if I stuck with women who had several references from other people who'd stayed with them, I'd reduce my chances of getting raped or murdered.

It was around 10PM when I got to her house, which normally would have been bedtime for me, but Amanda, my couch surfing hostess, was horrified that Stockyards City was the only part of Oklahoma City I'd seen. She declared she was taking me somewhere good, so I laughed when we walked into the bar she took me to, a smoky little hole in the wall. Amanda started tapping people's arms, explaining my adventure, and asking where they thought I should go before I left town the next day.

I got the best suggestions from Melissa, a Rachel McAdams look-alike, and her boyfriend Logan. They told me about a historic hotel that is supposedly so haunted that the New York Knicks blamed their loss to the Oklahoma City Thunder on their stay there the night before the game. They'd gotten no sleep, they said, because of the freaky things going on. The story goes that back in the day, a pregnant maid named Effie was locked up on the top floor to hide her away and not spoil an important man's reputation. After she'd had the baby, he still wouldn't let her out, so she jumped out the window, killing both her and the baby. It sounded creepy.

Amanda suggested something less spooky; she said she'd take me down a slide in a downtown building over her lunch hour the next day.

"It's a twisty slide, like the kind at McDonald's," she said.

"Why is there a twisty slide in a downtown building?" I asked.

"Well, it's an old fire escape. You're not technically *allowed* to use it, but if you sneak up there with a carpet square and jump in, it's not like they can stop you halfway down, you know?"

"Huh," I replied, losing interest. I pictured myself shooting out the side of some rickety old fire escape slide and plummeting thirty stories to my death. I thought it would be a bummer to end my fifty-state journey in state number three . . . in a body bag.

Melissa & Logan's cute friend Steve came in and they told him what I was doing. He flirtatiously asked if there was any chance I'd be coming through Oklahoma again at the end of the trip. I assured him there wasn't, but that didn't stop me from flirting with him for the rest of the night. They all agreed they would've loved to have heard about my adventure before I'd come to town so they could have helped me make plans. By the end of the night, I'd had much more fun than I'd imagined I could have in Oklahoma.

The next day I toured the Oklahoma City National Memorial & Museum and found myself wishing I had someone there with me. I didn't mind traveling alone. Having been single my whole adult life and loving to travel, I was fairly used to eating by myself, touring historical sites by myself, and navigating my own way from place to place. That didn't mean I wouldn't mind having someone beside me for all those things, though.

The museum was tragic; I was in tears several times, especially when learning about all the children who were killed in the bombing. I was struck by how each person who died that day thought it was just another day. They were just going to work, or dropping off their kids at day care . . . and then, minutes later, they were gone.

I always thought of the same two answers whenever I heard that question, "What would you regret if you died tomorrow?" I would wish that I'd seen more of the world, and I'd feel sad that I'd never gotten married or had children. Hopefully by the end of this journey, I would feel like I'd seen the U.S., and maybe, if everything worked out right, I might even have a husband with me the next time I traveled. Either way, I was pretty sure the long trip would be worthwhile.

I drove by the (reportedly) haunted hotel before leaving town but didn't have the time (or the guts) to go in and check it out. I craned my neck while driving through downtown, scanning the sides of the tallest buildings for a giant twisty slide. No dice. But I did find a place called Braum's where I stopped for ice cream (the best recommendation I'd received at the bar the night before, in my opinion), so I drove away from Oklahoma City a happy lady.

I had one more stop before leaving Oklahoma: two nights of rest and relaxation with family in Tulsa. My cousin's kids cracked me up. Four-year-old Trey beat me at every single game we played: Chutes & Ladders, Candyland, Uno Moo, & Forest Friends. Talk about a blow to the ego. It took all I had in me to restrain my competitiveness and not scream, "I challenge you to Scrabble, a game that takes real skill!"

On my last day there, my aunt and cousin and I wandered around the Gilcrease Museum, admiring the paintings and statues. While watching a short film about a featured artist, I noticed a little old couple sitting on a bench, holding hands and leaning into each other.

So sweet, I thought, *having someone to grow old with*.

But then I remembered a friend of mine once telling me about a great aunt in her eighties who was all a-twitter because her friend had just gotten married for the first time . . . at age eighty-five. I guess if you looked at the glass half full, at least they'd found each other before they died. I realized these two might not be growing old together at all; there was a chance they were on a dating adventure of their own. Maybe it's never too late to find love.

#4 – MISSOURI

I drove from Oklahoma to Missouri for a very quick stop. In hopes of saving some money for the pricier states (Seriously Hawaii and Alaska? Could you move a little closer to the rest of us?), I'd decided to just hit the corners of some states if I could find dates in those places. Whatever I didn't spend of the allotted $100 for that state could be banked for the more expensive states coming up.

I found Mr. Missouri when looking for someone to stay with on couchsurfing.org. I couldn't resist clicking on his profile, seeing his huge, bushy beard. Who has that? I'm a fan of unique. I didn't want to stay with him, because I'd decided that for safety, I'd never stay with single men, but I emailed him about my little adventure and he agreed to be my Mr. Missouri. We set our date for breakfast Friday morning since he had plans with his church group on the Thursday night I would arrive. He said I was welcome to join them if I had nothing to do, and not knowing anyone else there, I went.

That night, when one young couple asked the group to pray for them, then held hands and leaned into each other as their friends prayed, I couldn't help but remember a guy in my college small group that I'd once dreamed of praying with like that. Pretty much every girl had a crush on him, including me. When my dorm room phone rang one night, I answered, and a male voice asked, "Do you know who this is?"

"Jim?" I guessed. That was the guy I had a crush on, and that was who it sounded like.

"Yeah. Can I come over?" Holy crap. Jim wanted to come to my room? Jim the hottie? Jim the guy every girl on campus wanted to date? I almost screamed.

"Sure," I said casually, then hung up the phone and really did scream. I ran downstairs to breathlessly tell my girlfriends JIM IS COMING TO MY ROOM!, then frantically ran back upstairs to throw all the clothes strewn about my dorm room into the closet. I checked the mirror, popped a mint, sprayed on some perfume, then sat down and tried to look natural. I mean, this might be small-group related, but it might be that Jim had seen how funny and smart I was and was coming over to tell me he was totally into me.

He never came.

I probably could have avoided complete humiliation if I'd just taken some time and thought through the situation, but no, no. Not me. Instead I desperately called Jim's dorm room and left a message.

"Hey Jim, it's me . . . Tiffany . . . ummmm . . . I thought you were coming over? Ummm . . . call me!"

He did call. Several hours later. He was completely confused.

"Did I miss a meeting or something?" he asked. I emphasized that *he'd* called *me* and said he wanted to come over but then never showed up . . . and as I talked through it, I saw it for what it really was. The voice hadn't said, "This is Jim." The voice had asked if I knew who it was, and when I'd said, "Jim," he'd said, "Yes."

It was a prank call. I felt like a complete idiot.

I started to laugh it off, but somehow words flew out of my mouth without a filter. I admitted that I had been really excited that he wanted to come over and had thought that maybe he'd wanted to ask me to go out sometime. He stuttered for a few moments but amazingly – and likely uncomfortably, but I've blocked that part of the memory – agreed that yeah, we could go out sometime. I smiled through the entire showing of *Sabrina* that Friday night, sitting *thisclose* to him in the dark movie theater. He never asked me out again, but for one fabulous night, I had a date with the catch of the campus! (Oh fine, it was a pity date, but who cares? I had a date with JIM!)

Back in Missouri, this church small group was full of fun people with whom I had no past history of awkward crushes. I had a lot to talk about with Audra, who had recently relocated to Missouri from Colorado, and I was very entertained by a girl named Diana who said she wanted to marry a guy with the last name of Sossum so she could send out subliminal messages every time she introduced herself (say it a few times fast . . . you'll get it). We even played Bananagrams, one of my favorite games. I won the first two and thought maybe I should throw the third so these people wouldn't find me really annoying (have I mentioned I can get a wee bit competitive?), but then I lost legitimately. Good times.

    The next morning I met Mr. Missouri for breakfast, the first of two dates in two states in one day. That was a new record for me. My previous record, up to that point in my dating career, was three first dates in one month. (When I joined an internet dating website, I got my money's worth, by golly.)

    Mr. Missouri and I engaged in animated conversation at a local breakfast spot. We hadn't exactly gotten a chance to talk when all those people were at his house the night before, so we made up for it over breakfast, sharing as much of our life stories as we could squeeze into two hours. Having seen pictures of his out-of-control beard, I'd guessed that anyone who could rock that look had to be pretty cool, and I was right. He didn't have the mongo-beard anymore, but instead sported a well-groomed beard and a handle-bar mustache, which was also pretty unique. I was impressed by his ability to keep his breakfast out of it.

    He was a fan of traveling, too, and had wandered around Europe for three months at one point. He'd planned to stay longer but was ready to come home after about half the time he'd allotted.

    "I sometimes secretly wonder if I'll get through all fifty states," I admitted.

    "Think you'll get homesick?"

    "Mmmm . . . not in the traditional sense. I'm more afraid of getting tired. Like, sick of sleeping in other people's guest rooms or my tent . . . a missing-my-bed tired."

    "That would ruin your book title, wouldn't it?"

    "Yeah. I mean, who'd buy a book called *37 Dates in 37 States*?"

    He was really easy to talk to, but he had to get to work and I had to move on to my second date of the day. We said good-bye on the street corner and I drove off to find the giant fork of Springfield, Missouri. Yep. A giant fork. I set my self-timer, took a picture beside it, and then headed for Arkansas.

#5 – ARKANSAS

If anyone in their 30's tells you they've never tried internet dating, they are either a) already married, b) lying, or c) dateless. When dating websites first started appearing on the internet, people seemed a bit ashamed of using them to find dates, like they weren't good enough at meeting people through normal channels so they had to resort to this weird way of doing it. These days, though, pretty much every unmarried person in America has tried it at least once. It's no big thing. It's easy to shop for men at home in your pajamas, and a lot more socially acceptable than shopping for men in your pajamas in any other location.

I met Mr. Arkansas using Match.com. I'd venture a guess that it's one of the more popular internet dating sites in America, but sadly popularity doesn't always translate to quality. There were still a large amount of weirdos to sift through, trying to find a decent man. There were less there, though, than on the free dating websites, which I guess made sense. Freaks must be cheap as well as freakish. Men who are willing to pay to have you ogle them online are one step up on the food chain.

It's hard to write about yourself in an online dating profile. They ask all these questions and you feel this pressure to make yourself sound better than all the other women on there (without lying or making anything up . . . or coming off as haughty . . . or trying so hard to be humble that you sound like you have no self-confidence . . . it's so complicated!). I went with this for my attention-grabbing headline: "Smart, sassy, fun-loving Christian seeks same for laughs, long conversations, and future nursing home companionship." It seemed positive but not prideful, informative yet concise, and, if I do say so myself, more clever than a lot of other ones I read before typing mine. And I spelled everything correctly, so that set me apart from about half my competition. Good enough.

Arkansas was surprisingly scenic! After New Mexico, Texas, and Oklahoma's flat, boring highways, I rather enjoyed the twisty, tree-lined roads. I flew in and out of my new friend Jana's apartment (my friend Nina had asked her to host me for the night) to get to my evening date at a place called Wildwood. Considering the name of the place, I briefly thought about putting on my hiking shoes but instead decided to go with the cuter two-inch heeled boots. I wanted to look good for my date for the night, a teacher who conveniently had the same name as the guy I'd had breakfast with that morning. No worries about calling him the wrong name!

The festival they were putting on that weekend was "Lanterns," an annual event celebrating the first full moon of the year. I met Mr. Arkansas beside a giant blow-up blue moon, and he gave me a bouquet of daisies. How sweet! It was a brisk February night, so I was happy to see bonfires burning in several spots alongside the little lake. We started our tour of the world ("Like Epcot, but smaller," I said. He didn't laugh. Tough crowd.) in Asia, then wandered over to Mexico.

"Oh crap," he muttered as we walked across a bridge.

"What?"

"Nothing," he muttered again and then greeted someone coming across the bridge toward us. He didn't stop to make introductions.

"Crap," he said again when they were out of earshot.

"What?" I asked again.

"I was kind of hoping no one would know about this."

"It's perfectly normal for people to date," I reassured him. "If they ask you about it later, you don't have to tell them the fifty dates part if that's embarrassing."

"I hope none of my students are here," he said, looking around. One of the main reasons I'd chosen him was because he'd listed "teacher" as his occupation on his internet dating profile. To be hired as a teacher, he must have passed a background check. No history of jail time = good enough for me.

"Well, again, they're probably aware that their teachers are normal people who do normal things like date." He didn't seem convinced. I hoped he wouldn't shove me behind a tree if one of his students came strolling along.

We spent our first "WildBucks" (the currency for the evening at Wildwood) at the food stand in Morocco. We ordered lamb kabobs and couscous, quite a stretch for me. I showed sheep at the county fair when I was growing up in Iowa (I even have a trophy declaring me the Buena Vista County 4-H Master Sheep Producer of 1988!), so I tried hard not to think about my fluffy friends as I ate their descendants.

Next we stepped up to the palm reader. I don't buy into fortune telling or horoscopes, so I was a skeptic customer from the start. I didn't give her much to work with.

"You must be a teacher of some sort," she began. "The young people you work with really like you."

Well, I did work with teenagers until about a week ago when I quit my job to drive around the country. Close.

"You have a talent you really needed to explore . . . maybe art or music?" she tried.

"Definitely not art," I assured her, thinking back to that "F" I'd gotten in high school art class. I was hoping maybe she'd hit on writing and tell me lots of people would buy my book, but I wasn't going to lead her to it.

"You are going to go on a really long trip," she predicted.

Hey, maybe this isn't complete crap, I thought. *I'm just starting out on a really long trip.* But then she elaborated.

"Two or three years from now . . . out of the country."

"I'll put that on my calendar."

"You are going to have a great summer."

"Good to know."

"Do you have a sister?"

"Shouldn't you know that, with your psychic powers and all?" Okay, I didn't actually say that. I verified that I did indeed have a sister.

"She's going to need to lean on you a bit. Be there for her."

"Gotcha."

Overall, everything she said was pretty much believable but just vague enough to make me think she was full of crap.

We moved on to Americana, then Venice, then Shakespearean England. We were still hungry, so we went back to Asia for some spring rolls.

"You must be cold," I observed. I had my hat and gloves on but he had neither.

"You could keep my hands warm," he replied.

Cue the crickets.

Let me just put this out there right now: I'm not a very affectionate kind of girl. As the lead in our high school musical my senior year, I'd had to negotiate a scene where I was supposed to kiss a guy goodnight. Not looking at him, I crossed my arms and glared at the director.

"A hug?" she suggested. I shook my head.

"How about a goodnight pat on the back?" she tried. I agreed and the tense standoff ended.

As an adult, I'm still not touchy-feely. When it comes to dating, I'll make my interest known, but if I'm not touching you when I talk or brushing up against you as we walk or just grabbing your hand and holding it, take it as a sign that I'm not into you. Furthermore, suggestions about keeping you warm will more likely earn you a punch in the arm than a cuddle session.

We strolled back to the area deemed Mexico to get some churros for dessert and were pleasantly surprised to find a six-man mariachi band performing. They were awesome and my feet were killing me, so we sat and listened to them for a while before heading out. Stupid sexy shoes. Dumb, dumb, dumb. Yes, I'd looked taller and thinner for my date, but I'd wobbled on throbbing feet half the night along those romantic luminary-lit paths. It had been a very cool date, strolling from Asia to Morocco to Venice and sampling foods along the way, even if I was limping by the end of it.

When I got back to Jana's apartment, she had two of her guy friends over who wanted to hear all about this "experiment." I told them a bit about it, and then they wanted to hear about Mr.

Arkansas. I said I felt bad about the stereotypes I'd had about Arkansas, because my date had been a pretty classy guy and not at all redneck. They assured me that there were plenty of rednecks around Arkansas and they could find me one pretty quick, but I said I was happy with the date I'd just had.

Daniel, originally from Louisiana, was determined to set me up with a true Cajun when I got there. I already had a guy lined up, but after describing him, Daniel didn't think he represented the state well. I said I was fine with a city boy. Daniel responded by spitting tobacco juice into a Gatorade bottle. Gross. Mike noticed my repulsion.

"I stopped chewin' in fifth or sixth grade," he said proudly. I suppose my eyes popped at that. At what age had he *started* chewing tobacco if he'd given it up that young?

"Oh, I've given it up more than once," Daniel said, "but I started chewin' again right about dove season." My "what?" got me a lecture on various hunting seasons. I even had to friend him on Facebook so I could admire his albums of hunting photos.

"I hope you're not a vegetarian," Jana said. I shook my head.

"I been huntin' all my life," Daniel said. "My dad and his buddies thought it was cool to have me out there with 'em, seein' an eight year old chewin' and drinkin' Bud Light."

Jana & I gave him the raised eyebrows.

"It was an interesting childhood," he conceded.

Mike said that growing up in Arkansas had been interesting, too. He told me a (supposedly true) story that he thought personified the Arkansas stereotype. It seems that a case worker got a call one day from some of her clients out in the backwoods.

"We caught us a leprechaun!" they yelled. Because these two were mentally challenged, she didn't think much of it. The next day, though, she was still thinking about it and decided maybe she should drive out there and make sure everything was okay. When she got there, they were agitated.

"We caught us a leprechaun, but he won't give us his pot of gold," they said. She was confused, then got worried when she heard thumping. She followed the noise to the closet.

"That's where we're keeping him," they said. She opened to door to find a little person, tied up and gagged. Seems he'd come around to tell them about the Jehovah's Witnesses . . . I'm betting they crossed that address off their evangelizing list after that.

It was getting late, so the guys headed out. Jana told Mike she'd see him at a party the next night and asked what he was going to wear.

"I might wear my new hundred-and-fifty-dollar jeans," he replied.

"You paid $150 for jeans?" I asked incredulously. He didn't seem the type.

"The girl working at the store tricked me into buying 'em," he said, shaking his head. "She showed me her boobs and said I looked good in the jeans, and the next thing you know, I'm paying $150 for jeans and feeling too stupid to say no."

I was shocked. What kind of stores and salesgirls did they have in Arkansas?

"She showed you her boobs, right there in the store?" I clarified.

"Well, she was wearing this low cut shirt and they were just poppin' out . . ." He cupped his hands under his chest, then shook his head, embarrassed, and walked out.

Ah, men.

#6 – TENNESSEE

Growing up, the congregation at my Lutheran church in rural Iowa consisted primarily of farmers and retired farmers. If you're not familiar with the appearance of the average Iowa farmer, here's a pretty reliable generalization: they're all white. With my church-full-o-white-people background, I couldn't help but giggle as I sat in a Lutheran church in Memphis, the only white person in the entire building.

I wasn't all that thrilled about going to Graceland, but Tennessee was another state I was just hitting a corner of in hopes of saving some cash. I'd found a guy in Memphis willing to date me later that afternoon, and I thought as long as I was there, I might as well go see their #1 tourist attraction. I'd told my parents they should drive down from Iowa and meet me, or suggested that my mom wrangle her two sisters for a girls' weekend. I figured they'd love all the Elvis memorabilia. But if any of them had come down and gone to church with me that Sunday morning, just down the street from Graceland, they'd have been squirming in their seats. I don't think they've ever experienced what it's like to be in the minority. Having lived in Ghana for a few months, it wasn't my first time being the only white person in an all-black church. The only weird part to me was that it was nothing like an African church service. There was no dancing, no hanky waving, and no shouting, "Amen!" They were Lutherans, all right.

When worship ended, I pulled into the Graceland parking lot.

Honestly, I don't really care where Elvis lived. While I appreciate his contribution to the music world and understand his sex appeal to that generation, I was two when he died, so I'd never dreamed of him seducing me in the jungle room. I almost changed my mind about going in when I found out how much it cost – I had to pay $10 just to park, then $30 for the basic tour! For an extra $4, I could also tour his two private planes, but looking at the map, I decided I'd rather spend $4 on a strawberry shake at a little food stand called Shake, Split, and Dip, just around the corner from the ticket booth. It was closed, though, so I had to go to the diner instead. Everything smelled so good that besides ordering the shake, I also got a burger and onion rings. I passed on "Elvis' Favorite," the fried peanut butter and banana sandwich.

Before I got on the bus to be driven straight up through the gates of Graceland, I stopped at the little girls' room. I nearly puked up the $11.85 I'd just been robbed of for my greasy lunch. It reeked and my feet stuck to the floor. Seriously people? I just paid $10 to park, $30 for a tour ticket, and $12 for lunch, and you can't clean your freaking bathroom? Where, exactly, was my $52 going? I was beginning to hate Elvis. Well, not Elvis. Just the people who were making money off Dead Elvis.

Graceland was about as thrilling as I thought it would be, but even worse was the text message that came at the end of my tour. Mr. Tennessee was sick in bed with a 102-degree fever.

Crap!

Crap, crap, crap!

I weighed my options. Should I have a dateless chapter, or should I go find some homeless man, take him out for dinner, and call it a date? Could I still call the book *Fifty Dates in Fifty States* if I didn't have a date in Tennessee? I was leaving town that night to drive to Jackson, Mississippi. I didn't have a lot of options.

I'd crashed the night before with another virtual stranger; Jana from Little Rock had asked her friend Katherine from Memphis if I could sleep on her couch, too, and she'd agreed. In our get-to-know-you chitchat, Katherine had mentioned she played on a co-ed kickball team, so I texted her from the Graceland parking lot, begging for help finding a date. Within minutes, she had a man for me.

"Hallelujah!" I shouted in a wholly un-Lutheran manner.

An hour later, I stood on a corner of Beale Street, waiting for my new date and trying not to look too dorky. I realized I should have asked Katherine something other than the guy's name since I had no idea who I was looking for. Was he Black? Asian? Hispanic? Caucasian? Tall? Short? Clean cut? Shaggy? Tattooed? I saw a guy lurking across the street and prayed that wasn't him. He had old-school monk hair: bald on top, encircled by a strip of hair, then shaved at the bottom. I didn't think he was really a monk, though, since he was wearing jeans and staggering a bit, presumably from whatever was inside the brown paper bag in his hand. *That's probably my guy*, I sighed. *I've had good luck until now; I was bound to be lined up with some losers somewhere in the fifty.* But then my actual date rounded the corner, looking sober and sporting a fabulous head of hair. I liked him immediately.

We meandered up and down Beale Street, asking each other typical first date questions, and deciding eventually to pop into B.B. King's Restaurant and Blues Club for a drink. A band was in the middle of a song, and it didn't take long for my vocal chords to start hurting, shouting to be heard across the table. I remembered those greasy onion rings I'd had for lunch at Graceland and prayed I wasn't grossing the poor guy out with stinky breath as I yelled at him. We got there at just the right time, I guess, because after a rousing extended rendition of "Proud Mary," the band thanked everyone for listening, then left us to talk in reasonable tones. (I was also very relieved and happy that the near-elderly woman who'd been singing lead and doing her best Tina Turner impression had not collapsed from exhaustion.)

We split the Soul Sampler – wings, potato skins, BBQ ribs, and fried pickles – and I manned up and tried one of the fried pickles. I grimaced and gagged a little bit but did not throw up – yay me! Mr. Tennessee Take Two turned out to be funny and talkative, and though I felt bad that my originally scheduled date was home in bed sick, I was pretty happy with his replacement.

There was another place down the street he wanted to show me, but I needed to use the bathroom first. It was then that I decided there was not a clean bathroom in all of Memphis. Okay, okay, that's a really broad statement, considering I didn't visit them all, but whereas my feet had stuck to the floor in the last one, I was sliding on the floor in this one. As I came out of the bathroom, a woman coming in literally fell down in front of me. She was wearing cowboy boots, which I suppose didn't have the traction that my hiking boots did, and whoops, there she went. I wondered if she got anything free, like an appetizer or a dessert, as a way of apologizing. I considered trying that. With my budget, free food as compensation for falls might be a great game plan.

Back at the table, the waitress brought our bill and apologized for not being around much. Sir Charles Barkley had come in and her boss had sent everyone running to serve him like a king. We looked over and sure enough, there he was, big as a barn. People were interrupting his dinner to ask him to pose for pictures with them and sign autographs. Fame had to suck sometimes. Cold ribs aren't nearly as good as hot ones.

We headed down the street to the place Mr. Tennessee had told me about – Earnestine & Hazel's. Some sources say it was a sundry store, and some say it was a juke joint, but everyone agrees that you could rent a room upstairs . . . by the hour, if you know what I mean. It supposedly continued to be a brothel until the early nineties, if you can believe it, and rumor has it that the Rolling Stones' song "Brown Sugar" was written about the ladies of the night they met there. Nowadays it's a bar and *the* place to get a burger at 2AM. It was pretty dead when we went in, being early in the evening, but Mr. Tennessee said the place is always packed after midnight. We creeped around the seedy upstairs rooms and I wondered how the health department hadn't shut the place down. The plastered walls were cracking and the floors groaned; supposedly it's even haunted, but I didn't see anything in the dimly lit rooms.

I had to hit the road, so I thanked Mr. Tennessee for filling in on short notice and for being adventurous enough to say yes and help out some crazy dating traveler. I wished him luck in life and love and kickball, then pointed Cherry Cherry south.

#7 – MISSISSIPPI

I am going to marry this man, I thought. *We're going to adopt kids from all over the world and grow old together on some plantation in the middle of nowhere.* I floated to my car after dinner with Mr. Mississippi. This was amazing.

We'd met for dinner and it was kind of like a movie. I don't enjoy fine dining at fancy places on a regular basis, so I was a little intimidated walking into this restaurant in Jackson. I wasn't wearing fleece, my usual attire, so in my mind I was pretty dressed up. Everyone inside, though, was wearing skirts or jackets. I didn't have those wardrobe choices, living out of my car.

Self-doubt came slinking around again, and I worried that Mr. Mississippi would be disappointed. I was staying with a girl named Ashley, a friend of a friend of a friend, and I'd been at her house earlier as she was getting ready to go to a fancy awards banquet. A co-worker of hers, a former Miss Mississippi pageant contestant, had loaned her two different-sized curling irons and two products to make her hair look big and fabulous. She'd even written out detailed instructions on how to use the products, like, "Hold bottle ten inches from your head and spray onto roots." I walked toward the restaurant with my normally flat hair getting flatter by the second in the misty night. Miss Mississippi I was not.

He was waiting for me inside and we sat at the bar until our table was ready. Being pretty frugal, I don't get out much, even when I'm not driving around the country and living out of my car, and on those rare occasions that I do, I never darken the door of places this ritzy. I saw the charge slip when we moved from the bar to the dining area: $17 for two drinks!! I was a little afraid of how much dinner was going to cost.

Over steak (me) and fish (him), we talked about Mississippi and college and careers and travel. I quickly formed the general opinion that he was a good guy. He was even a Big Brother and had recruited several of his friends to be Big Brothers, too. He was close to my age but had an old soul aura that made him seem mature while still looking good.

"I want nine kids," he said. My ears perked up.

"You'll have to start dating twenty-two-year-olds if you want nine children," I teased.

"I could adopt," he retorted.

Ding, ding, ding, ding! The magic word – adopt!!

I first started thinking about adoption when I was about ten. I don't know if we had a snow day or what, but I remember being home from school on a weekday with my whole family, sitting in our living room, watching *Donahue* on TV. (For you young'uns, think pre-Oprah.) On that day's show, he was interviewing kids in the foster care system who were hoping to be adopted. I especially remember one freckle-faced boy. Donahue asked him what kind of parents he wanted – parents who liked sports or music or animals? The little boy thought about it for a few seconds, then shrugged his shoulders.

"I just want someone to love me," the little guy responded, tears filling his eyes. He didn't care what their hobbies were as long as they loved him. I begged my mom for months afterward to call *The Donahue Show* and ask for info on adopting that little boy. My brother is two years older than me and my sister is four years younger; the boy from TV would have been two years younger than me and two years older than my sister, creating a perfect every-two-years spacing among us kids. It was meant to be! But she never called.

I have friends who were in the delivery room, watching the birth of the child they would add to their family through adoption. I have friends who have gone to far-off countries to bring home children to their forever families. I've volunteered at orphanages in Africa and Central America and fallen completely in love with children in each and every place. I admit that like most childless people, I'm curious to see what a child with my DNA would look like, so I'd love to have a few biological children, but I also have this huge longing in my heart to bring home kids who just want someone to love them, like that little boy on *Donahue*. A guy who was open to that seemed instantly more attractive.

Mr. Mississippi suggested moving to one of his favorite bars, so I said I'd follow him there. I think it's a bad idea to get into a car with a stranger, even if you do plan to marry him and raise nine kids together. At the bar, we continued our great conversation, agreeing on everything from fiscal responsibility to stay-at-home moms. I'd never dreamed of living in Mississippi, but this was going fabulously. I might have to acquire an accent.

Then the conversation turned to faith. The Titanic dreams I'd been building up all night hit an iceberg and slowly started to sink. He said he had taught Sunday School and led Vacation Bible School and sang in the church choir . . . but then he'd started reading. The more he read, the more he doubted what he'd grown up being taught. Now he considered himself a theist, or maybe an agnostic, or maybe an atheist. Our nine future children who'd been dancing happily in my head suddenly vanished.

We still had fun. He just wasn't the man of my dreams. I thought about how hard it was to find someone who has all the qualities you're looking for in a partner, and how close someone can be while still being miles away. And how maybe, despite saying it shouldn't be that hard to find a guy with just the three qualities I was looking for – Christian, smart, and funny – it might actually be harder to find than I'd thought. On the way home, I checked in with Alicia, my Chief Safety Officer, and shared this sadness.

"You'll find him," she said. "He's out there. I've got this feeling you're going to meet him before this is over."

This was only date number seven. I knew there were forty-three more chances to meet someone who would be a better match for me, but that night, all I really wanted was one guy; I didn't necessarily want fifty dates, just one perfect-for-me man.

As I left Jackson the next day, *Layla* came on the radio. I decided that whether or not I'd call Mississippi a good date or a bad date would depend on whether or not they played the song all the way through the instrumental ending. They did.

As I drove along, snacking like I always do when I'm bored, I wondered what would happen if something I ate went down the wrong pipe while I was behind the wheel. I snacked a lot as I drove: cashews, granola bars, Jube Jel Cherry Hearts. (Side note: if you've never tried Jube Jel Cherry Hearts, *you must*. Brach's puts them out at Valentine's Day, and I'd bought four bags of them before leaving Colorado. I stashed one away in my trunk so I could enjoy it in May or so.) But back to my question: if I choked, would I lose consciousness and drive off the road and die in a fiery crash? Because it would really make me mad, if you can be mad when you're dead, to know that everyone thought I'd died because I was a bad driver. I took pride in being a good driver! But then again, would having everyone know I died choking on a Jube Jel Cherry Heart be better?

#8 – LOUISIANA

Daniel, Jana's Louisiana-native friend back in Little Rock, sent me a Facebook message when I said I was headed for his home state. He had a cousin, he declared, who would "carry me frog gigging." I stared at my computer screen for several minutes, wondering what the heck that meant, before asking for a translation. He said it meant his cousin and I would go out in a boat and catch frogs, maybe see some alligators, and enjoy the moonlight. I pictured being clubbed over the head and dumped in a swamp, leaving the gators to eat the evidence. I went with the safer bet and headed for my pre-arranged date in New Orleans.

My citified Mr. Louisiana declared he wanted to give me "a true New Orleans experience." He succeeded; when I'd finished all fifty dates, I would definitely remember where I went on a vampire tour. We started the evening a little less dramatically with some local food. I ordered the jambalaya and he had red beans and rice. I wasn't a big fan of either one, but I gave myself credit for trying something new.

Mr. Louisiana had some interesting internet dating nightmares to share. (You know how it is – you "meet" someone online who seems great, but then actually meet, face to face, and find out they're completely different than they'd advertised themselves to be.) I would give first runner up to the lady who decided not to meet him alone for their first date. Instead, she brought along her best friend. And her son. And her ex-husband. But she loses out in the Making-a-Crazy-First-Impression Pageant to the woman who, before they even met, was asking Mr. Louisiana some pretty personal questions, like "How much money do you make?" When they met in person for the first time, she talked about her plans for their wedding, including which church it would be held in, where the reception would be, and where they would honeymoon.

Oh fine, I'll admit I've been guilty of a little daydreaming myself, but everyone knows you don't say the M-word too early! Men get scared and run away! And on the first date? No. No, no, no. That just makes you look crazy.

After dinner, we strolled over to the St. Louis Cathedral. By day, it looks like your everyday, ordinary cathedral. At night, it was a little spooky, looming over us as we began the vampire tour. It quickly became apparent that Rene, our tour guide, loved this vampire stuff. Me? Not so much. I'd never seen a vampire movie in my life. (Neither the stupid trendy teen vampire movies, as he called them, or the real vampire movies, whatever those may be. And oh, Mr. *Twilight* hater?? At least the kids who loved those books were reading instead of wandering around dark alleys at night.)

We poked around the French Quarter while vampire man pointed out different places where scenes from *Interview with a Vampire* had been filmed. People nodded their heads excitedly . . . I tried to smile and not shiver. It was freezing. And I may not believe in vampires, but the stories he told were creepy enough to give me the shivers from fear as well as cold. Blood and gore gross me out. I was pretty glad when it was over and Mr. Louisiana and I went to the Cafe Du Monde. Beignets and hot chocolate are way more my style than hearing about dead people and the monsters who sucked the blood out of 'em.

Mr. Louisiana was forty-two, which, as far as I could remember, was the oldest man I'd ever dated. I generally date younger men. It might be because I look (and maybe sometimes act) younger than what I really am; more likely, it's because most men my age and older are already married with kids. It may also stem back to being freaked out by an older man many years ago.

When I first got out of college and was a teacher, one particular dad decided I was the woman of his dreams. I did the math and figured out that if he'd been a promiscuous seventeen-year-old, I could be his daughter. I endured his flirtations as professionally as I could during parent-teacher conferences, but got really freaked out when he sent me a card saying how wonderful I was and how thankful he was that his children had me in their lives. He ended the card by writing that he hoped I'd go with him to the local park where we could sit and play our guitars together. I was mortified. He started finding excuses to come see me when he dropped his kids off for school, so I started sprinting for the teacher work room every time his blue mini van pulled up outside my classroom window, yelling at the history teacher next door to come get me out of my hiding place once he'd left.

On the last day of school, I got a message from the secretary saying I needed to stop by the flower shop on my way home that day. They had a bouquet for me to pick up. I got a little excited, thinking maybe they were from that cute new assistant track coach I'd talked to a few times; he was a poor college student, though, so it didn't seem likely. The reality of who they were more likely from slowly sank in. He'd been sending me notes the entire semester. While I'd never been brave enough to tell him no to his face, I thought he'd take the hint. I started to feel a little sick as I went to the teacher work room and called the flower shop.

"Can you tell me who the flowers are from?" I asked the woman who answered.

"He wanted it to be a secret," the lady giggled. I asked if they were from the man in question.

"Well . . ." she seemed to debate whether or not to confirm my suspicions, " . . . you're spoiling the secret, but yes."

I sighed. I thought about it for a moment, then came up with a good solution.

"Could you please deliver them to the closest nursing home?" I asked.

"What? They're beautiful!" She sounded hurt, like I was personally insulting her floral design skills. I tried to assure her that yes, I was sure they were lovely, but no, I definitely did not want those flowers.

"You don't know the whole story . . . " I started, but I didn't burden her with it. Why did the florist need to know that I was creeped out by a man seventeen years older than me with three kids and a mini-van? Did I really have to explain that I was freshly out of college and wanted to find a man my age who didn't already have teenagers? The residents at the nursing home would love to have some pretty flowers on their dinner table that night. They would get much more enjoyment out of them than I would.

Looking across the table at Mr. Louisiana, I realized he was about the same age as that parent had been years ago. Now the age gap wasn't nearly as wide. And let's be honest: George Clooney is fourteen years older than me, and I would not be at all creeped out if he wanted to date me. Heck, he could even pick me up in a blue mini van if he wanted to. Older men don't seem so bad once you get kind of old yourself.

I have an unfortunate history of waking up in frightened confusion, not knowing where I am. The first time anyone noticed this was on a camping trip with some friends. Natalee, Stephanie, and I had just settled down in my cozy little tent when I began dreaming about chaperoning a church lock-in. I dreamed we were playing Cops and Robbers and I'd hidden in a cupboard, but then the kids locked me inside and wouldn't let me out. When I came to, I was clawing at the top of the tent, the small opening of my mummy-style sleeping bag tight under my armpits, like a strapless prom dress.

"Help, help, help!" I cried as I clawed. "Help, help, help! Where am I?"

Natalee put a hand on my leg and gently said, "I'm Natalee, and you're Tiffany, and tomorrow we're climbing Mt. Evans." She explained later that she wasn't sure where exactly we were camping, so that seemed like the best response to my question.

I was immediately embarrassed. I didn't say a word, but quietly slunk back down and tried to go back to sleep. (Our friend Naveen, who'd been sleeping in another tent next to ours, said the next day that he'd heard me and wondered if I'd gotten lost coming back from the outhouse. Nope, just dazed and confused *inside* the tent, thank you.)

Most of our friends heard about the incident, of course. A few years later, while camping on the edge of the Ngorogoro Crater in Africa, I dreamed I was stuck under a tent platform and couldn't sit up or move in any way or I'd knock my head on the wooden beams.

"Help, help, help!" I urgently whisper-pleaded, frozen in fear.

My friend Cheryl reached out and touched my leg.

"I'm Cheryl, and you're Tiffany, and tomorrow we're going on a safari," she parroted. Oh geez.

I'd had wild dreams in my own home, too. I once came to after I'd jumped out of bed and whipped back the covers because I'd been dreaming about a snake slithering in the bushes. I'd also woken up standing in my closet with no idea how I'd gotten there. And once I woke up precariously perched on the corner of my bed; I'd been reading before I went to sleep about Teddy Roosevelt exploring the Amazon River by canoe after his presidency, and I'd been dreaming that I was on a raft, fearful of going down a tributary instead of the actual river. I woke up on my knees, leaning off the bed, looking at the four doors in my bedroom: one to the hall, one to the bathroom, and two to closets . . . but no routes to the Amazon.

So it's not entirely surprising that I found myself thinking, *Oh crap, I hope that didn't wake up Joe and Daphne.* These two very kind people had never met me until the day before, but we had a mutual friend and they'd agreed to let me stay there for a couple of nights. The first night had been uneventful, but on this, the second night, I'd been dreaming that someone was breaking into my car, which was parked right outside the guest room window. The loud thud of my feet hitting the hardwood floor when I leapt out of bed woke me up. There I stood, looking out the window at an untouched car in a perfectly quiet neighborhood. I slunk back into bed and prayed there wouldn't be a knock on the door followed by a worried, "Are you okay in there?"

I'm amazed at how I can always seem to find ways to embarrass myself . . . even when I'm asleep.

#9 – ALABAMA

The drive from New Orleans to Mobile was beautiful. Well, once I got out of New Orleans it was beautiful. That took a while. Like an hour. Let's just say that I wanted to take the scenic route, so I turned off the GPS when it kept barking at me to get on the interstate. So yep, I took a scenic route . . . in the wrong direction . . . straight into a baaaad part of town. I'm pretty sure I saw a part of the city most tourists never visit.

Once I actually got onto the right road and headed east instead of whatever direction it was that had landed me in the ghetto, I felt as free as a bird. I love driving alone. I know some people hate it, but I don't. I like making my own decisions (thus my love/hate relationship with the GPS), stopping when I want to stop, and listening to whatever I want. I found that Mississippi had the same tree-lined roads along the coast that they'd had through the central part of their state and I smiled. I'm a fan of good planning, even if I do fly by the seat of my pants pretty regularly. Bravo, state-wide landscapers!

When the trees opened up to white, sandy beaches, the view took my breath away. I stopped and had lunch (maybe a banana with a spoonful of Nutella doesn't count as lunch for most people, but it had become a pretty regular meal for me) sitting on a park bench overlooking the water. The area had been hit hard by Hurricane Katrina, and many homes were still in the process of being rebuilt. It was a strange contrast of beautiful and broken.

Crossing the border into Mobile, I obeyed the GPS as it led me to Anita's house. Anita and my Chief Safety Officer, Alicia, were long-time friends, and she'd agreed to take me in for a couple of nights. As I pulled into the driveway, I knew I was in the right place. She's made and posted a big sign that read, "Homeless Shelter: We pay rent so you don't have to."

It's good to have friends. (And friends of friends.)

I have to admit that I wasn't very excited about dating someone in Alabama. The possibility of a Southern gentleman had been built up by Alicia, my CSO and the craziest football fan I knew. (How many ways can "Roll Tide!" be used? It's like "Aloha" for Alabamans.) But when thinking about potential Alabama dates, I pictured a . . . ummm . . . less sophisticated sort. Think wife-beater tank and missing teeth. This mental image wasn't helped by my first Mr. Alabama "applicant." I got an email from someone who had seen my website. He asked if I had sex after each date; if so, he was interested. To quote Julia Roberts in *Notting Hill*, one of my favorite movies, "Tempting, but . . . no." I deleted his email without responding.

The second email I got from an Alabaman sounded promising. He was a former Iowan, like me, and knew one of my friends from Colorado. Unfortunately, between the time I'd sent out my first email asking friends to set me up with their friends and the time I got to Alabama a month later, he'd started dating someone. He emailed again, saying he'd decided it would be best not to go out with me while trying to woo her. I was disappointed and also a bit worried; I'd gotten emails from several guys in various states who sounded great – what if they were all taken by the time I finally got to their states?

Luckily Jana, who had hosted me for the night back in Little Rock, had a friend who was married to a guy from Mobile. She said she knew four of his friends who were single and started firing off emails. She got an interested response from one of them and voila, I had my Mr. Alabama.

If you're looking for a way to get someone excited about your upcoming date, take a tip from this guy: intriguing text messages. I got a couple the day before asking questions like, "Do you get queasy on carnival rides?" and "Ever had motion sickness?" I spent the entire day guessing what we might be doing. Riding a Ferris Wheel at a street fair? That would be fun. A swampboat tour? I'd seen billboards advertising those as I drove into Mobile, but I'd puked on a ferry once, so that might be bad. A helicopter ride? That would cost a ridiculous amount of money. Whatever it was going to be, I was curious and looking forward to it. I like a little mystery.

He also sent some texts saying we'd be changing locations four times over the course of the evening, so it would be easier to pick me up than have me following in my car the whole night. I was uneasy with the whole getting-into-a-car-with-a-stranger idea, so I consulted Jana, who consulted her friend Amelia, the one who'd set up the date. The all-clear was given, but I was still a little nervous about not having control of the situation. I'd seen a lot of swamps driving from New Orleans to Mobile, so it would be pretty easy for some crazy man to dump my body into one of them. I didn't want my tale of grand adventure to end up on *48 Hours* or *20/20*.

I made the mistake of experimenting with make-up just before he picked me up. I'd been having a problem with breakouts around my chin, which seemed totally unfair since I also had wrinkles around my eyes. (Shouldn't your face only be allowed one or the other? Am I old? Am I young? Pick one!) I'd never worn much make-up since it just didn't feel natural to me. I'd brush on some eye shadow and hit the lashes with mascara and call it good. But, in hopes of covering up the "blemishes" ('cause Southerners speak so delicately and would never use harsh words like "zits" or "pimples"), I bought some foundation. I thought it seemed a tad too light when I first dabbed it on, but I figured maybe it would look better once my whole face was the same color . . .

. . . and that, my friends, is how I ended up looking like a mime five minutes before Mr. Alabama was scheduled to pick me up. I grabbed some tissues and started furiously rubbing at my face, trying to get it off. Ugh. I should have known better than to play with make-up like some twelve-year-old at a slumber party. The doorbell rang right on time (of course!); looking in the mirror, I was horrified by the splotchiness of my face. Parts of it were ghostly white from the make-up while other parts were ruby red from the rubbing. How did those girls on *The Bachelor* look so good every dang day?

Mr. Alabama didn't look like a serial killer when he picked me up, but I texted his license plate number to my Chief Safety Officer just in case. We then took off for what he said was our first destination.

"Is this the thing that might make me sick?" I asked.

"I'm not telling," he said.

"Well, I just think you should be warned that if I get sick at our first destination, I'll probably want to go home instead of go to your other destinations," I kidded.

Half kidded.

I wasn't really kidding.

"I've planned a very memorable evening," he assured me. "Someday when Oprah asks you which date was the best, I want you to instantly say, 'Alabama!'"

"Oprah's retiring soon," I reminded him, "so that will never happen."

I thought the fact that he was planning on me being alive in the future boded well for me, though. Whatever it was we were doing, he obviously didn't have plans to kill me and dump me in a swamp.

He told me his entire office had gotten involved in this date, advising him on where to take me, what to wear, and what I was into, since he was representing the entire state. They'd done some internet investigating (stalking) and knew everything about me, right down to where I'd gone to college. He even had a Dave Matthews Band CD playing on his car stereo. I didn't know whether to be flattered or freaked out.

As we exited the highway, I saw a building marked "aerospace" and thought, *Oh wow, we're going up in the air!* The field outside the small airport was dotted with little planes and helicopters, so I asked which we were going up in.

"We're going up in a Skyhawk 172," he said.

"And that would be . . ." I led. I didn't know if it was a plane or a helicopter.

"One of those little planes," he laughed, pointing to an aircraft.

"Are you going to be flying it?"

"I could, but I asked one of my friends to take us up tonight," he explained. Wow.

We climbed inside, then sat on the runway as the pilot did what seemed like a thousand safety checks before we took off. I sat there getting more and more nervous, thinking, *Don't throw up, don't throw up, don't throw up.* I'd flown a lot, but never in such a small plane. And when I'd gone paragliding in Peru a few years before, what should have been the experience of a lifetime turned into desperation to get out of the sky when I'd started puking. I was praying I wouldn't now. How horrible of a date would I be then? Blotchy face + smelling like vomit = probably too much to ask a guy to deal with.

The take-off was easy, but then I started worrying not about puking, but about dying. I remembered hearing about two little planes like this that had crashed into each other, and every year some little plane or another seemed to crash into the mountains in Colorado. I tried not to freak out.

There are no mountains here, I reasoned with myself. *There is, however, a whole lot of water to go down in.*

I tried to think of something else. It was March 5, my mom's birthday, I remembered. God wouldn't let me die on my mom's birthday. That would be tragic, to be reminded every year on her birthday that her beloved daughter had died in a freak plane crash while out on a date with some stranger in Alabama on that very same day. I took deep breaths, feeling like I'd found the magic answer.

It was a beautiful flight. We saw the sun set over Mobile Bay and looked at the twinkling lights of the city below as it got dark. The pilot let me take control of the plane for a few minutes as we flew over Dauphin Island, then took over again to make sure we landed safely on the other side of the water. I was happy I hadn't puked or died, but I was confused as to how we were going to get home, now being on the opposite side of the bay than where we'd left Mr. Alabama's car. Then I saw a driver step out of a sleek black car and hold up a sign with Mr. Alabama's name on it.

Holy crap. He had hired a freaking driver!

I slid into the car, simultaneously amazed and horrified, thinking about how much he'd spent on this date. I tried joking about it to ease my guilt. He said he'd sold a kidney to finance it, but hopefully it would be worth it. I chortled, uneasily wondering what "worth it" translated to for him.

The chauffeur dropped us off on Main Street in a sweet little town called Fairhope. They were having an art fair that night, and we meandered the streets under trees strung with twinkling white

Fifty Dates in Fifty States

Christmas tree lights. We popped into shops and galleries here and there to look at art and sample wine.

"Wow, I love this one," I said as we looked at one particularly lovely piece, "but I could never afford anything so extravagant."

"I'd sell my other kidney and buy it for you, but I'm pretty sure I need at least one to live," he said. "I'll look into selling a lung."

Later on as we turned down a side street, my ears perked up. Was that Neil Diamond I heard? I love Neil! I walked faster and there, at the end of the block, some old guy was singing on a street corner, karaoke style. A crowd had gathered around him as he sang his heart out to "Brother Love's Traveling Salvation Show." As entertaining as he was, even better were the women in their fifties and sixties, dancing wildly as he sang. I laughed at first, but then thought, *Oh geez, that'll be me in twenty years, shakin' it on a street corner while my husband stands a few yards away, sheepishly holding my purse.* I don't embarrass myself on a regular basis by holding back, you know.

We found our way back to the town car and our chauffeur, and he drove us along the shoreline to a fancy restaurant. Mr. Alabama's officemates had debated which restaurant in the area would be the most impressive, and this was the place they had decided on. My first inclination was to go for the steak, but remembering where I was and wanting to branch out, I decided to try the sea bass. It was a delicious choice, far better than I'd ever guessed fish could be, and while we ate, we talked and laughed for a long time.

On the way home, we stopped and walked out onto a pier. It was one of those moments that's perfectly romantic, and part of me thought maybe I should kiss him, since he'd spent a lot of money on this date. That seemed a bit prostitute-ish, though, and a really bad reason to kiss someone. Kissing someone I didn't have feelings for, despite the really great, memorable date, felt like it would be cheapening my kisses down the road with someone I was really crazy about. I turned away, hoping he wasn't horribly disappointed, and walked back to the car for the ride home.

Mr. Alabama planned an amazing date that I knew I'd never forget, and it made me wonder how many guys plan wildly romantic dates like that for women in their regular, everyday lives. I think sometimes we're afraid of going all out, fearing we might scare off the people we're crazy about if we're over-the-top, but if I were a few dates into a new relationship and someone planned a night like that just for little ol' me, I would definitely feel wooed. Maybe even loved. And that feeling only comes along once in a while.

Anita insisted we tour Bellingrath Gardens before I left Alabama, and I'm so glad she did. Our tour guide for the historic home was a no-nonsense older woman named Velma. I had to strain my ears to understand her, because she had that syrupy drawl I'd been dying to hear from some Southerner. She was very proper and I intrinsically felt that I'd better not mess with her. At one point she must not have been happy with where I was standing, because she pointed at me, then pointed at a spot next to her on the floor. I quietly moved over, feeling like I'd been caught doing something bad in school. After the house tour, we wandered beside the river and through the gardens. If I'd had more time, I would have stayed all day, walking the grounds and soaking up the sunshine. It was lovely.

Driving back to Anita's house, we almost hit a battered minivan that pulled out in front of us. After slamming on the breaks, Anita had to eventually pass the slow driver. I gave the driver a glare on Anita's behalf as we went around, then gasped and giggled. The woman driving had few teeth, but what she lacked in enamel, she made up for in ink. She wore a wife-beater tank top and had a confederate flag sticker on the back window.

Ah, my Alabama stereotype, come to life, I thought. *So glad you could make an appearance for me before I left.*

I stopped in Gulf Shores on my way out of the state and was pleasantly shocked by how stunning it was. I felt guilty for ever thinking bad thoughts about Alabama. Between Bellingrath Gardens and this amazing stretch of shoreline, Alabama was the prettiest state I'd driven through so far. Roll Tide!

#10 – FLORIDA

I stopped in Pensacola to arm myself. I was going to be camping that night for the first time during this road trip, and I thought I'd better have some sort of protection. No, I didn't get a gun. Honestly, I had considered it back when I'd started planning the trip months before, but I pictured myself rolling over onto it in my tent in the middle of the night and somehow setting it off. I preferred not to die during my great American adventure, especially not in a stupid self-inflicted accident like that. I thought about getting a taser, but those things were pricey. So there I was, in the camping aisle at Walmart, disappointed that I only had two choices: a knife with a four-inch blade or a machete. I debated the pros and cons of each, thinking I wouldn't have to get so close to my would-be attacker with the machete, but I'd probably have better control with the smaller weapon. I chose the knife. Then I went over to the pest-control aisle and picked out a bottle of wasp spray. I'd been told it had better long-range accuracy than pepper spray.

The drive along the coast was slow and boring. Luckily I have a mind that is easily entertained, so I got a kick out of random stuff I saw along the way. Driving past the Bayside Inn, I wondered if it was run by Zach, Kelly, Screech, and Slater. A bit down the road, a "For Sale" sign in front of a house encouraged me to call Shelley Elley for a tour. Seriously? Did her parents hate her or did she make a really unfortunate choice by taking her husband's rhyme-y last name? And the guy on a bike pulling a tented kid cart . . . with an adult woman sitting inside? Oh, America. I love you so.

    I stopped at Panama City to hike around Gator Lake. I had imagined a lovely boardwalk with a fence on either side so you could look down and see the alligators without them actually snapping your foot off. Instead I found a dirt trail and a sign that marked the start of what they called a "Self-Guided Nature Walk." I had hiked by myself for years in Colorado without worrying about my safety; at Gator Lake, though, no one was close enough to hear me scream. I was constantly looking toward the lake, wondering how far out of it gators would crawl. I was also keeping my eyes peeled for random mounds in the sand. My friend Laurie had warned me about red ants, saying some people have horrible reactions to their bites. Having dropped my health insurance to a bare-bones plan when I left my job, a visit to the ER was not in my budget. And yet, once I finished the loop and was back at my car, I was pretty mad that I hadn't seen an alligator.

    I headed out of town, aiming for the place I planned to camp for the night: Apalachicola National Forest. Yeah, it appeared to be out in the middle of nowhere, looking at the map, but with a name like that, how could I *not* go? My enthusiasm dimmed as I wasted an hour, growing more and more frustrated with every minute that passed while I drove around lost and looking for it. I finally pulled up to the gate as the sun was setting . . . only to find the gate locked. I let a few choice words fly as I pounded my head against the steering wheel a time or two. Now what was I supposed to do? I'd passed by a sign a little further back that pointed out a primitive campsite. That would have to do, I guess. I'd been driving all day and I was ready to be done. I chose a camp site, got my new tent set up without any problems (hallelujah!), cooked myself a lovely meal of spaghetti and meatballs (just add boiling water!), and got everything cleaned up and put away just as it was getting dark.

    I came out of the "primitive toilet facility," as the state webpage called it (translation: a hole in a plank above a pit of human sewage), and stopped short when my headlamp lit up two eyes. Surprisingly, my first thought was, "Aw, how did a little kitty-cat get out here in the middle of nowhere?" I shuddered when it started scampering up a tree and I realized it wasn't a friendly feline but a (probably rabid) raccoon. I've heard those little beasts are fierce and can claw your face right off. I walked back to my campsite but turned around when I realized I'd left my backpack on the picnic table. I froze. The raccoon was right behind me.

"Yuhuhuuuuh!" I uttered and flailed. Then I told myself to calm down. What's that saying? *It's probably more scared of you than you are of it.* I collected myself and waved my arms at it.

"Shoo! Get out of here!" I said. It didn't move. Obviously reason was going to get me nowhere. I jingled my keys at it. Nothing. I lunged at it like I was going to chase it. It scampered back a couple of steps, then lunged at me. I did that Scooby-Doo move where your feet are moving but you're not going anywhere as I fumbled around in my pocket, trying not to scream as I hit the unlock button on my key fob. I jumped in and took deep breaths. *You know, I'm behind on postcard writing*, I thought. *I think now is a good time to do it. Right here. Inside my car. With the doors locked, just in case he's agile enough to open doors.*

Twenty minutes later, I figured he would have sniffed around and found nothing (I had enough camping experience to know not to leave food outside), then gone on his merry way. I swung my headlamp around the area, saw nothing, and quickly moved from my car to my tent.

I changed into my pajamas, snuggled down into my sleeping bag, and looked at my travel alarm clock. 7:30PM. I read for half an hour, then turned off the light. I made sure my big knife and my wasp spray were within reach, just in case anyone tried to attack me in the middle of the night. As I tightened my mummy bag around my neck and my face, I realized that I'd have some trouble getting to my weapons should someone enter. I took solace in the fact that the intruder would have just as much trouble getting through three zipped areas: the rainfly, the tent, and my sleeping bag. I figured he wouldn't know where my weapons were, and I would still have time to unzip myself from my sleeping bag and use them on him before he violated me. I drifted off but woke up several times during the night, hearing rain (a lovely sound) and some other unidentified noises (owls? rabid raccoons? rednecks?). It was a long night.

The next night I checked into a hotel. Call me a wuss, paying for a room after only one night of camping, but I had well-thought-out reasons. First, I needed a shower. I smelled. There hadn't even been sinks in the "primitive toilet facility," let alone showers. Second, I was going to go swimming with manatees the next day, which was probably going to be the most freaking awesome experience of my life, but it meant that I'd be in a lake or a stream or some other dirty body of water and would need to wash that off afterward, being a bit of a germaphobe. Third, my tent was wet. Everyone knows you don't put away a tent when it's wet or you'll have a stinky, moldy, unusable tent. I had paid a huge wad of money for that thing, so I wasn't about to let it become unusable after just one night in the forest. Also? *LOST* was on that night, and though I wasn't a huge TV fan, it was the one show I was completely addicted to. With so few episodes left before the series finale and no TV in my tent, I was pretty excited to head off to a hotel.

    I checked into a Days Inn near Crystal River and immediately strung up my tent between a lamp and the bathroom mirror. I draped the tent's rainfly from the mirror to the shower. Then I spent the rest of the evening ducking under and between them to get to various objects like the sink or the TV or the toilet.

    I got up really early the next morning and headed to the river with my guide from River Ventures. My friend Naveen, who had moved to Florida a couple of years before, had told me that swimming with manatees was the coolest thing he'd done since moving there. I was a little bit worried I wouldn't see any since it was pretty late in the season, but I'd only been in the water for a few minutes before the manatees started swimming by. They were absolutely huge. I guess the water in the Gulf of Mexico gets too cold for them in the winter, so they come into these warm springs. The babies were the most playful; one kept swimming in circles around me. So cute! My guide and I were the only ones there for an hour and a half, snorkeling and playing with the gentle giants. Then a boatload full of people came by and that was the end of the adventure. It's hard to get close to a manatee when twenty other people are trying to get close to it, too. Half my Florida budget was gone with one short experience, but it was worth every penny; I'd probably never swim with manatees again.

    After showering off and checking out of the hotel, I found a movie theater to kill some time. I'd like to say I saw something thought-provoking or something that had been nominated for an

Oscar, but to be honest, I saw *Dear John*. What can I say? I'm a sucker for that Nicholas Sparks.

When I walked out two hours later, I pondered the phrase, "It's better to have loved and lost than never to have loved at all." I wondered if it was true. I'd loved, but I'd never loved someone so much that I'd married him. I couldn't imagine how much it must hurt to lose your spouse. It sounded cowardly, but I thought I'd be saving myself pain down the road if I just stayed single.

The other deep thought I thought, walking from the theater to my car, was *I'm not wearing a single thing that matches*. I had on a dark pink t-shirt, khaki pants, and black Crocs. Maybe my mom was right. My fashion sense stunk.

I drove into central Florida and set up my tent for the night. I jumped when I heard a noise that made me think someone was killing babies or strangling cats; looking around, I discovered that was the call of peacocks. Who knew? It was going to be a long night if they kept that up. I sat in my tent, plugged in my wireless internet card, and watched the previous week's episode of *The Office*. I wasn't exactly roughing it.

I checked in with my Chief Safety Officer, thinking I'd better let her know where I was, just in case I went missing.

"I hate the thought of you camping," she said.

"It's not like I'm in the middle of nowhere like I was the other night," I said. "This place is closer to civilization. I can hear traffic on the turnpike."

"That's even worse! What if someone running from the law sees your tent and decides to come on in? You can't lock the doors on your tent."

"Why would someone running from the law want to get into my tent?"

"Um, hello? They've been in prison and haven't had sex with a woman in who knows how long?"

"Well, how would they know there's a woman all alone in this tent and not a burly, well-armed man?"

"Is Cherry Cherry parked in front of your tent?"

"Yeah."

"How many burly, well-armed men drive a red, four-door

Toyota Corolla?"

"ALICIA, IN THE FUTURE, IT WOULD BE NICE IF YOU WOULD NOT PUT HORRIBLE MENTAL IMAGES IN MY HEAD WHEN I AM ALL BY MYSELF OUT HERE!" I yelled into my cell.

Of course, after that conversation, every little noise freaked me out. I sat there reading and swore someone was walking around my tent. Sure, it could have been one of those peacocks strutting around, but listening to the crunch of the leaves, the stride sounded longer, like man-steps. Oh fine, I'd never studied peacocks to know how long their stride was, but it sounded more man-like than peacock-like to me. And this expensive new tent didn't have a single window to look out and see which it was.

I eventually turned out my headlamp and snuggled down into my sleeping bag. I didn't mummy it up. For one, it was pretty muggy in central Florida, so I was warm enough half in/half out, and two, I wanted easy access to my knife and the can of Raid. Trying to fall asleep, I visualized what I would do when that man who'd been circling my tent tried to get inside. First, I'd spray the Raid in his eyes. Next, while he was temporarily blinded, I'd slice his Achilles tendon with my new knife so he couldn't run after me. Then I'd kick him in the nose, get out of the tent, and kick him in the groin. I'd call 911 while standing over him, giving him a little shot of wasp spray or a kick to the crotch anytime he tried to get up. He would never try to violate anyone ever again. Of course, I looked more like Reese Witherspoon than myself in my vision. I mean, why not improve yourself when you have the chance?

It was a loud night. No one tried to get into my tent, but the traffic on the turnpike was unrelenting and those stupid peacocks were cawing all night long. It rained. And rained. And rained. I woke up a little after seven and read for as long as my bladder could stand. I wished I'd gone for a walk the day before. The sunshine was gone.

Relief flooded me when I arrived at Naveen's house. My friend Krystal and I had stayed with him a year before; we'd flown down for a long weekend and had received the royal treatment. After the previous rough night of camping, I was excited to have a soft bed, indoor plumbing, and no peacocks or imagined prison escapees circling my tent. Naveen is also a great cook, so I knew my granola bar and fruit diet would be on hold for a few days. The first thing I did, though, was string up the wet tent again. I had no idea what I was going to do when I wouldn't have a place to dry it.

After a day of R&R, it was time for my date with Mr. Florida. I'd found him on Match.com and he was a hottie. I'm always a little suspicious of the attractive, popular types though. It stems back to a little incident in college with an attractive, popular guy. I was neither attractive nor popular in college. That might be a little harsh, but looking back at photos from that period of my life, those years weren't my finest. I had fully embraced the grunge look. Everything I wore was XL and flannel. I was definitely not popular. Going to a small high school, I'd been a starter on the volleyball team, a soloist in the choir, and a captain of the dance team. Once I got to college, I was smart enough to know I wasn't good enough to play volleyball, but I thought I might have a chance auditioning for the choir or the dance team. Nope. Turned out no one thought I was good at anything. Instead I focused on studying and went to chapel a lot, 'cause Jesus still thought I was awesome, even if no one else did.

In the fall of my sophomore year, I saw a poster announcing auditions for West Side Story. I'd had the lead in the school musical my senior year of high school, but after my earlier rejections at college, I knew better than to aim too high. I tried out as a dancer and made the cut. I wouldn't have to attend every rehearsal, which was a plus since I was working three jobs and was terrified of losing my academic scholarship. I'd been declared good enough for something, though, and I was ecstatic.

It didn't last long. At the first rehearsal, I got bumped from a Shark Girl to a Jet Girl. That meant I wouldn't get to dance and sing "America" with Anita and the other girls. The director said it was because I'd only auditioned as a dancer and not as a singer as well, but I've a sneaking suspicion he took one look at me and realized there wasn't enough make-up in the entire state of South Dakota to make this pasty white girl look Puerto Rican.

The upside of being a Jet girl was a certain Jet guy who flirted with me. He was a popular upperclassman. I loved rehearsals more and more. Another girl made it obvious that she was into him, but he ignored her. Me, though? He paid attention to me. At first I told myself he was just being brotherly; he probably thought of me as a kid sister. But one night he gave me a ride home, and there was a moment when I was almost certain he was about to kiss me. And, I'm ashamed to admit, I wanted him to. I didn't care that he had a girlfriend. In my romantic, fairy tale world, I pictured him breaking her heart, telling her he'd fallen for someone else, then declaring his love for me. I knew it was going to happen. I just had to be patient.

When the show ended, I nearly cried. He still hadn't even asked me out, let alone declared his undying affection. The bright side was that he was in one of my classes. He didn't come much, but there was a chance I might see him if he decided to show up. Then, one magical night, he called.

This is it, I thought. *He's going to tell me he's missed me and he broke up with his girlfriend and he wants to go out with me.* He made small talk for a minute, then cut to the chase.

"So, I missed a test in class today, huh?"

"Oh . . . yeah, you did."

"What were the essay questions?"

Realization dawned slowly and painfully. He wasn't calling to ask me out. He was calling to ask what had been on the exam so he'd know exactly what to study. He thought the nerdy girl would be happy to help out the hottie. That was the moment when I started being suspicious of hot, popular guys showing interest in me.

And the next day, when he sat down to take his exam and found that none of the questions I'd said were on the test were actually on it, I'm guessing that's the moment he realized you shouldn't mess with smart girls.

Getting ready for my date with Mr. Florida was comedic. He said we'd be going out in his boat, so I figured I should put on swimwear. I'd been wearing nothing but jeans and sweaters for the month I'd been on the road, so I had to walk down to my car from Naveen's second-story apartment and do some trunk shopping. After a little digging, I found my black bikini, some capri pants, and a t-shirt. I'd also need some footwear other than hiking boots, so a little more digging produced my shoe bag. I pulled out some flip flops and headed back up to the apartment.

A swimsuit is not my typical date attire, but I'd actually had a date at a water park a year before. I decided to use the same tactic I had that time: distract him with the goods up top so he doesn't look anywhere else. I hadn't seen the inside of a gym in a couple of months, so things were even worse than normal. Plus I was really white. Like, glow-in-the-dark white. I looked at myself in the mirror and decided it was not a bikini day. I vowed to a) stop eating junk food as I drove, b) start doing sit-ups, and c) buy some of that tan-in-a-bottle lotion. Yikes.

I decided to just wear the t-shirt and capris, but felt that even the v-neck showed too much pasty whiteness. I trekked back down to the parking lot to find a shirt that covered more of me, then went back up to the apartment and blow-dried my hair. I noticed a little perspiration on my upper lip and worried I'd be sweating like crazy out on the boat. I went down to my car a third time and pulled out a darker colored shirt that wouldn't show sweat quite so badly. Huffing and puffing my way back up, I realized these stair climbs were the most exercise I'd gotten in a long time. My body must hate me.

Mr. Florida already had the boat in the river when I arrived at the dock, and I jumped into it, praying I hadn't misjudged how far away it was. I landed safely inside and we took off. It was a gorgeous day. I love water. I loved the mountains when I lived in Colorado, but if I could pick (and if I won the lottery to pay for it), I'd live right on a lake with a ski boat and a little Sunfish sailboat and a kayak of my very own. When the Dave Matthews and Kenny Chesney duet "I'm Alive" came on the radio, I thought it was the perfect song at that very moment. I felt completely content.

It's funny how my previous date had planned out every detail of the evening but this date seemed to wing it. Mr. Alabama took me to the best restaurant his coworkers could think of; Mr. Florida took me to an impromptu lunch at a place on the river called the Swamp House. Two different styles, two fabulous dates. There was something about Mr. Florida, though, that made me comfortable from the very beginning.

"I'm hungrier than a hostage," he declared, then suggested I try some new foods. I looked around to see where the nearest bathroom was, just in case I puked. The alligator bites were surprisingly good. They were deep-fat fried and looked like popcorn chicken. Not bad at all. The raw oysters, however, were gross. I tilted one off its shell and down my throat; he insisted I eat another. I almost gagged, trying to choke the second one down. I'd never had anything so slimy in my mouth before. I'm not sure, because this is just a theory I haven't actually tested, but I'm guessing that if you vomit on a man, he will probably not be attracted to you. It finally went down, and that was the end of new food tasting for me.

Mr. Florida was easy to laugh and easily made me laugh. I love people who are easy to talk to and who you can just be yourself with. We talked about past dating experiences, and he had some fun ones. My favorite was a woman he'd found on the internet. They met at a restaurant, and when he got there, she was already at the bar and already drunk. She made some completely inappropriate comments over dinner, then laid down in the booth and *went to sleep*. He was mortified. He got her up and out, but then she said she needed a ride home. She lived with her ex, and she hadn't wanted to tell him that she needed the car so she could go on a date with someone else. I laughed sympathetically at his story and said that's one of those fun surprises in internet dating: they may look good on paper, but in person, they might be a train wreck.

We got back in the boat and kept cruising up the river. I kept my eyes peeled for an alligator, but we never saw one. After several hours, we pulled over on a little beach alongside his friends' boat. Someone had left the remnant of a fire barely glowing, so the four of us gathered up wood and got it raging. Another boat pulled up and we welcomed some locals (a nice way of saying "crackers," which is what the city folks called the country folks) to our fire. They had a boom box strapped to their boat, and as we stood there by the fire with country music blasting and the sun setting off in the distance, I smiled; it was one of my favorite moments of the trip thus far.

Let me reiterate that I'm not touchy-feely. I'm not a big hugger, and I like my personal space. One summer at the camp where I took the teenagers I worked with, there was a theme dance; my students all wore signs that said, "FREE HUGS." My sign said, "$1 Hugs for World Hunger." No one hugged me the whole night. I felt a little bad about hungry kids not getting any donations, but I was happy that strangers weren't hugging me. That's just weird. I don't like people touching me, especially people I don't even know or like. But standing around the campfire on the side of the river, Mr. Florida put his arm around my waist and I didn't mind it one bit.

We climbed back into our respective boats and headed back to the dock. I texted my Chief Safety Officer to let her know I was alive and well. Very well, indeed.

"I think I might let him kiss me at the end of the night," I texted. Yeah, yeah, yeah, I know I'd just said on my last date that I wanted to save my kisses for someone who meant something to me, but things were really clicking with this guy. He was totally into me. And heck, I *wanted* him to kiss me.

I wonder sometimes if married people forget how great kissing is. It had been a year since I'd kissed anyone. I knew this because I'd broken up with my last boyfriend on my thirty-fourth birthday, and I was turning thirty-five the next day. I was definitely ready to be kissed. I read an article once that said to keep romance alive in your marriage, you should kiss your spouse for at least ten seconds every day. Ten seconds? Are you kidding me? I couldn't imagine having someone in my house who I could kiss every day and having to *force* myself to kiss him for ten seconds.

Back where we started, Mr. Florida asked me to hold the boat against the dock while he backed up his trailer. He stepped up onto the dock, then turned around and kissed me on the forehead. So sweet. I felt a little bit melty inside. We got the boats out of the water and went to a restaurant to grab some food. All in all, we spent about nine hours together, which was by far the longest date of the ten so far. At the end of the night, Mr. Florida walked me to my car, being the gentleman that he was, then planted a light, sweet kiss on my lips. Perfect.

Driving down the interstate on the way home, I started thinking about how I should have kissed him earlier in the day so I could've kissed him more. And then I thought, *Man, why didn't I just kiss him more in the parking lot?* It'd been a year since I'd kissed anyone, and what if I didn't get to kiss anyone again for another year? That little two-second kiss hadn't been nearly enough. I sent him a text.

Me: Are you still on I-4?
Him: Yep. Why?
Me: I'm not sure I was quite done saying good-bye to you yet.

I was trying to be flirtatious and coy, but being the one-woman comedy show that I am, I got all mixed up in the neighborhood where I exited after telling him to meet me there. I found him eventually, thankful that he hadn't just given up and driven away.

I hopped up into his SUV and he was ready for me. He wrapped his arm around my head in what I can only describe as a headlock. He mashed my face into his and stuck his tongue further into my mouth than I thought was humanly possible.

He's trying to make me bulimic, I thought. *And I can't pull my head away. Is this one of his moves? Does this actually work on women? Am I odd? I mean, is this a move that all other women love?*

I'm probably not the best kissing judge. I mean, it wasn't like I had kissed all that many men in my lifetime. Of those I had kissed, some were good kissers and some were not, but none had ever come so close to playing tonsil hockey for real.

I was able to maneuver his arms lower, around my back, so I could pull my head away and get some air. Things improved after that. Well, the giant console between the driver and passenger seats was a little awkward, but still. I wasn't going to complain about making out with a hottie. I checked in with my Chief Safety Officer on the way home and she could tell I was really happy.

"You know, you're setting your own rules," she said. "It's not like you're only allowed one date. See him again if you want to."

I thought the next day about what she said. *Maybe*, I thought. *Maybe I could fly down sometime this summer and see him again. Go fishing. He said he likes that. Or in the fall . . . we could go to an FSU football game.* I tried not to think about it too much. I waited anxiously for him to call or text or email me.

I friended him on Facebook, which probably wasn't a good idea. Sometimes ignorance is bliss. On my Facebook page, you'll see pictures of me surrounded by the teenagers I used to work with, or my family, or the orphans I love in Africa. In his Facebook pictures, he was surrounded by beautiful women. He was obviously a popular guy and people loved hanging out with him. I couldn't get over how beautiful all the women were. I thought, *This is what he's used to. This is what women in Florida look like. And I'm not enough. Not blonde enough. Not tall enough. Not thin enough. Not surgically enhanced enough. Not fashionable enough. Not wild enough.*

And honestly, for a day I felt pretty bummed about it. He had been fabulous, and the nerdy girl inside me couldn't help but be awed by the hot, popular guy.

When I talked some sense into myself, though, I remembered that I am enough. For someone I would be more than enough. Someone someday would think I looked hot whether I was in stilettos or I'd slept in a tent for a week. He'd love my big heart and want to go visit orphans in Africa with me. He wouldn't care if my hair was flat when I took off my ski helmet. He'd love how easily I made him laugh. He'd overlook my flaws and see my inner beauty. He was out there somewhere. And when I found him, I was going to make him one happy man.

The next day was my birthday – thirty-five big ones. I went with Naveen and some of his friends to the Strawberry Festival in Plant City, but we didn't see many strawberries. We mainly saw carnival food: corndogs, funnel cakes, and just about anything you could deep fat fry. Also? "Chocolate dipt bacon." (I guess spelling rules are different in central Florida.) We continued on to an NHL game in Tampa, which was an awesome way to celebrate my birthday. I love hockey! The funniest moment of the night was when they did the "kiss cam." You know how the "kiss cam" works – if they point their cameras toward you and show your picture on the jumbotron, you're supposed to kiss your date. They showed several couples who willingly played along, but the fourth couple wasn't as cooperative. The woman screamed and covered her face and jerked away from the guy. He looked at the camera for a few seconds, then pointed to the other side. The camera panned to his left, and there sat his wife, not looking very happy. He kissed her anyway.

I kept checking my phone, thinking surely Mr. Florida would shoot me a text wishing me a happy birthday. I mean, geez, we'd made out in his SUV the night before. Didn't that mean anything to him? I texted him the next day, hinting that I'd welcome a second date and making it clear that I was in town for another two days. He didn't ask me out, though. I caved and asked him out, but he said he had to get up really for work the next morning.

That's the problem with thinking your kisses mean something: when they don't mean much to the other person, you end up feeling pretty stupid for thinking it meant something more than it actually did.

#11 – GEORGIA

Mr. Georgia was twenty minutes late for our date, but don't judge him. I was thirty minutes late. Let's just say Atlanta rush hour traffic was unlike anything I had ever driven in before. I'd toured the ghetto (thanks, GPS, for suggesting that route . . . seriously?) and nearly rear-ended someone who stopped abruptly in front of me (which left me digging under the front seats later, trying to find everything that had gone flying off the back seat). Mr. Georgia and I had started out texting each other about potentially being late, then moved to phone calls about potentially becoming definitely. In the end, we both found the date location and walked in late together. I thought it was sweet of him to wait for me so I didn't have to go in alone.

The Viking Cooking School in Atlanta hosted our date for the evening. We were in the Steak, Roast, and Chop Workshop, and it didn't take us long to figure out we were completely out of our league. We'd missed the tutorial on making Cabernet Butter, being late, but I'm not sure it would have mattered. Mr. Georgia didn't cook at all, and I'm no Julia Child myself. We kept giving each other that raised eyebrow look that says, "Are we the only ones here who don't know how to do this?" The guy next to us was taking notes while Mr. Georgia and I whispered like remedial troublemakers in an honors class.

Besides showing us how to do stuff, the teachers, Chip and Peggy, asked for volunteers to slice and chop. (Our new friend Michael, the excessive note-taker, had a lovely drawing in his notes on how to properly slice an onion. I whispered to Mr. Georgia that I have a Pampered Chef chopper that does the job nicely.) He was ready to participate, though, so they handed him an apron and put him to work slicing sausages. Chip's example was a lovely, even slice; Mr. Georgia mutilated the meat. I sat giggling, even though everyone else was still looking uber-serious. The mashing didn't matter in the end, though; everyone loved the sauce Mr. Georgia helped make, even if it didn't look pretty. We also loved the Pork Chops that the sauce went on top of, the New York Strip with the Cabernet Butter, and the Prime Rib with Horseradish Cream. Oh, and Peggy's Roasted Garlic Popovers. And the Chopped Salad with Three-Peppercorn Buttermilk Dressing. And the Chocolate Mint Cheesecake Bars. It was pretty much a never-ending feast. I'd never seen so much food on my plate. And it was soooo good. Between blissful "mmmmms," I thought, *Is this heaven? No . . . and it ain't Iowa, either, despite the plethora of meat.* I was loving Georgia!

We talked a bit with Michael, the note-taker, and it turned out he wasn't a brown-nosing nerd. Get this – he wanted to impress his wife by learning how to cook her a gourmet meal!

"We've been married ten years. You gotta do something to keep things fresh, you know?" Nice. Go, Michael!

We wandered around the Viking store afterward, checking out stuff we didn't know we needed, like cheese slicers and hot chocolate makers and $7000 refrigerators, then went down the street to a coffee shop where I could get to know Mr. Georgia a little better. I knew, since he was a friend's younger brother, that he was young, and I honestly wasn't interested in trying to make a love connection with a 24-year-old. With the pressure to be impressive off, I relaxed and had fun just hanging out and chatting.

Mr. Georgia, I found out, had a history of planning romantic, memorable dates. He said if the Viking Cooking School hadn't given us the free cooking class, he would have planned something cool and memorable for us.

"Like what?" I asked.

"There was this girl I really liked, so I rented out the rooftop of a hotel. The hotel staff had started a fire in a fire pit for us before we got up there, so the two of us hung out, roasting marshmallows and making s'mores."

"Oh my gosh! How cute is that?" And why had no man ever

liked me enough to plan something that cool for me??

He also shared that when one of his friends said he was going to propose in a week but didn't really have a plan, he jumped into action, putting up thousands of twinkle lights around a gazebo so they would have a romantic engagement story to tell. Awww! I flipped through my mental rolodex, trying to think of who I knew in his age range to set him up with. What a catch!

He was thinking of set ups, too; he asked if I needed help setting up my remaining thirty-nine dates.

"How have they been going?" he asked.

"Honestly, the past month has been rather weird and confusing."

"How so?" I got the feeling he wasn't just making polite conversation, but actually wanted to know. It was refreshing to be able to talk to someone honestly, so I confided in him.

"Well, with some of them, I wasn't sure if the guys planned awesome dates to impress me or to impress every woman in America."

"What do you mean?"

"I mean, I'm not sure if they were interested in me or just putting on a good show, knowing I'd write about them."

"Not your normal dating experience, huh?"

"I've been dating for twenty years, and this is totally new."

"Let me give you a little insight into the male mind," he advised. "With guys, everything is a competition. Don't be surprised if every guy you meet wants to outdo whatever you did with your previous dates."

"That's not the point!" I countered.

"Every guy will want to be the most memorable."

"But this isn't a dating competition!"

"If he plans a great date, you'll remember him."

"Even if he took me up in a hot air balloon, which would pretty much be the best date ever, if he couldn't make me laugh or carry on an intelligent conversation, the excellent, memorable date would be for nothing. Just because the *activity* was memorable, that doesn't mean the *guy* will be."

He shook his head. He understood my point, he said, but that didn't mean I was going to magically change the chemical make-up of the male mind.

It was nice to have someone to laugh with, be honest with, and just be casual with instead of trying really hard to make him like me. He was a good guy and would've been one heck of a catch if I'd been ten years younger. I feared that every guy like him in my age range had already been scooped up.

While in Atlanta, I couch surfed with an intriguing couple named Ken & Linda. They'd bought a big farm house that was over a hundred years old and were in the process of renovating the whole thing. They said they were eight years into their major project and figured it would probably take another eight years to completely finish it. I found it an amazing undertaking, especially after I saw the "before" pictures. I applauded their vision. If I had seen that house in its "before" state, I would have told the realtor to forget it. It proudly stood in the middle of a neighborhood, the city having grown all around it; what had once been a farm was now the heart of the city.

Ken and Linda shared pictures and stories of their travels to Kenya, Greece, and Albania. It was like vacationing in foreign places without leaving the U.S. They'd met ten years before and had been having the time of their lives together ever since. I found it encouraging that she was thirty-five when they got together; it gave me hope that I could possibly still find a good guy at my age. They'd endured some tough stuff, too. I found out she'd almost lost him when he casually commented one day about recovering from surgery.

"What kind of surgery?" I asked.

"I got shot," he responded. Looooong pause from me.

"Where?"

"Here," he said, touching his upper chest near his shoulder.

"No, I mean, where, like, geographically? A drive-by?" I'd seen some rough parts of Atlanta in the two days I'd been there.

"It was out front," he responded. Another loooooong pause.

"You mean, in front of your house?"

"Yes."

"A drive-by shooting in front of your house?" I clarified, trying not to act too freaked out.

"No, no," he said. Oh good. I was starting to get a little worried about what kind of neighborhood I was in. But then my brief feeling of reassurance went out the window.

"I was out doing some lawn work in the front yard, and a car pulled up . . ." Long story short, it wasn't a drive-by but an attempted robbery that left him in the hospital for a long, long time.

I thought of them, finding each other a bit later in life, then almost being torn apart, while wandering through Oakland Cemetery. I'd gone to see Margaret Mitchell's grave since I loved *Gone With The Wind*. Her grave was pretty obscure (I walked past it twice, expecting something more prominent, before I finally found it), but the cemetery was full of many more elaborate resting places. Some had statues on their tombstones, and there were several large vaults. I peeked through the windows of one and saw what appeared to be several generations of couples in a family vault. Most had Bible verses or Christian phrases etched beneath their two names, like "I Know That My Redeemer Lives" or "The Lord is My Shepherd, I Shall Not Want." But above the names of one pair was etched a single word that struck me: "Reunited." I looked at the dates and realized that she had died nine years before he had. I was struck again at how devastating it must be to lose your spouse. How do you find the strength to go on when the person you live with and love is suddenly no longer in this world? I couldn't comprehend it.

I thoroughly enjoyed my stay in the guest bedroom of Ken and Linda's rambling suburban farmhouse, except for the night Ken gave me a stale marshmallow right before bed. I chewed on it, sucked on it, and did my best to soften it up, but that dang thing was just not edible. It wasn't dissolving in my mouth at all, so I spit it out and set it on the edge of the bed. A few hours later, I woke up when I heard Ken and Linda getting ready to go to work. I realized one of my ear plugs had fallen out, so I lifted a corner of my eye mask and ran my hand over the sheets, feeling for it in the mostly-darkness. I saw something over on the edge of the bed, but when I picked it up, it was all wet.

Nope, that's that stale marshmallow, I thought.

And then realization slowly and horrifically dawned: I'd only been dreaming about a marshmallow! That was my earplug I'd been chewing and sucking on in the night! Sensitive gag reflex . . . sensitive gag reflex!! I ran for the bathroom.

After brushing my teeth 'til my gums bled and rinsing with Listerine three times, I packed up Cherry Cherry and headed out for my grand finale in Atlanta, climbing Stone Mountain. It didn't exactly qualify as "getting into nature" since there were hundreds of people walking the same path, but it was "getting off my ever-softening backside," which hadn't been happening much since I'd left Colorado. A young Asian tourist was climbing the trail in a mini skirt and heels, which made me think maybe it wasn't as steep as it seemed (but I didn't see her at the top, so I'm guessing she got smart and went back to her car after a while). A large woman sitting and resting on a rock had a similar thought. When an old man with a cane passed her, she took a deep breath, stood up, and muttered, "If he can do it, I can do it."

As I climbed the mountain, I saw several examples of men who, to me, exemplified what I wanted and didn't want in a husband. The man carrying his son in one of those backpack kid carriers? Yes! Yes, yes, yes! I wanted to be with someone who strapped our kid in a backpack and took off for a hike, introducing our child to nature. The man running down the trail, jumping from boulder to boulder with his daughter on his hip? No! No, no, no! The poor girl looked terrified as she desperately clung to his shirt and got bounced around like a ragdoll. What would have happened to her if he'd tripped? I wanted to be with someone with a little more common sense than that. Maybe my "three things" theory was a little off. Maybe I was pickier than I thought. New list: Christian, smart, funny, and not likely to cause brain damage to our offspring.

I picked up my friends Krystal and Ginger at the Atlanta airport later that night. Both worked at an elementary school back in Colorado and were joining me during their spring break to see the sights of Charleston and Savannah together. I was deliriously happy to have people in my car with me. They were probably less excited, since whoever sat in the back seat had to share that space with all of their luggage, my trunk being filled to capacity.

They looked at some of my date options for upcoming states and tried to help me decide who I should go out with. Since all three of us were single, we thought it would be really fun to do a triple date in South Carolina. We had two problems with that idea, though.

First, I was having problems finding one man in South Carolina to go out with me, let alone find dates for all three of us. And second, what men would believe us when we introduced ourselves as Tiffany, Krystal, and Ginger? They'd either think we'd made up those names or we'd gotten the night off from working the pole at the strip club on the corner.

I wasn't accustomed to considering the needs of others after driving solo every day for over a month. First they teased me that it took me forever to get out of the car. (Um, hello? Thieves might break in if it looked like there was something worth breaking in for, so I had to unplug my GPS and my iPod, tuck them away in my purse, then hide the chords in the little box between the seats. That process took time!) Then they teased me that despite the fact that Ginger asked me several times to pull over so she could get something to drink, I never actually pulled over. (In my defense, I was so enjoying their company that I got caught up in conversation and forgot about her multiple requests to find a gas station. And really, being thirsty isn't an emergency like, say, having to go to the bathroom.) And finally, they teased me because we very nearly got hit more than once. (Hey, I'm a good driver! Those close calls were always the other person's fault! And statistically speaking, the more time you spend on the road, the more likely you are to get in an accident, right? So far, so good. Cherry Cherry was scrape-free. Make fun all you want, friends, but all evidence points to me having skills on the road.)

Having friends along meant doing things I wouldn't have done if I'd been by myself. The three of us went on a ghost tour in Charleston and it was actually pretty fun. I believe in ghosts about as much as I believe in vampires (nada), but the tour guide on the ghost tour was a lot more laid back than the guy in New Orleans. The vampire guy had been so excessively obsessed with vampires that I had almost laughed at times. Our ghost tour guide, John, was much more easy going. When I told him about what I was doing and the book I was writing, he told me about a memorable woman who'd once been on one of his ghost tours. She had very obviously been drinking before she arrived, and throughout the tour, she was constantly pawing at him, asking stupid questions. As they walked down a dark alley, she tried to hold his hand and rest her head on his shoulder. Never mind the ten other people in the group. Or the fact that he was trying to work. Or that he was wearing a wedding ring. I didn't find the tour quite as romantic, I guess, because I had no problems keeping my hands to myself.

We drove out of town one day to tour the Boone Hall Plantation. I will readily admit that I wanted to see it less for its history than because some of *The Notebook* was filmed there . . . sue me. I decided that one day I'd have my very own Avenue of Oaks alongside the long driveway to my big old house. I'd have a wrap-around porch where I could sit at sunset and drink sweet tea. (Okay, fine, you got me again: tea is gross and I'd rather die of thirst than drink it. I'd have to sit and wave at the passing neighbors while drinking a big ol' glass of cold milk in Wisconsin instead of sweet tea in the South, but whatever.)

Back in town, we lazed away a morning walking along Charleston's Rainbow Row. A park at the end of it was home to a quaint little gazebo, and I couldn't resist entertaining my friends with a reenactment of a movie classic. I sang/shouted the lyrics of "Sixteen Going on Seventeen" as I twirled and spun around the gazebo . . . until I thought, *whew, I'm getting out of breath* . . . . and then *gosh, I'm not feeling so good* . . .

I've heard dancers talk about "spotting," a technique where you focus your eyes on one point so you don't get dizzy when doing turns. I never took dancing lessons, though, so maybe I shouldn't have been twirling around that gazebo. My singing stopped abruptly and I clung to the railing for dear life.

"You okay?" Krystal called out through her laughter.

"Uuhhhh," I moaned, trying to keep my breakfast down. This never happened to Liesl.

We drove from Charleston down to Savannah, the quaintest little city in the South, if you ask me. We filled our days touring the historic district, climbing to the top of the Tybee Island lighthouse (where Ginger cutely hugged the wall rather than look down), and taking a little ferry ride on the river. Never one to miss an opportunity, I struck the *Titanic* "I'm the king of the world!" pose at the bow of the boat and belted out the opening lines of "Come Sail Away," channeling Styx.

Krystal turned to Ginger and said, "You know that episode of *Friends* where Phoebe wants to turn everything into a musical? That's kind of what life with Tiffany is like."

"I don't think I ever saw that episode," I retorted. I can't help it. It just comes bubbling out of me.

We visited a candy shop and I eagerly took every free sample they offered me. I stood salivating over the caramel apple display for a good five minutes, desperately wanting one but being unable to justify the price. Eight dollars. Eight dollars! I'd sat in the car back in Charleston while Ginger & Krystal toured some historic building, saving myself $8. I was trying so hard to be good with my limited amount of money, but sometimes it just sucked. The caramel apple was covered with chocolate and nuts and could easily have been a meal, but I turned and walked away. Stupid budget.

If I ever win the lottery, I thought to myself as I sadly trudged away, *I am coming back to Savannah and buying that stupid $8 apple.*

We did have a bit of trouble in our otherwise blissful five days: Ginger's wallet disappeared. She didn't know if it had fallen out or if she'd accidentally left it somewhere or if some petty thief had gently snagged it out of her purse as we wandered about. We called every place we'd seen, revisited several of them to look for ourselves, and finally ended up at the police station to file a report. She couldn't get past TSA checkpoints at the airport without some sort of official paperwork. It got me worrying about what would happen if I lost my purse. I kept everything in there. Since I feared someone might break into my car, I kept my GPS, my iPod, and my cell phone with me wherever I went. I'd be in bad shape if I lost all that with thirty-nine states to go. Plus my driver's license? Cash? Credit card? Library card? I became even more OCD about keeping all my valuables together.

As we wandered around Savannah the day before I took them back to the airport, I thought, *This isn't so bad. I mean, sure I'd like to have a husband and kids, but having single girlfriends to vacation with is pretty great, too.* But then a couple crossed the street at the same time we did, and the baby in the stroller they were pushing was in that cute "I just discovered my feet" stage. My heart melted as I watched him grab his little socked foot and try to get it into his mouth. I wanted that.

On our way to the airport, I said maybe I'd name a daughter Savannah someday because I'd loved it. That made Krystal think of the movie *Savannah Smiles*, which we both remembered from our childhood. I told them that even though the bums in that movie, Boots & Alvie, were completely harmless and nothing but good to the little girl, I'd had a recurring nightmare as a child that they were trying to kidnap me. Instead of running away, though, I'd been frozen in place and unable to move. They'd get closer and closer, and I'd just stand there, paralyzed . . . and then I'd wake up. I also had a recurring nightmare about Jaws having the ability to come up out of the water and onto shore. I'd run from door to door of the waterfront motel, begging people to let me in, but no one would.

From the backseat, Ginger piped up about a scary childhood dream she'd had.

"I dreamed about Freddy Krueger. He was killing everyone, but I realized he was probably just lonely, so I stopped running from him, turned around, and asked him, 'Are you sad that you have no friends?' And he said, 'Yes, I have no one to do anything with, so I kill people because I'm sad.' So we went to the mall and got manicures and he stopped killing people."

She's pretty much the nicest person in the world.

#12 – SOUTH CAROLINA

I've heard the same complaint over and over from single women: all the good ones are taken. I had even declared it myself a time or two (or two hundred), but I was beginning to realize that wasn't the case at all. There were still a lot of good guys out there; unfortunately, I just couldn't seem to meet one who had the right combination of qualities *I* was looking for. Mr. South Carolina was a great example of one of the "good ones" who had to be right for someone. I really did need to fire up my matchmaking service.

I met Mr. South Carolina at Frankie's Fun Park in Columbia. A week before, I'd emailed them about my little adventure and they'd agreed to give us a free night of fun; when we got there, they handed us a card loaded with *a hundred dollars* of free play! That meant we'd get to try every attraction at least once, so off we went. We started out at the batting cages. He went first. I was a little intimidated, watching him nail hit after hit; I hadn't swung a bat in years. I did pretty well, though. I only completely whiffed on a couple of pitches, and I had some pretty good hits, considering how rusty I was.

Next we headed over to the super-fast race track. The signs posted said you had to be 16 and have a driver's license to race these carts, so I maybe should have taken that as a cue to be a little more careful. I spun out on the first curve. Luckily we were the only two on the race course and he was able to dodge my wreckage. He beat me (dang it!) but I was having a lot of fun because (and I think I may have told you this already, but . . .) I'm slightly competitive. Okay, fine, I am *really* competitive. Competing in just about anything is my idea of a good time, so this date was right up my alley, even if I didn't win. I did better on the regular go-carts, but he still beat me.

There was a giant arcade inside and that's where I broke even. We played a trivia game, and since I seem to have endless brain space available for useless knowledge, I beat the pants off him.

"How did you know that?" he asked after I successfully answered one completely random question.

"Cause I'm brilliant," I said dryly.

"Modest, too," he said. Yep, that's me.

He beat me in basketball and laser tag; I beat him in mini-golf and guitar hero. We both stunk at Dance Dance Revolution, but overall we had a fabulously fun night. It was the kind of date I'd always thought would be a blast but, like most people, had never planned since I tended to fall into the dinner-and-a-movie rut. I'm sure racing go-carts and swinging baseball bats isn't everyone's cup of tea, but it was a lot more fun than sipping coffee and looking at each other uncomfortably during awkward silences. We had plenty of time to talk while we waited in lines or wandered around the mini golf course, so it was a good way to get to know each other, too. Solid date. Now I just needed to work on that matchmaking service idea.

I had flawless skin growing up. In college, one of my friends told me she was envious of it, which made me amazingly happy since I'd always bemoaned my pasty whiteness.

"It's like porcelain," she'd said. Aw. Thank you, new best friend!

In my thirties, though, my face decided to go crazy. I started having horrible breakouts around my mouth. I frequently washed my pillowcase in scalding hot water. I kept my hands off my face. I cut back on junk food. I spent more money than I cared to remember trying every different acne product on the market. Nothing seemed to help, so I was dating my way around the country with fresh zits popping up at least once a week. Despite the fact that I was on an extremely limited budget, I made an appointment for a facial before I left Columbia. I was obviously desperate; $80 buys a lot of gas.

The girl who did my facial was super sweet, but I'm thinking I should have asked to see her license. She was horrible. I'd only had one other facial in my whole life, but the experiences were vastly different. My friend Wendy gave me a free facial when she was just getting started in her new career. She worked in a posh salon with hot towels and soft music. The place I went to in Columbia left me with goosebumps and frozen toes.

The new girl washed my face twice and then brushed something onto my skin. "This may sting a little," she said. A little? I gritted my teeth and wished I'd had a baby so I knew that Lamaze breathing stuff. Whew.

"Do you have . . . a magazine?" I panted through gritted teeth. "If I . . . could just . . . fan . . . my face . . . a little . . ." I was having trouble speaking. It hurt. Holy crap, did it hurt.

"Oooh, it's not supposed to sting that much," she said worriedly and started wiping it off. Good Lord. Sweet mercy. Ow, ow, ow.

"Are you familiar with extractions?" she asked. My friend Wendy had used a little tool to push out blackheads, so I said yes, expecting the same treatment. This woman pulled on some rubber gloves and *popped my three zits*. I couldn't believe it. I'd paid eighty dollars to have someone wash my face twice and then pop three zits? I could have done that myself for free! Oh, but how could I forget the added bonus of that severe acid burn? Couldn't have done that by myself at home!

When I slid behind the wheel of my car afterward, I pulled down the visor and looked in the little mirror. My face looked awful. I'd thought it was bad before with three big zits, but now it was worse. Much worse. My forehead was especially burned. That was where she'd started, so I guessed it had been burned the worst, having had the acid stuff on it the longest. There was another spot under my eye that was really bad; it kind of looked like I'd been punched. I couldn't tell if it was a burn from the acid stuff or a bruise from where she'd used my eye socket as leverage while popping one of the zits. And, of course, there were the three bloody scabs where she'd popped the pimples. Yikes. I prayed the whole mess would clear up before my next date.

#13 – NORTH CAROLINA

I was lucky enough to find another great place to couch surf, this time in a beautiful home on Emerald Isle, North Carolina. Ken and Sue had retired from jobs in upstate New York, relocated to the Carolina coastline, and were now living it up, post-kids and post-careers. They told me about all their social activities and volunteer work and new hobbies. Retirement sounded fabulous.

They'd invited some friends over for dinner and celebrated "Earth Hour" by flipping every switch to "off" and eating by candlelight. Fresh off that facial, I'd never been so happy to sit in the dark. My face was an embarrassing mess. I'm sure they wondered if I'd spent too much time out in the sun, but I didn't explain – anyone who spends $80 on a facial could have afforded a hotel, right?

Their dinner guests had only been retired for a year, and while Don was loving it, Kathy was having a harder time adjusting. The four of them talked a lot about reinventing yourself after retiring, and how everyone they knew there had done it. One guy, for example, had been a doctor in his pre-retirement life; now he was a fishing instructor and loving it. Sue talked about volunteering her time to guard sea turtle nests before they hatched, then helping the little creatures get to the ocean. Kathy and Sue both volunteered at an agency that helped low-income families pay their bills. They all seemed to have more to do than they had time for, and they all seemed very, very happy.

I kind of felt like a faker. There I was, without a job and

enjoying a retirement-like phase of my own. But had I earned it? These four had all worked hard for forty years to get to this place in life, and I had worked only twelve years before taking a little hiatus from the working world. It made me feel I was enjoying something I maybe didn't deserve quite yet.

The next day Ken and Sue drove me around to show me the beach side of the island. We had fun watching their lab play in the surf. When we got back to the car, though, I almost lost it. I'd heard the term "wet dog" before, but I guess I'd never experienced it for myself. When the dog and I climbed into the backseat, I could only think of five words: *Wet dog! Sensitive gag reflex!*

"Wow, it's warming up, huh?" I said, breathing through my mouth and hoping I was faking them out. I rolled down the window and stuck my nose in the fresh stream of air.

When we drove around to the other side of the island, I found a place where I'd love to live someday – the sound side of Emerald Isle. The water was calm, not crashing on the shore like the ocean on the other side, just a mile away. People had long docks going out into the water, and I pictured myself sailing a little Sunfish or kayaking across the sound. I tried not to think about how many banks I'd have to rob before I could afford to buy one of those houses.

After saying good-bye, I made my way up the island to Cedar Point. Cherry Cherry and I were about to experience a new adventure: car ferries! I drove her onto the boat and away we went to Ocracoke Island. I'd be camping again that night, out there at the National Park Service campground. People had told me I wouldn't need reservations that time of year, so I wasn't too worried about it being full. And it wasn't. In fact, there wasn't a single person there. I instead found a lovely surprise: the campground would open for the season in *five days*.

Crap. Crap, crap, crap, crap, CRAAAAAAAAAAP!!

I started looking through the pamphlets I'd picked up at the North Carolina Visitor's Center when I'd crossed the state line a day earlier. I called some campgrounds and couldn't believe the crazy prices they were charging.

"To sleep on the ground?" I rudely asked one lady when she quoted the nightly charge as $45. I was incredulous. And mad. I feared this whole "flying by the seat of my pants" thing might have a downside I hadn't anticipated. I ended up booking a campsite in Rodanthe, which meant I didn't get much time to explore Ocracoke. I drove onto the next ferry, heading to Hatteras, with just minutes to spare.

When I was in high school, I was, for some reason, drawn to lighthouses. Maybe the thought of living beside the sea was romantic to me as a land-locked Iowan. I had folders and calendars, pencils and binders, all of lighthouses. A friend had even drawn me a picture of a lighthouse that I still possessed. I dreamed of living beside a lighthouse, or at least visiting one. So when I came around a curve and saw the Cape Hatteras light, I got tears in my eyes. I know it might sound crazy, but here was the lighthouse I'd seen in pictures for twenty years, and in my mind, it somehow made sense that if I was finally seeing this lighthouse, there still existed the possibility of meeting a good man yet, too. I walked around it, seeing it from different angles, trying not to scare off the deer that were quietly grazing nearby. It was the perfect place to spend the twilight hour.

I got to my campsite well after dark. I put up my new tent for the third time and gave myself a pat on the back for how quickly I snapped it into shape. I unloaded what I'd need for the night and went to sleep. I woke up terrified a few times in the night, thinking my tent might blow away with me in it. I'd never slept near the ocean before and had no idea how windy it was.

I shot up in my mummy bag when the beep-beep-beep of a garbage truck backing up woke me the next morning. Why didn't this stupid tent have windows? I hoped it wasn't as close as it sounded, because it sounded like it was about to run over my tent. The next sound I registered made me groan: raindrops. Ugh. So far on this trip, I'd camped three nights. Each night I had camped, it had rained. I'd paid a lot of money for a very good tent, so I wasn't having any problem staying dry. The problem was taking it down: a) I got soaked, taking down the tent in the rain; b) the rain was cold, which meant that even though it was fast to take down, my fingers were still numb by the time I finished; and c) you can't put away a tent when it's wet, so that meant I had to find a place to string it up to dry. Why did it have to rain every stinking time I camped?

I wriggled into my clothes, crawled out of the tent, and made a dash for the bathroom. Then I sat in my car and stalled for hours –

reading, eating breakfast, using the free Wi-Fi – before I finally accepted the reality that the rain was never going to stop. I ripped the tent down as quickly as I could, but even after just five minutes, I was soaked. My rain jacket had kept my upper half fairly dry, but my khaki pants hadn't fared nearly as well.

 I decided that since I was going to have to change my pants anyway, I might as well go out in the rain to see the main draw of the Outer Banks. I climbed the wooden stairs to a rickety bridge over the dunes and stood staring out at the ocean. It was pounding mercilessly onto the beach. I started walking, staring out at the waves. It looked like there was a wall about twenty feet out, it was churning so high. For those who have grown up along the ocean, maybe that's common, but for someone who's lived her whole life in land-locked states, it's freaky. I thought about picking up some shells but feared a rogue wave snatching my feet out from under me and pulling me out into that sure, swift death. There wasn't a soul on the beach, so I'd have to save myself; I'm not a strong swimmer, so I knew my chances weren't good. I stayed a safe distance from the water.

 I saw nice houses further down the beach and headed that direction. My completely saturated pants clung to my legs; it felt like I'd waded into the sea fully clothed. After half a mile or so I turned around and headed back. I giggled as I walked, thinking it was probably a good thing no one was there to see me. You know that Coldplay video for *Yellow*, where Chris Martin is walking along the beach, just getting soaked? That's pretty much what was happening for me. I was a mess, but I didn't mind.

 I returned to my car, changed into dry pants, and headed out. The roads were flooded in places, and I was honestly a little freaked out. Poor Cherry Cherry. What does that much water do to a car? I pulled over once to look at another lighthouse, then continued on to civilization.

 I decided to get out of the rain and cold by hiding out at the local library. I'd been sitting there working on my laptop for about half an hour when I noticed a lady staring at me. She soon came over and took the seat next to mine.

 "I was in an abusive marriage for twenty-two years," she whispered.

 I stared blankly at her. How do you respond to that? And why was she telling me?

"I'm . . . so sorry," I said. She looked back at me intently.

"I can help you get out."

"Um . . . I think you're confusing me with someone else," I tried, baffled.

"I see the signs," she continued. "You're wearing long sleeves and a hat. Trying to cover bruises, aren't you? Maybe some cigarette burns? Bumps on your head? And your eye . . . looks like it's healing, but it must have been pretty bad."

Oh, no. It slowly dawned on me and my mouth dropped open. That stupid facial!

"Actually," I started, shaking my head, "it's cold outside, so I'm wearing long sleeves, and since I camped last night, my hair is a mess and I'm covering it with my hat, and my eye – "

"Don't make excuses," she cut me off. "You'll end up dead. I almost did. Is he here with you? Is that it?" She looked around the library. A few people were looking at us, probably because her whispering was getting more hiss-like the more agitated she got.

"Is that him?" she jerked her head at a man standing a few feet away. I pictured the poor man getting accosted by her.

"I've never seen him before. I'm here alone," I urgently whispered back, growing a little panicked. "And I'm not in an abusive relationship! I just got a really bad facial!"

She leaned away and looked hard at my face. "Honey, no one leaves a facial looking like that. Take this card and call the number when you're ready to get away from him. We'll get you out."

As she walked away, I collected my things and hustled out to my car. I guess two days isn't long enough to avoid people after some idiot burns part of your face off.

I couch surfed the next two nights with a guy named Alan (yeah, yeah, I broke my own rule about couch surfing with men, but he was the only decent-looking person with strong references who lived on the Outer Banks and I was cold . . . and I needed a place to dry out my tent). The second night there, he suggested we go out to a local bar for Dollar Taco Night. I love a screamin' deal (and my face was looking better, the scab under my eye having fallen off), so we went. The place was packed, but he knew a couple of guys sitting at a table in the corner. We went and joined them, saving us a who-knows-how-long wait for a table. It turned out that both guys worked at a local radio station, and as we talked, my trip came up. They suggested I come in the next day for a live interview.

"Your website says you're a Christian," Matt asked on the air. "How far do these dates go, physically?"

"Not very far."

"Can you elaborate?" he urged.

"Well, I've kissed one guy so far out of the twelve dates I've been on," I replied, "so not very far."

They seemed disappointed. Why did it seem like half the people who heard about this project were hoping for more smut?

After the interview, I headed inland. I had a date in Raleigh the next night. I was hoping for a good connection with Mr. North Carolina because I was growing a little discouraged. Yes, I was getting to see the country and I knew I should be content with that, but I'd gotten my hopes up that maybe the man of my dreams was out there somewhere, just waiting for me to show up. I heard the old Indigo Girls song "Love Will Come To You" and almost cried. I'd loved that song when I'd first heard it, but here I was, fifteen years later, still waiting for love to come to me.

A car drove by with personalized plates that said, "BE GLAD," and I reminded myself of all I had seen and done that I would have missed if I'd gotten married young. I was on an adventure, and life in general had been pretty fabulous up to that point. I needed to be glad. Then an old man tried to change lanes without checking his mirrors. I swerved into the turn lane to avoid a collision and laid on the horn. There went my temporary gladness.

They say opposites attract, but Mr. North Carolina was pretty much the male version of me and we had a blast! I was told to meet him at the church where he worked, but I didn't get much information beyond that. Jana, who'd let me stay with her in Little Rock, had come through for me again. She'd recruited her parents in North Carolina to help me find a date there, and they set me up with a guy from their church, so I was comfortable not knowing the exact details of what was going to happen. It was actually really fun to be surprised since that was the opposite of most of my dates. I might be a *little bit* of a control freak, I admit, but it was mostly a safety issue. I couldn't just hop into a car with a random stranger; I had to tell my Chief Safety Officer where to look for me should I go missing. But since Mr. North Carolina was the youth worker at a friend's parents' church, I figured he was safe. He would never have been hired to work with teenagers if he hadn't passed a background check, right?

We met mid-afternoon and headed to downtown Raleigh. The first surprise? A rickshaw ride! A little two-seated covered cart was hooked up behind a bicycle. The driver, Donald, handed me a long-stemmed red rose, filled our champagne glasses with Sprite, and turned on the romantic music. Mr. North Carolina & I clinked glasses and off we went.

We pedaled around the downtown area, checking out the historical sights. We saw the first skyscraper in Raleigh (a whopping four stories!), the governor's mansion, and the Capitol building. And statues. Lots and lots of statues. I guess there are a lot of famous North Carolinians. (Carolinans? Carolinians? We debated.) Looking at one statue, I said, "Is this the bronze version of the eternal flame?"

Mr. North Carolina instantly started singing "Eternal Flame." Jackpot! I'd found a "randomly-bursts-into-song" kindred spirit! I complimented him on his Bangles cover as we toodled along.

At one point we drove right between two big museums where a massive amount of elementary school children were obviously enjoying a field trip. Cue the open-mouthed stares!

"Who is that?" I heard one kid ask another.

"They probably think I'm Jackie Chan," Mr. North Carolina said. Kids pointed and waved. It felt a little weird, but then I thought *why not?* and waved back. Some of the chaperone moms awwwed at us. I bet they wished they'd get taken out for a rickshaw ride with someone who'd give them a long-stemmed red rose and some champagne. Well, Sprite . . . but seriously, who drinks champagne at three in the afternoon on a Thursday?

We had a memorable time being peddled around the downtown area, and Donald was a fun tour guide. We went back to the church for the Maundy Thursday service, then headed back out for dinner afterward. We ate at this cool little place Mr. North Carolina was a fan of. It was in a converted warehouse and specialized in Asian cuisine. He ordered for us – heat seeker shrimp, dumplings, scallion pancakes, and crispy green beans – and not only did I try everything, but I did it all with chopsticks! That's right, the farm girl learned how to eat without a fork. Yay, Mr. North Carolina for making the date both fun and educational!

"You know how you got 'Eternal Flame' stuck in your head earlier?" I asked. When he nodded, I continued. "Well, during the sermon, the pastor was talking about the final this and the final that during Jesus' last week, and all I could think was, doodaloodoo, doodaloodootdoo, doodaloodoo, doodaloodootdootdootdoo . . ."

"Yes!" he declared, then joined me in singing, "The Final Countdown!" Finally! A man who totally appreciated my dorkiness and unending knowledge of random song lyrics!

"Hey, do you know what was the best show ever?" he asked.

"Arrested Development," I shot back. We silently high fived over the table. ("The Final Countdown" was one character's theme song for his magic show. If you've never seen it, you won't get it. Just know we were basically sharing a brain at this point in the date and it was awesome.)

I waddled out of the restaurant, absolutely stuffed. We drove down the street, picked up vanilla shakes and apple turnovers, then drove to a really tall building. Two of his friends were waiting in the parking garage to let us into the building, and for a moment I feared Mr. North Carolina was going to make me base jump off of or rappel down this building as some kind of grand finale . . . but nope – we just enjoyed the view. We ate our tasty apple turnovers (I know, I know, I said I was stuffed, but there's always room for dessert, right? And yes, my thighs *were* beginning to hate me, thanks for asking.) while he pointed out different things from our eagle-eye view.

On the way back to the church, where I'd left my car, we talked a lot about youth ministry, something we obviously had in common. It made me miss the students I'd worked with and loved back in Colorado, and I hoped I hadn't made a huge mistake by leaving them. I admired Mr. North Carolina for being passionate about his work. I'd met so many people who worked just to pay the bills rather than doing something they loved or that they felt made a difference in the world. He was doing both. I had been doing both, but now I was driving around the country, dating. I wondered how that was serving the world.

#14 – VIRGINIA

I'd been looking forward to Virginia for a long time. It had been one of my top destinations originally, before this whole fifty-date thing took over the itinerary, and I couldn't wait to see my friends Andrew and Sheri. They'd left Colorado four and a half years earlier, and after a bit of bouncing around, they'd recently landed on a farm in southwestern Virginia. I planned to stay for nearly two weeks, catching up with them, bonding with their boys, and enjoying two weeks off from dating.

I never expected a traffic jam in rural Virginia, but there I was in stop-and-go traffic on the interstate. I passed a sign that said, "Speed limit enforced by aircraft." That seemed like a waste of taxpayer dollars when I wasn't going more than thirty. I was bored, sitting there stuck in traffic, so I fiddled around with my GPS to see if I could switch up the voice. I chose the Australian option, picturing Hugh Jackman sitting in my passenger seat as my new travel companion. He would certainly spice up the long days on the road. Unfortunately, the Australian voice sounded nothing like Hugh Jackman and was a whole lot more annoying than the American version. The way he said "recalculating" in a completely condescending tone made me feel like I was the dumbest driver out there. I did not need a critical co-pilot; I switched to the British voice.

Once I made it to the farm, I breathed a sigh of relief, knowing I could relax for a while. Bouncing from house to house every night or two had left me feeling rather discombobulated. I'd traveled quite a bit in the past, but I always had a home to go home to. Out on the road with no end in sight, and with my actual house sold and being lived in by someone else, I didn't have the option of going home. It was strange. My friends, though, made me feel right at home. I played with the boys during the day and slept comfortably in my little basement guest room at night.

The boys were a hoot. Micah had been a baby when they'd moved away, and although I'd seen him a few times over the years when they'd visited me or I'd visited them, at five he was outgoing and adorable. One day, as we drove into town, he sweetly invited me to go with him to Walmart.

"What's Walmart?" I asked, playing dumb. "What do they have there?"

"Oh, fishing poles and guns and stuff," he said. I laughed.

"He may have been born in Colorado, but he's a Virginia boy now, huh?" I asked Sheri.

I loved hanging out with them, hiking and reading stories and playing Superman (using a clothespin to secure a towel around our necks, turning on the REM song of the same name, then "flying" around the house). We made cookies and blew bubbles and kicked soccer balls and had a grand old time. It was nice, not worrying about dating or finding dates or blogging about dates. I hated to complain, knowing many single women would have happily lined up to take my place, but being so completely focused on dating had gotten a little sickening.

I tried to be as helpful as I could while I was there, not wanting to just mooch off their generosity. One day Andrew and one of his friends needed to be dropped off along the river for a three-day canoe trip, so I drove them over. He recommended a scenic hiking spot on the way back to the house, so I stopped in for a solo hike. The peace and quiet was a refreshing change after hanging out with two energetic little boys, but I couldn't seem to shake the morbid thoughts that came with hiking alone.

I wonder if I'm still on the trail.

I really hope this is the trail.

I haven't seen anyone for an hour. If I break an ankle, I'm going to have to find a stick to use as a crutch and hobble myself out of here.

Do I have cell coverage out here? (Pull out the cell phone and check.)

Nope.

If I hobble myself out of here with a broken ankle, that should be an automatic ticket to be on Survivor. *No application process or tryout for me. I'd be one tough chick.*

I wonder if there are bears here? (Start clapping to scare off bears.)

I haven't seen anyone for a long time. No one would hear me scream.

Maybe bears are still hibernating. No, it's spring. They'll be awake and looking for food.

Oh my gosh, I slathered myself in coconut-scented sunscreen! They are soooo going to eat me!

(Clap. Clap. Clap. Frantic clap-clap-clap-clap.)

Well, they say that if you meet a bear, you should lay your pack at their feet and let them eat whatever you've got in there.

Oh, let's get real — what bear is going to work his way through a backpack and a cellophane wrapper to get that measly little granola bar when I am big and juicy-looking and smell like coconuts?

Hey wait, coconuts aren't native to Virginia. Bears wouldn't be attracted to that scent.

But bears are probably more adventurous eaters than I am. They'd probably be willing to give coconut-scented hiker girl a try.

Whoo, just rolled an ankle and it didn't even hurt. You rock, ankle. Way to be strong. I wonder if it's all the milk I drink? No, that's for strong bones and teeth. What gives you strong ankle muscles? I should have paid attention in high school science class instead of writing and rewriting the names of my six future children. Christopher, Catherine, Cami, Cory . . . crap, I've forgotten the other two. What kind of mother am I? I can't remember the names of my phantom children!

Oh, like it matters at this point. I can't even find a father for my children.

A husband would be convenient right now. We could be hiking together. That would be fun. And he could scare off bears for me. (Clap, clap, clap.)

Actually I kind of like being alone. It's nice to have quiet time to think.

But man, if I hiked the entire Appalachian Trail alone, I would be certifiably insane by the end of those five or six months.

I need some chapstick. (Pull out and apply chapstick.)

Oh no! My chapstick is peppermint scented! Do bears like peppermint? If a bear bites my lips off, will I still be able to scream? Maybe I should put some on my ears, too, so he'll bite them off and I won't have to hear myself scream . . .

I have to pee. I haven't seen anyone in three hours now, but wouldn't it just beat all if about the time I pull down my pants, someone wandered right past my chosen tree 100 feet off the trail . . .

Please, please, please don't let any ticks have jumped up on me while I was squatting in the bushes. I seriously only had my pants down for thirty seconds, tops. I do not want a tick in that area.

Hey, look! Wild ponies!

After a week of not thinking about it, I had to get back to the business of finding dates in the nearby states. I didn't know anyone in Kentucky or West Virginia, so I had to do some internet shopping.

I would never claim to be a dating expert, but I did feel compelled to write emails to some of the guys in those states to give them some internet dating profile tips. They needed help. Shopping around for dates in Kentucky and West Virginia, I would have sent the following messages to five men in particular:

1. You love your dog. I get that. But ten pictures of your dog and only one of you? Are you trying to find a date for yourself or for your dog?

2. Yes, women want honesty in a relationship, but the statement "Just looking for someone for no-strings-attached sex" probably isn't what women join an internet dating service hoping to find. Try a virtual chat room instead, dude.

3. Your abs rock. I get that. And I appreciate that you probably do three hundred sit-ups a day to keep them looking like that. Awesome. But during our date, I'm not going to be having a conversation with your abs. Unless you're in the Witness Protection Program, put a picture of your face on your page.

4. A shot of your tractor as your profile picture? For real?

5. When taking photos, try to remember that you're not in a frat anymore. Holding an object to make it look like it's coming out of your fly? Juvenile. Grow up. (Ditto for pretending to violate an animal statue. Seriously? *Seriously?* There is not a woman in this world who finds that funny.)

West Virginia and Kentucky were killing me.

You know what stinks about having a really, really great time on a first date? The day after. The waiting and wondering. Will he call? Text? Email? Did he have as great a time as I did, or was he happy when the night was finally over? I had misread Mr. Florida. I'd thought we'd connected well, but despite my flirtatious texts afterward and flat out asking to see him again, he'd said he had to get up early for work, the modern-day equivalent of "I have to wash my hair."

Mr. Virginia had been hard to find. For weeks I'd looked forward to arriving at Andrew & Sheri's house, but I hadn't planned anything beyond getting there and crashing after nearly two months on the road. As my time hiding out in their basement dwindled, I realized I couldn't put my dating project on hold forever. I had to find a Mr. Virginia.

While dropping them off for their canoe trip, Andrew asked Patrick if he knew any single guys who'd be willing to go out with me. I winced at how pathetic that sounded, but the offers weren't exactly pouring in and beggars can't be choosers. Patrick texted one of his old buddies, saying he was smart and could do more push ups than the average construction worker (this comment was made as we drove by a large gathering of construction workers, two of whom appeared to be having a push-up contest along the side of the road).

As I drove away, leaving them there with the canoe, he hadn't heard anything back.

When they came home three days later, he said it sounded like it was probably going to happen. Not for sure, but maybe.

Later that night, I got a text saying this was definitely going to happen. Their friend would be calling me soon.

Eighteen hours later (but who's counting?) I got the call as I was hiking solo again, this time through a more populated (and thus less likely to make me think a bear was going to eat me) place called Hungry Mother State Park. I found a place to sit down and talk (I thought huffing and puffing through the phone might not be attractive), and we talked and talked and talked. And then he asked if I was free that night.

Have you ever read *The Rules*? Me neither. I know the basic theme of the book, though: don't make things too easy for guys. Make them pursue you. Only answer one of every four emails and don't say yes to a date unless he asks you out three days in advance.

But playing hard to get? I definitely did not have time for that. And considering the fact that I was not a big fan of talking on the phone and this guy had kept me talking for forty-five minutes while I sat around, hot and sticky and swatting at bugs three miles into a six-mile hike, seemed to me a good sign that this could be a good night. Screw *The Rules*.

I had to drive an hour and a half to get to where he was, and we started out by walking around the campus where he and Sheri and Patrick had all gone to college together. He was much the same in person as he had been on the phone, laid back and easy to laugh. Oh, and he looked good. Really good. I was, of course, wearing a t-shirt, jeans, and flip flops. I began wishing a fashion consultant would take pity on me and give me a makeover.

We drove to a restaurant and ate and talked and talked and talked and talked. About an hour in, I realized my face hurt from smiling and laughing. I couldn't stop. The next day, when I checked in with my CSO, she asked me what had been so funny and I couldn't even say. It wasn't like he was telling jokes, but everything we talked about seemed to make us laugh. Maybe it was the drink I'd ordered that tasted like blue Kool-Aid. I didn't really know.

We talked a lot about dating and relationships and our hits and misses in love. He poo-pooed the theory that a woman can grow more attracted to a man if he's really funny or a great conversationalist or whatever; for men, he said, a woman is either attractive or she's not. She could be the funniest or the smartest or the kindest woman in the world, but if he's not attracted to her from the start, he's never going to magically become more attracted to her. He had a theory of his own about the difference between men and women: men marry hoping the woman will never change, while women marry hoping they'll be able to change the man. I laughed and admitted there *might* be some truth to that.

"So what is it you're hoping to find, going on a date in every state?" he asked.

"Well, really there are just three basic things I'm looking for in a guy; I want to find a man who is smart, funny, and Christian."

"That doesn't seem like it would be that hard."

"You'd be surprised . . ."

"Are you sure there's not more to your list than just three things?"

"I don't know," I mused. "Maybe. I mean, I guess there must

be, because despite meeting and even being good friends over the years with several different guys who met my basic three criteria, I wasn't attracted to them for one reason or another."

"There's that indefinable thing," he said.

"Yep," I agreed, smiling at him and thinking, *You have that indefinable thing!* I didn't tell him that, of course. I'd hate to scare a guy off before he had a chance to fall in love with me.

We swapped stories of bad set-ups we'd endured over the years. I told him about the guy from Alaska who'd asked me to move there with him after one date, the Baptist minister who made me feel like I was in a counseling session instead of on a date, and the guy who'd walked into our date carrying a studly-looking motorcycle helmet . . . because he'd been knocked off his scooter twice already and had decided he'd better invest in some extra-protective headwear. Mr. Virginia's worst blind date was a double date with a friend. From the very beginning, he wasn't interested in the girl at all, which made things rather awkward the entire time. While the women were in the bathroom at the end of the night, his friend (who recognized his lack of attraction but his girlfriend's friend's definite interest) warned him that the women would probably suggest getting together again. He recommended having an excuse ready.

"We should do this again," one of the women said when they returned to the table.

"I can't; I have to go to a wedding," he quickly replied.

"Oh . . . well . . . we were thinking maybe Wednesday night."

"Um . . . yeah," he stammered. "That's when the wedding is."

"On a Wednesday?"

"Yeah . . ." he stalled, racking his brain for something. Anything. "My family's weird."

Note to self: for credibility, make sure you hear what day they want to go out again before giving your made-up excuse.

I thought about that later, wondering why honesty, supposedly the best policy, is so hard. I'd much rather have a guy tell me he's not interested in me than sit around waiting and wondering if he's going to call. And yet, when the tables are turned and I'm not interested in the guy, I have a horrible time just telling him that. I say it's because I hate to hurt anyone's feelings, and while that may be true, it's also true that I'm a chicken.

Mr. Virginia asked about my previous thirteen dates, and after hearing about the Cessna in Louisiana and the gondola in Texas and the rickshaw in North Carolina, he laughed about blowing it and making Virginia look bad. I disagreed and assured him he was representing Virginia very well.

We drove up a mountain that my friends had laughed about when I'd told them earlier that this was part of his plan for the night. "That's totally a make out spot!" Andrew and Sheri had laughed. As we wound our way up the hill, I debated. Should I kiss him? I definitely could. I was very attracted to him. But I had kissed Mr. Florida and that had turned out rather disastrously. Maybe it would be better to not kiss this guy. I could avoid the inevitable emotional roller coaster that came with kissing someone if I chose not to get on that metaphorical roller coaster in the first place. It turned out I didn't have to make the decision, though; when we got to the top, the gate was locked. We drove back down.

"This date is horrible compared to flying in a Cessna," he muttered. I assured him it wasn't a competition and I was having a fabulous time.

We headed to a little coffee shop he knew of and ordered hot chocolates and a piece of white chocolate raspberry cheesecake to share.

"We're closing!" the girl behind the counter yelled, three bites in. We couldn't catch a break. We shoveled down the cheesecake and headed back out onto the street. We wandered around the downtown area, talking, laughing, and making fun of scantily clad college co-eds. We popped into a bar and fed quarters into a trivia game, but it didn't work. Mr. Virginia just shook his head. Nothing was going right.

A girl caught my eye as we left the bar. She was crossing the street with her dog on a leash, and among the many young women out that night, this girl really stood out, despite her lack of make-up or poofy hair or skimpy clothes. I honestly thought she could be a model. And then she walked past us and I noticed the giant backpack she was carrying. She walked half a block down the street and started unpacking and laying out two blankets in an alcove in front of a store. She was homeless.

We walked past her, going back to Mr. Virginia's car. It was sobering. I wanted to turn around and go back and talk to her . . . ask her if she was okay or if she needed anything. Maybe it was because I was traveling alone myself. Maybe it was my years of working with teenagers. I wasn't sure what caused it, but my heart was aching to get her off that street. I wondered again what I was doing, driving around the country without a care in the world while people like her slept on the street. What kind of person was I?

I couldn't believe it when we got into his car and the clock read 1:30AM. It was way past my bedtime. As he drove me back to my car, we were quieter than we had been earlier in the evening. I suppose we were both tired, but the laughter was softer and the conversation had long pauses. The comfortable kind. I started thinking about how nice it must be for married people to lie in bed at the end of the day, mixing those long, comfortable pauses with quiet words that are harder to say in the light . . . worries, fears, and secret hopes for the future.

Why does the female mind jump instantly to marriage? Maybe it's not the female mind; maybe it's just my mind. I'm pretty sure that after a first date, guys are usually thinking, *Do I want to go out with her again?* I've already moved on to, *Would he make a good husband?*

He walked me to my car; I hugged him and said I'd had a great time. I drove to Andrew's parents house, where I would be spending the night, and snuck quietly in the door and up the stairs like a naughty teenager who'd missed curfew. When my alarm went off the next morning, my first thought was, *I am soooo gonna need a nap today.*

Andrew, Sheri, and the boys arrived in time for lunch, and when they asked how the date had gone the night before, I said Mr. Virginia was one of my favorites so far.

"Yeah, we don't know for sure what time she got home, but it had to be pretty late," Andrew's dad chimed in. "She came down alone to go to church with us this morning, but we don't know if anyone snuck out after we drove away."

My mouth dropped open at Richard's comment. I wasn't used to being teased by a sixty-something-year-old man. I'm pretty sure I turned ten shades of red.

When the boys were out riding the ATV and we women were alone in the house, Mary Ann said, "Don't tell Richard I told you, but he was like a mother hen last night, waiting for you to get home."

"Oh, no," I said, hating that I had worried them.

"We waited up a little while, hoping to hear how it went, but then we went to sleep," she said. "Richard woke up around 1:30 and then woke me up and said, 'All the lights are still on. Go upstairs and see if she's here. Do you think she's okay? Should we call someone?' I told him you were a grown up and to go back to sleep."

"And he acted so nonchalant when we asked him when she got in!" Sheri said. "He was like, 'Oh, I don't know . . . long after we went to bed.' That's so sweet; he only had sons and not daughters to worry about!"

Sheri urged Mary Ann to tell me their love story, and my mouth fell open again as I listened. Richard and Mary Ann had met when she was visiting Virginia from Florida. They wrote letters back and forth to each other; he went to visit her once and she came back to visit him once. They got engaged, then married. This happened over the course of *three months.*

"Wow," I said, not able to think of a better response. Who does that? I started thinking about Mr. Virginia and what a great time we'd had. Maybe we could write each other.

So did he call? Text? Email?

Nope.

I was so disappointed, even if I was slated for thirty-six more dates around the country.

Sheri said that was intimidating. What guy would want to deal with some girl who was about to date thirty-six more men?

I said maybe he had to go to a wedding.

I got my hair cut before leaving Virginia. I considered just letting it grow because that stupid facial back in South Carolina had cost me an arm and a leg and left my budget in shambles. Sheri said her hairdresser, Amanda, charged only $15 for a haircut, though, and I wasn't sure when I'd get an offer like that again. And really, that bad haircut I'd gotten before leaving Colorado had been growing out for two months now and was very much in need of help. I booked an appointment.

Amanda cut hair while teaching cosmetology to high schoolers at a VoTech school. She had one student in particular who made me laugh, the only boy in the room. He didn't do a thing while I was in the chair but walk around, talking to people with a flamboyant twang and avoiding work. He put on a long blonde wig and totally pulled it off. I caught what was obviously the tail-end of a conversation when I heard him say, "I broke up with her because her scab smelled like pennies."

Okay, A) that's just gross, but B) I had a moment of panic when I thought, *Maybe I can't read guys at all. I mean, maybe that's why these guys who I think I have a connection with don't call me. I'm misreading them. I thought this kid was gay, but he's talking about breaking up with a girl. Maybe I suck at reading men.*

And then he clarified that this was in the first grade.

Phew.

Amanda suggested highlights for another $15, so I left for Kentucky looking good and feeling much more confident.

Mr. Virginia showed a little promise. After a few days, I sent him a text thanking him for taking me out. I would have preferred him initiating contact, but I got tired of waiting. It took three days before I got something close to getting asked out again.

Him: On the road for work right now. Are you headed my way at all before you leave town?

Me: Have you read the blog about our date yet?

(I feared my rave review of him might scare him off. That and some of my friends had bashed him for not calling or texting me. One had called him a fool. Better than a tool, but still, probably not super flattering.)

Him: Hmmm....for now, I will put my question in a holding cell. I'll read the blog first.

Me: Fair enough . . . but I'll be hoping you re-ask. :]

He texted again the next afternoon.

Him: Just read thru the blog! I guess I should've told you that I had to be out of town for work (and not a wedding!) sooner . . . then I wouldn't have been such a "fool" as one comment said! ;-)

Me: They're all living vicariously through me, so they can be a little harsh. Don't mind them. :]

Him: No wonder they live thru you...you are like a rock star...going out with fifty men...and making out with 49 of them!! Not a bad life.

Me: That is so not true! You're just mad that mountain overlook was closed. ;]

Him: Sure it's not true! Should have gone up the mountain much

earlier... ;-)
Me: Yep! Guess you'll know better next time! ;)
Him: You're right. What was I thinking?! Mr. Florida was much smarter than me!! ;-)
Me: Ugh. I was stupid with Mr. Florida. But I was only 34 then. I'm older and wiser now. Well, trying to be wiser. I thought I exhibited a good amount of self control with you. :)
Me: And Sheri led me to believe you were innocent and would be turned off by someone overly flirtatious. But then she heard about your wild weekends in Vegas...
Him: Wild weekends in Vegas...not me! Sheri was right...I am sweet and innocent!
Me: Sweet for sure...I'll have to withhold judgment on the innocent part until I can investigate further...
Him: That's fair. Only 36 more guys, and then you can investigate further! :-)

My stomach flip-flopped. Was he serious? He was an hour and a half away from me and he wasn't going to ask to see me again before I left?

Me: Do I really have to wait that long?
Him: Yes, you do have to wait...that's part of the rules of your adventure!
Me: Says who? I thought I made up the rules. :(I think you're playing hard to get. And the worst part is that it's working! Grr!
Him: According to your blog, there is a whole book on "the rules"!! And even if I'm not playing hard to get, I'm glad it's working!
Me: You're infuriating. If you were here right now I would punch you. You're gonna be so sorry when Mr. North Dakota sweeps me off my feet....
Him: What a temper! I'm putting my money on Idaho...you are a meat and potatoes kind of girl, and Idaho is the potato capital!!
Me: Mmmmm, you're so right. I'll send you a postcard from my honeymoon in romantic Boise. :)

And that's how things ended with Mr. Virginia.

When I left Sheri and Andrew's house, I strongly considered pointing Cherry Cherry east instead of west to go convince him it was a bad idea to let me drive away. I mean, yeah, I got it. Who wants to date someone who's dating fifty guys? But I didn't want fifty guys. I just wanted one. And driving away, I wondered why I was leaving behind the one I'd connected with more than any other so far.

#15 – KENTUCKY

I hadn't had much luck finding a date in Kentucky. Two days before leaving Virginia, I'd gotten an email from a guy who hadn't sent a picture (always a little scary) but said he would be honored to be my Mr. Kentucky. With no other options, I planned to head toward a town called Prestonburg. He said it was the closest big town where we could meet; it wasn't even in bold print on my map, though, so I wondered just how big it actually was. He described himself as recently divorced and a fan of NASCAR, fishing, and hunting. He didn't sound like my dream man, but I was at the point where I couldn't exactly be choosy. I shot back an email saying I'd be there Thursday night and would love to meet up either for dinner that night or breakfast on Friday.

On my way through Kentucky, I pulled over to use the bathroom at a McDonald's. I started wondering what was going on when traffic slowed to a crawl, and then I saw a big sign declaring "Hillbilly Days." Oh boy. Once inside, I asked a few different people what exactly Hillbilly Days involved, and everyone said the same thing: pretty much any food you could want, like funnel cakes and corn dogs and stuff. Huh. Sounded like a party.

Here's another interesting phenomenon I noticed in the McDonald's: groups of teenagers were coming in, which seemed like a normal teenager thing to do, but every so often a kid would yell "Daddy!" or "Mommy!" and one of those teenagers would turn around and talk to their kid. Wow.

I started wondering which would be worse, being an old maid or a teen mom. I guess the perk of being a teen mom would be that you have kids before you're old enough to realize how much work they are. The older I get, the more I think, *Whoa, life as you know it is pretty much going to end when there are little people depending on you.* But I guess they'll be empty nesters by forty, so then they can do all the things I'm doing before forty. But still, it's gotta be a pain to have to find a babysitter so you can go see the new *Twilight* movie.

I pitched my tent in a state park and noticed a guy a few spots down from me setting up his grill beside a nice RV. I considered walking over there and chatting with him since I hadn't made definite plans with my supposed Mr. Kentucky yet. I could make Mr. RV Man my Mr. Kentucky if we chatted around the campfire for an hour. I wondered what kind of guy camps alone in an RV, though. That just seemed a little odd. Plus he had this fluffy white dog that was not at all manly; I wondered if I could count him as a date if he wasn't actually interested in women. He was there, though, which was more than I could say for the divorced no-picture man who hadn't emailed me back yet. I decided I'd say hi when I walked past his RV to go to the bathroom. Well, maybe I'd say hi. Being kind of shy made set-ups a whole lot more comfortable for me than pick-ups.

As I got closer to his RV, I noticed a handicapped tag hanging from the rear-view mirror. He looked perfectly healthy to me. Then I noticed a woman inside the RV. She was the handicapped one. And old. His mother? I looked at him again, more closely now without the two campsites between us. Ohhhh. Yeah, he was probably in his 70's. Not gay, but old and married. Definitely a no-go on the back-up plan. I had to hope my pre-arranged Mr. Kentucky would come through.

I checked my email one last time, found nothing from the man who was supposed to be my date, then went to bed early. I wasn't sure what I was going to do if this guy didn't get back to me by morning. I didn't have time to be sitting around a campground waiting for him to get in touch. If we didn't meet for breakfast, we wouldn't be able to meet at all. I had a date in West Virginia lined up for the next night.

I was mad when some rednecks drove in and woke me up with their hollering. I thought about yelling at them to shut up, but I figured it was best not to let them know there was a single woman alone in a tent ten feet away. Who knew how much they'd been drinking? I looked at my cell phone. It was 10:04. I was shocked. When had I become such an old lady that I flew off the handle when people woke me up at 10:04?

The next morning I checked my email again. Nothing. I walked around the campground area. I took a shower and got as date-ready as I could in a campground. I read a book. I checked my email again. Nothing. I gave myself a mini-pedi, minus the polish (it didn't make the necessities list when packing) since I planned to wear flip-flops on the date if he'd ever get in touch. I packed up the car. I checked email again. Still nothing. It appeared I was being stood up.

A lady walked by and asked if I'd seen anyone in the tent a couple of spots down from mine in the opposite direction of the man I'd thought was maybe gay but was really just an old married guy.

"No, I haven't," I said. It did seem kind of strange that I hadn't seen anyone go in or out of that tent the night before or that morning, but I hadn't thought much of it. Once, when camping with a group of teenagers from my church youth group, we were in a site next to a woman who slept in her car with the doors locked. When I hadn't seen anyone come in or out of the tent last night, I just assumed the person here was maybe like her, afraid of traveling alone as a woman. I figured maybe she just stayed in her tent so no one would know she was alone. Or it might be a man who needed a lot of sleep and had only gotten up to pee in the woods in the middle of the night when I hadn't seen him.

"Well, they never registered at the front entrance. They snuck in the night before last, pitched that tent, and haven't been seen since. I think it's odd," the old lady said.

"Maybe they went hiking and they got lost in the woods somewhere," I offered. Then I thought, *Man, how long would it take someone to find my car and send out a search party for me if I were sitting in the woods alone, hurt? And/or partially eaten by a bear?*

"I think I'll call the ranger and make him come look in the tent. Who knows, maybe he's dead in there," she said. Ew. I didn't want to think I'd slept fifty yards away from a dead guy.

Maybe that was my Mr. Kentucky in there. Bummer for him, but it would make me feel better knowing there was a good reason I'd been stood up.

Heading for West Virginia, I saw a sign that said, "Loretta Lynn Homeplace" and thought, *why not?* I tried to picture her but wasn't sure if I was actually picturing her or Sissy Spacek playing her in the movie version of her life. The homeplace, unfortunately, wasn't right off the highway like the sign had led me to believe. I drove and drove and drove. I stopped seeing signs after about fifteen minutes and figured I'd gone too far. I considered pulling over and asking some guys who were sitting on their porch if I was lost, but I wasn't sure it was a good idea to admit I was lost and alone. I was about to turn around and go back to the highway when I saw a sign declaring this the home of Loretta Lynn and birthplace of Crystal Gayle. I drove up, not sure what I'd find.

What I found was a charming old man, a brother of the two famous ladies. He lived nearby, showing the house to anyone who stopped in. Honestly, I wasn't all that interested; I couldn't even remember if Loretta Lynn was still alive. It wasn't like I was a big fan. But the older I got, the more I appreciated old people, and the more I realized that I would one day be an old person, too. It seemed to me that old people loved company, so after the quick tour of the house, I sat on the porch with Herman and listened while he talked. I didn't understand some of what he said, between his accent and my lack of knowledge about life in the holler and country music, but he was fascinating. He had lived up there as a child when there was no road, just a creek bed you walked up. His childhood teacher walked over the nearby mountain every day to come down to their one-room schoolhouse. He'd met his wife when they were in second or third grade. That was the story I most loved to hear.

"I lost her a few years back," he said. He showed me a picture in the house of them holding hands.

"Wow, you both look so young!" I said.

"She was thirteen in that picture. I was a year and a half older. I had to wait a while to marry her, but she was the only one I wanted." He told me how they'd both grown up there, how they'd known each other for years, and how they'd finally gotten married when she was eighteen. After a lifetime together, she'd been diagnosed with Lou Gehrig's Disease, he said. He'd taken care of her, right up here in the holler, while it progressed over five years.

"I'd'a done anything to save her," he said, looking off into the distance.

I almost cried. If I couldn't imagine how hard it would be to finally meet someone and then lose him, how hard must it have been for him to love her his whole life, only to lose her? And yet a part of me was jealous, because I'd never known love like that. A part of me wanted that, no matter how much it might hurt.

His phone rang.

"Hey darlin,'" he said. "Yep. I'm just up here on the porch, flirtin' with a pretty girl."

He hung up and said, "That was my daughter."

Looking at him, I decided he was my Mr. Kentucky. That hour we spent on the porch of his childhood home, him talking and me listening, was time better spent than dinner or breakfast would have been with the guy who'd stood me up. Maybe more than any of my dates so far, this sweet and sad old man had given me a glimpse of what it was I was looking for.

#16 – WEST VIRGINIA

I had two options for Mr. West Virginia. The one that made me laugh the most wasn't the one I picked. I guess I wasn't clear on my website when I said guys who wanted to be my date in their state should send a photo. This guy sent a photo, alright . . . of his tractor. I'd already seen the same shot on the internet dating website where I'd been trolling for dates, so I wasn't completely surprised. I thought maybe he was *inside* the tractor in the picture, so I enlarged it . . . but nope, it was just his tractor. I passed.

The guy I chose instead had me a bit worried. I'd responded to his email and gotten no reply. I didn't want to sound desperate, but let's be honest: I was. I emailed him again, asking if he'd changed his mind. He quickly replied and said he hadn't gotten my first email, but he definitely wanted to be my date. Phew.

He texted me as I drove toward Charleston, saying I was going to want to stay in West Virginia after meeting him. I texted back that many had tried to persuade me to stay in their state but none had succeeded. He fired back, "Amateurs." I liked his confidence! (And just in case any men are reading this, please note that there's a fine line between confidence and cockiness. One is hot, the other is repelling. Just a little public service announcement.)

Upon meeting, though, I could tell right away I wouldn't be dying to stay in West Virginia with him. He wasn't a bad looking guy, but I wasn't attracted to him. I know I'd just argued with Mr. Virginia that guys can become more attractive, like when they're funny or have some hidden talent you fall in love with later, so I tried to keep an open mind. And he was holding a gift bag, which I thought was an interesting tactic. Who doesn't like presents?

"A little road-tripping package," he said as he handed it to me. Aw. I took a peek inside and found the most random assortment of gifts I'd ever seen amassed in one bag: a West Virginia t-shirt (logical, since that was where we were), two boxes of candy (I do love to indulge my sweet tooth while driving!), a little stuffed monkey with freakishly huge eyes (whaaaat?), and finally, a box of eight assorted candy-flavored chapsticks. (Did he think I was eight? Or was he hoping to taste my soft, Reese's Peanut Butter Cup-flavored lips later?)

"Thanks," I said and stuffed the bag into the backseat of my car. I'd read *The Five Love Languages* once and found that one of my primary love languages (what makes me feel loved) is receiving gifts. That might make me sound greedy, but it's not like that. It just means that I like little reminders that a guy is thinking of me. Like a little love note. Or flowers for no reason. Or a text in the middle of the day just to say he misses me. But candy-flavored chapstick and a creepy stuffed animal? I appreciated that he'd put together a little gift for me; it was sweet . . . just a little odd.

We walked to the minor league ballpark nearby to cheer on the Power. I thought that was the most random mascot name ever, and I couldn't get that 90's song, "The Power" out of my head all night. (Don't worry, I only sang it in my head. For the most part.) We sat in the bleachers beyond center field until it started to rain. We moved to some seats just behind the left fielder, and Mr. West Virginia said it was the perfect spot for some trash talking. It seemed a little unnatural to me, since I wasn't really invested in one team or the other, but he encouraged me to give it a try.

"You stink, Number 12!" I half-heartedly called. "You're gonna miss it when they hit it to you!"

"You're horrible at trash talking," he observed.

"I save my good trash talking for things I actually care about. Like Scrabble."

It's not that I didn't care about the game, but I wasn't a superfan of either team, so I wasn't really interested in hurling insults at the other. Unfortunately, Mr. West Virginia didn't seem to be a baseball fan at all. We ended up walking around the stadium a few times and didn't see much of the game. I was disappointed, because I love sports and I think games are great dates – you can watch the action but you can still talk to each other. Instead this date wanted to go into the bar to grab some food and chat. It was an okay option, I guess, considering it was rainy and windy.

Mr. West Virginia was a decent guy, but I didn't grow any more attracted to him as the night went on. I appreciated that he was brave enough to volunteer to take me out, but that's about as deep as my feelings for him went. He seemed to be successful in his career and had been raised well in a smaller town not far from the capital. I asked what dating was like around West Virginia, and he told me a bit about his past relationships. He mentioned that most of his old girlfriends were already mothers when he'd met them.

"Are you okay with that?" I asked.

"Well, most women around here have kids," he said, "so if I said I wouldn't date women with kids, then I wouldn't date at all."

I said I wasn't sure I wanted to marry someone who already had kids. Although I generally like kids, I'm not super keen on the idea of becoming a wife and a mom on the same day. I always thought it would be beneficial to have some time alone as a newly married couple to enjoy each other before the kids came along. I used to want five years with just my husband before getting pregnant, but the older I get, the less time I know I'm going to be able to wait. Pushing forty, I have a feeling I'm going to go from saying "I do" to peeing on a plastic stick within a week.

I asked Mr. West Virginia if he'd had much luck with internet dating, the way he'd found me. He said he'd been on some good and some bad dates. None were as bad as one his friend had been on, though.

"They had arranged to meet in a centrally located parking lot, then go somewhere for dinner," he explained. "When he pulled up, she came over to his window and said hi. He realized the pictures on her internet dating profile were not pictures of her. Well, they might have been of her, ten years earlier and fifty pounds lighter, but she was definitely not as she'd advertised herself to be. When she walked around the back of the car to come get in on the passenger side, he hit the gas and took off."

"Are you kidding me?" I said, chin on the floor. "He just drove away and left her standing there in the parking lot?"

"Yep."

"That's horrible." Geez. I can't imagine how I would feel if a guy took off after getting a good look at me. I mean, yeah, I guess she might have brought it on herself, but still. Ouch.

"Well, when you post old pictures of yourself on your internet dating profile . . ." he started, then looked at my hair and stopped. I cocked my head to the side and looked pointedly at him.

"Are you implying *I* pulled a bait and switch?" I asked.

"Well, you had long hair in your picture . . ." he said. I got ready to read him the riot act and declare it wasn't my fault some lady had chopped off more than I'd wanted her to, but then I thought, *Eh, screw it. This ain't no love connection.* I wasn't interested in wasting my breath defending my hair . . . but I did make a mental note to add a picture of myself with shorter hair to my website. I didn't want guys thinking I was dishonest.

He shared his umbrella with me as we walked home in the rain. Later on I thought about how that should have been romantic, but I wasn't thinking that at the time. He was a decent guy, but I just didn't feel that spark that I had with Mr. Virginia. I knew I shouldn't compare, but it was really hard not to. And really, what guy would want to be with someone who wasn't crazy about him? Probably none. *Hopefully* none.

Mr. West Virginia suggested we go to a bar to hear some live music, but I said I needed to get back. I was couch surfing at the home of an older woman and I wanted to spend some time chatting with her before it got to be too late.

She and her boyfriend offered me some much-needed wine when I walked in the door. (Can you call him a boyfriend when he's in his mid-sixties? Manfriend? Male companion? Ugh. I guess the dating lingo gets more complicated the older you get.) They were nearing retirement and making plans to sell everything and leave the country for a grand adventure in a couple of years. I felt a little jealous that they were in a relationship and I wasn't, being thirty years younger. We talked about their trip plans and my dating project, and I grew a bit uncomfortable as the night wore on. She couldn't stop touching him. I was a little grossed out, to be honest. Aren't you supposed to mellow out a little as you get older? Not these two.

Geesh. I excused myself, saying I was tired, and went to get ready for bed. Half an hour later, as I laid in bed reading, my phone buzzed. It was Mr. West Virginia.

> **Him:** I feel like u were cheated out of a good WV experience. Sure you're not up for some good music?
> **Me:** No thanks. I'm too tired to go out.
> **Him:** Well come over and we can chat some more.

A big no. I was already in my pajamas and settled in for the night. Also? Guys don't text you at midnight to come over and *talk*. I'm not stupid.

Ten minutes later, though, I found myself wishing I was anywhere but there. I could hear moaning coming from the room beneath mine. Gross. Gross, gross, gross. I wrapped the pillow around my ears and tried to go to sleep. Because really? Soon-to-be retirees having sex when I'm not? So not fair.

I had been looking forward to a couple of days out in nature, all by myself. Most of the people I met while driving around the country assumed I was a people person, because who drives around the country meeting new people every day if they don't love people? I probably should have thought about that before I started out. Truthfully, I can be a bit introverted. I really like spending time alone. I left Charleston and headed out on a scenic route, happy for some time to myself.

I meandered my way back into Virginia and started up the Blue Ridge Parkway. There were overlooks every so often where you could pull over and drink in the scenery; it was beautiful. The speed limit on this road, however, was not so beautiful: it was just thirty-five miles per hour. Looking at my map, I realized that at that speed, there was no way I was going to get to the campground I'd planned to stay at before dark. I quickly changed my plan and found a campground in a national forest. I felt bad as I pitched my tent, poor thing. Didn't she deserve a name like Cherry Cherry? She? Or was it a he? Or was I losing my mind, thinking my tent needed a name? I took a little stroll down by the lake as it got dark, but I stopped short before going out on the dock. A couple was out on the edge of it, arms wrapped around each other, occasionally turning in for a kiss. They weren't being grossly affectionate, just enough to make me jealous. I went back to my solitary existence in my tent.

It got pretty cold that night. When I woke up, packed up, and got into my car at 8AM, the temperature was forty degrees, so it was probably somewhere in the thirties overnight. I was glad I'd invested in a warm (if insanely expensive) sleeping bag before I'd left. My nose, the only part of me that had not been mummy-ed up, was frozen.

I drove into Shenandoah National Park and headed straight for a waterfall hike. The great thing about long hikes is that most people don't bother. They want to get out of their cars at the scenic overlook, snap a few pictures, and continue on their drive. It was nice and quiet as I wandered down this trail. I passed a few people with backpacks who had obviously camped out somewhere along the way, but because this wasn't part of the Appalachian Trail, I knew they weren't thru-hikers. I was hoping to run into one at some point, though, and hear what it was like. I'd read Bill Bryson's *A Walk in the Woods* three times, and although a part of me really wanted to hike the whole trail from Georgia to Maine, the more rational part of me knew I probably couldn't hack hiking over 2,000 miles.

I did well on the hike to the waterfall, mentally – no thoughts of bears eating me alive. Here was the bad part, though: it was all downhill . . . which meant that coming back, it was all uphill. I got back to my car a couple of hours later with a massive blister on the back of my right heel. And I had to pee like crazy. I drove down the road and found a picnic area with a vault toilet. For those of you non-campers, that means you get a toilet seat and some scratchy paper, but there's no flushing. Basically it falls down into a stinky pit. I had definitely peed in worse places, though, and I had to go so bad at that point, I couldn't have cared less.

I need to pause here, however, to say a word to you hoverers. Yeah, you ladies know who you are. You think that by setting your germ-free butt on that supergross toilet seat, you are going to contract some God-awful disease, so you squat a few inches over the toilet instead. But here's the issue: you sprinkle when you tinkle. And when I've just ingested a gallon of water out on a hike and I've got to pee like nobody's business and I'm already doing the pee-pee dance while trying to undo the triple knot in my drawstring-waist pants that I hope will deter any would-be rapists in the woods (or at least force them to use two hands to try to get the knot undone and my pants off, giving me open access to poke them in the eyes and run away), and then I see the seat has been peed on and I have to get a big wad of toilet paper and kill a tree to wipe off your pee-splatter before I can sit down, I curse you, woman who came before me! If you'd do two minutes of internet research, you'd find that your cell phone is a bigger harborer of bacteria than that toilet seat, and you touch your cell phone to your face every day! Do the rest of us women a favor and just plant yourself on the seat! Heck, I'm a germaphobe and I sit on toilet seats, for Pete's sake. Or if you can't bring yourself to actually sit down, then at least be a sweetie and wipe the seatie when you're done!

Back out on the winding road, I passed a young guy trying to hitch a ride. I mouthed "sorry" as I sped past him. Well, not really sped, going thirty-five miles per hour, but you know what I mean. But then I realized he had the shaggy beard that all the AT hikers grow when they're out on the trail. I felt bad, remembering from the book I'd read multiple times that Appalachian Trail hikers have to hitch rides into town occasionally during their six-month trek to buy more food or get a shower. I'd want someone to stop if it were me with my thumb out, and this might be my only chance to talk to a thru-hiker. Plus he was carrying nothing but a bottle of Gatorade and a park map. It didn't appear that he was going to kill me.

He thanked me profusely for pulling over as I pitched everything that was piled up on the passenger seat into the back seat so he could sit down.

"Most women don't stop," he said, "and I can understand. But thank you so much for pulling over."

He said he'd gotten used to begging for rides since he had to hike into town whenever he needed supplies. We talked about what it was like, doing the entire Appalachian Trail, and he assured me I could do it if I tried. He was taking a semester off of college at JMU to do it. He said this was the prettiest part of the trail so far, but he hadn't seen some parts of it completely due to the fog, clouds, and snow . . . and I thought I'd been cold the night before!

"Do you ever get lonely?" I asked.

"Well, there are quite a few of us out there hiking it, so you meet people you can walk and talk with if you want."

"Do you ever get scared?"

He told me about an older couple who'd been shot a few days before, just sitting at an overlook, watching the sunset. We both admitted that it was a little scary, traveling alone, when there are people in the world who will shoot you for no reason, but agreed that if we were afraid of everything, we'd never do anything.

"What's your name?" he asked as he hopped out a few miles down the road.

"Tiffany," I said. He shook my hand.

"Uncle Frank," he said, then shrugged. "Well, that's my trail name. Everybody gets one."

As I drove away, I felt really bad for not offering him anything from my food crate. Sheri had sent me off with two big bags of homemade chocolate chip cookies and a bunch of candy, too. I could have given him some of that or some fresh fruit. Instead I just dumped him on the side of the road. Sorry, Uncle Frank.

I couldn't find anywhere in the park with good cell phone reception, but I finally found a spot with a signal near a turn-off for a highway close to a town. I had a voicemail message from my very worried mother, wondering where I was. I called her to let her know I was okay but didn't mention anything about the hiker/hitchhiker I'd just given a ride to. Sometimes it's best to be selective about what you share. It's not lying, it's just not sharing *everything*.

I got to my next campground that afternoon. It was only forty-five degrees; I couldn't imagine how cold it would get overnight. I stalled, popping into the Visitor's Center and watching a movie about how the park became a park. I plodded back out to the car, dreading having to go set up my tent and endure another cold night. I noticed a giant raincloud hovering above me and remembered what Uncle Frank had said about snow. I wondered how comfortable my car would be to sleep in instead of pitching the tent. I debated the intelligence of paying $25 to sleep in my car, parked at a campsite. My mind was made up. I was finding a hotel for the night.

Once I made the decision, I was shocked at how fast I wanted to get out of nature and into civilization. I sped down the curvy roads (yeah, yeah, it was beautiful, but I'd taken enough photos for a while) and slowed down only when I started feeling carsick. I passed by a little white church with a sign that read "Normal Baptist Church," making a mental note to find a Baptist and ask what makes a Normal church normal and what the heck goes on at the Abnormal Baptist Church.

I found a hotel near the National Park but got that *oh crap, I really should plan ahead sometimes* feeling when they wanted $110 for a room. I sat in my car and used their free Wi-Fi to find a hotel with a cheaper rate. I'd have to drive another twenty minutes down the road, but I was ready and willing to do that if it meant saving fifty bucks.

Driving along, I realized I smelled. I wondered what guys expected me to be like when they agreed to the dates I was meeting them for. One of the men had asked me if it was like being on *The Bachelor* and I'd laughed. Those women wore dresses and spent lots of time doing their hair and make-up. I showed up for most dates in jeans and t-shirts. If they were lucky, I even took a shower before meeting them. There was a reason I was writing a book and not doing a TV show.

I sometimes wonder if everyone has as active an imagination as I do or if I'm the only one who creates elaborate, romantic scenarios in her mind. As I drove toward the hotel, I pictured myself checking in alongside a handsome stranger. Not male model handsome, but ruggedly handsome; handsome enough that I would find him attractive but not so attractive that he wouldn't find me attractive.

"I've been camping," I'd say to the front desk attendant, loud enough for the attractive man to hear and understand I didn't always look this greasy. Or smell this bad. "It was so cold, I had to come find a hotel."

"Where were you camping?" he'd ask, jumping into our conversation.

"Shenandoah."

"I've heard it's beautiful," he'd say.

"You should go sometime . . . if you don't mind girls who smell a little and haven't washed their hair for a few days."

"Maybe that's the kind of girl I like," he'd shoot back. Oooh, the flirtatious type!

"You'll be in room 412," the hotel clerk would say.

"Did you hear that? 412," I'd tell Mr. Handsome. "I'm going to go wash off everything you find attractive, but give me a call and maybe we can go grab some dinner . . . but don't actually come by my room 'cause that would make you look like a creeper and I'd probably call the police."

I'm bold in my daydreams, but still cautious.

Back in reality, I found no handsome man at the hotel, only a woman with unfortunate hair behind the desk (and you know that if I, with no fashion sense, thought her hair was bad, it had to be bad). I was surprised at the size of my room when I walked in. It was a suite with a couch. I never actually sat on the couch, because who knows what filth might be on there and when it had last been steam-cleaned (probably never), but it was quite a lovely room, nonetheless.

I watched the news before going to sleep that night, trying to catch up on what had been going on in the world while I'd been out driving around the country. A cloud of ash from an Icelandic volcano had halted all European flights, stranding people all over the world. Russia had stopped all adoptions after a woman had put her adopted son on a plane with a one-way ticket back to the country of his birth. And a freeze warning/frost advisory was being issued for Virginia. I thanked God I wasn't in my tent.

#17 – MARYLAND

The next day I stayed in the hotel room for as long as I possibly could. I'd paid over $60 to sleep there, so I was going to milk it for all it was worth. It had been a long time since I'd sat in front of a TV, so I lazed around watching *The Today Show* and *The Price is Right*. I took a very long, very hot shower. I caught up on my blog, then called down to the front desk and got permission to stay an extra hour. It was bliss.

I met Nora and Steve that afternoon. I grew up going to school with Nora's nieces, and Erika had asked her aunt if I could stay with them. They were sweet folks who took me to Annapolis to see the state capital and walk along the harbor. It was a cool town. They also took me out for dinner where I tried some new foods: crab dip, crab balls, and seafood pasta. I started thinking that someday I might actually become an adventurous eater if I kept this up.

I kind of cheated in Maryland. I'd met Mr. Maryland before. He was a friend of a friend, but if I was the one making up the rules, who said I couldn't go out with someone I'd met before? No one. Besides, my other options sucked.

One option, presented jokingly, was to go out with someone Steve knew. He was eighty, but it could work if I didn't mind helping out with his air tank and wheelchair. Oh, and his false teeth clicked when he talked. Steve advised me not to ask about his ex-wife.

"Bad divorce?" I asked.

"Well . . . more complicated than that," he said. "When they were seventy-five, she told him she wanted a divorce. She said she didn't want to spend the last years of her life pushing around a wheelchair and taking care of him. Ironically, two weeks after he moved out, she fell down the stairs. If he would have been there to call 911, she might have lived. Instead she laid there until she died."

Yikes. Note to self: keep the old man around, for better or for worse.

I opted against the old guy. I was really excited about another option, but he'd declared he didn't want to be my date. I kind of understood his reasoning, but I also hoped he'd change his mind. I had winked at him on Match.com, prompting him to email me. He said he thought the idea was interesting but he didn't want to be part of what he called my "cross country dating circus." I ignored him. He was persistent, though, and sent me a second email a few days later. I caved. I couldn't help it. He was a hot, Christian man who wanted to do Doctors Without Borders and adopt twenty kids. How could I resist? He was pretty much my dream man. We sent a flurry of emails back and forth, long paragraphs outlining who we were and what we hoped for in the future. For a week we found each other in cyberspace every night, having long conversations via instant messaging. He was amazing. I was smitten. I asked him again to be my Mr. Maryland, but he physically couldn't; he was leaving town for ten days, going on a medical missions trip to Southeast Asia. Melt, melt, melt.

Luckily my friend's friend is the nicest guy in Maryland and agreed to be my date there. I met him in a small town outside of Washington D.C. after a couple of fun days there exploring the city. (Although not in any of the brochures, my favorite attraction was a fly guy who'd slowly driven past the park bench where I was sitting; he was blasting, dancing to, and singing along with JT's "SexyBack." On a scale of 1 to 10, I gave him a 4 for attractiveness but a 9 for enthusiasm.)

Frederick, where I met Mr. Maryland, didn't have any Justin Timberlake wannabes, but it did have a unique bridge that appeared to be made of stone; it was actually a giant mural with lots of little paintings blended in. We walked along the creek, checked it out, and walked up and down the quaint little main street. It was a pretty long street, and after we'd gotten to the end, turned back, and returned to where we'd started, there were four fire trucks blocking the street. All the firefighters were standing around talking to each other, so there must not have been any big emergency. There was a fire truck just sitting there with the driver's side door open and no one near it, so I reached for my camera and told Mr. Maryland that I was going to go jump in it and he should snap a pic of me. Right about that time, though, a firefighter came along and spoiled my fun. I'm gonna guess that bailing a girl out of jail is probably not a fun date for most guys, so I took my camera back and slunk away.

We went and got ice cream at a local place. I'd thought maybe I'd lose weight while driving around the country, since I was pretty much living on fruit and granola bars; instead I took every opportunity to eat ice cream or any dessert, always saying something like, "When in my life will I ever again have the chance to eat at this ice cream shop in Maryland? Never!" The result? Moo.

Checking my email that night, I remembered what Mr. West Virginia had said about not getting one of my messages. He'd said something about a spam box, so I poked around the Gmail account I'd set up before starting the trip until I found the spam box: 232 messages. Yikes. Most of them were advertising penis enlargers (no, thank you) or travel deals (I'd love to, but I'm kind of on a tight budget right now), but one appeared to come from an actual person. I clicked on it. Oh, crap.

No, no, no! It was the guy from Kentucky – the one I'd thought had stood me up. He'd written back, saying he'd love to meet for breakfast if I could wait until he'd gotten his kids off to school. His wife had taken off with another man a year ago, leaving him and the kids, and he'd been too upset since then to date. I seemed like a safe bet, he said, since I was just passing through. It was time to get back in the saddle.

And then, it turned out, *I'd* stood *him* up. I felt horrible. I quickly shot back an email explaining the stupid spam box and repeatedly saying how sorry I was. He never wrote back. I wasn't surprised.

#18 – DELAWARE

States in the Northeast are conveniently close together; I moved on the next day to Delaware. I'd set up a date with a cute guy I'd found on a dating website. He said he liked to golf, so I asked if he could teach me. We agreed to meet at a driving range near Dover.

I had a small dilemma: what in my trunk/closet could I wear to golf? I'd seen golf on TV. I had no polo shirts, no pants, and no fancy golf shoes. The t-shirts I'd packed didn't seem good enough, but I feared the nicer date shirts I had would look out of place on the golf course. I made a quick stop at Target and grudgingly handed over $16 for a green polo, hoping that maybe I'd just blend in with the golf course and no one would notice how bad I was.

Couchsurfing.org had come through again with a place to stay, and the woman I was going to be staying with said she could get me a date if I needed it. She knew of two guys who'd be willing. One was married, and she thought that would make a great story for the book. I said that wasn't really what I was looking for and I'd stick with the guy I'd found on the internet.

When I got to her house and called her, she said she wasn't close by but she'd send over a friend who had her spare key to unlock the door for me.

"He's one of the guys you passed on . . . the married one," she said. I groaned. Yeah, this wasn't going to be awkward or anything.

"Call me crazy, but I'm just not into married guys," I replied.

He drove up a few minutes later and let me in. He seemed normal. After a few minutes of small talk, I just couldn't resist.

"How is it that you're married but available for dating?"

"We have an open marriage," he replied.

Crickets.

"So . . . um . . . how does one go about having an open marriage?" I pressed. "I mean, why did you get married if you wanted to be with women other than her?"

"Well, one person just isn't enough to meet all your needs," he replied matter-of-factly. *Um, shouldn't you have figured that out before you got married? 'Cause it seems to me the kind of information that would make you go, yeah, I'd better just stay single.*

"Huh. So how does one approach the topic?" I asked.

"Well, we were out people-watching one night, and it turned into, 'Which of these people would you sleep with?' And then that turned into, 'Who would you *let me* sleep with?' Of course, we were both pretty drunk at the time. But the next day she asked if I'd been serious, and I asked if she'd been serious, and we both said yes."

"Huh." That was about all I could muster.

I had a different outlook on marriage. I'd been waiting a long time to get married, so to have my husband think I "wasn't enough" would kill me. And if he went and had sex with someone else, there was a good chance I would kill him.

I took off for the golf course to meet someone who might be interested in being with just one person rather than a steady rotation of flavors of the week. He was waiting for me in the clubhouse wearing, naturally, a polo shirt. I was glad I'd stopped and bought one, too, because a sign said, "Collared shirts required." Yikes. These golfers were serious. I worried they might kick me out for wearing jeans, but I'd already spent half a tank of gas to fit in here. No more. We chatted for a bit and then I followed him out to get his clubs and a basket of golf balls. After showing me a couple of times how to hit it, he handed me the club.

The results were mixed. I'd nail one and watch it sail, but then barely hit the next one and watch it dribble four feet away. Consistency probably comes with practice, right? I'd say I did pretty well, considering the only other time I'd ever tried to hit a golf ball was during a one-day P.E. session back in high school. We chipped a few out of a sandpit, then putted a few times on the putting green. Then we were off to try a hole.

I didn't do so hot the first time around. I kind of lost count, but I think I got a six. Not bad, really, right? I mean, I've taken more than six shots to sink a ball at a putt-putt course. But on the second hole, I shot par. How amazing is that? Three hits and I was done. I doubted that the LPGA would be calling me anytime soon, but I walked off the green feeling pretty good.

We swung down to a restaurant on the wharf and had the dining room all to ourselves. All the other customers were in the bar, and it was so loud we didn't think we'd be able to hear each other speak in there, so we opted for the empty room. We had lots of time to talk, and he was a good guy. Like a lot of the others, though, I just wasn't feeling it. And honestly, I kept thinking about that guy from Maryland I'd been chatting with via email. He'd only been gone a couple of days, which meant I had to wait another week to hear from him again. Why was I out on a date with someone I wasn't interested in when I'd already found the man of my dreams?

I liked Mr. Delaware's response, though, when I asked the question I'd asked several men during this journey.

"What is it you're looking for in your ideal woman?"

"Someone like you," he said. "But near me."

Aw. Good answer.

"Dancing Queen," my ringtone, interrupted my in-car concert the next day. I punched a button on my GPS.

"How are things going?" my friend Julie's voice echoed through my car.

"Just a second . . ." I mumbled. I'd been cruising a back road, singing along to Duffy's "Distant Dreamer," my new theme song. I fumbled with my iPod, trying to turn it off so I could hear her, and then poked at the GPS, trying to switch it off of Bluetooth mode. It had seemed like a smart idea originally, that whole hands-free talking thing, but no one could hear me when my voice got tunneled through the GPS.

"Is that better?" I asked, holding my cell phone up to my face. I hoped this wasn't one of those states that had the no-talking-while-driving rule.

"Much," she replied. "Where are you?"

"Somewhere in Delaware, I think."

"And how's it going?"

"Not too bad," I replied.

"Met the man of your dreams yet?"

"Ummmm . . . possibly."

"Really?" she said, excitement in her voice.

"No, probably not. I mean, there's this guy I've been emailing, but he's currently in a another country, and one of my dates this month was great, but he said to call him when I was done with the rest of the dates, so that doesn't sound too promising."

"What state?"

"Virginia."

"You liked him more than Mr. Texas?" Julie asked. She knew he'd been the previous leader of the pack.

"Yep."

"Better than the guy you made out with in Florida?"

"Let's try to forget that ever happened."

"So if he was the best, why aren't you making something happen?"

"I can't stop already!" I declared. "Besides, what am I going to do, say, 'Hey, I don't want to sound like a stalker, but I've decided to drop everything and stay here in Virginia so I can date you'? I mean, the average guy would freak out."

"So you're going to wait until you're done, and then go back and find him?"

"It was one date! I mean, yeah, it was great, but do I really want to fly to Virginia or Texas or anywhere at the end of this for a second date? I mean, I'm not exactly made of money. How am I supposed to develop a relationship with someone who lives in a completely different part of the country than I do?"

"So basically you're saying this is the worst possible way to find a husband."

I sighed. Originally I'd thought I could go anywhere and stay anywhere and do anything for love. And really, that was possible. I'd do anything and go anywhere *with* someone I loved and was married to. It was the idea of moving somewhere just to *date* someone that seemed a little bit crazy.

"Potentially, yes. This may be the worst possible dating idea ever. I guess we'll have to wait and see."

#19 – PENNSYLVANIA

Erika, who'd already found me a place to stay with her aunt in Maryland, also asked her college friend Megan if she knew of any single men in Pennsylvania to hook me up with. It just so happened that her husband knew a guy who thought it was an interesting idea. I'd found my Mr. Pennsylvania!

I stayed with my old Colorado friend Laura and her husband Steve in the new house they'd just built out in the country. It was quiet and beautiful and not really close to anything date-like. Mr. Pennsylvania was accommodating, though, and said he'd meet me in the nearby Cabela's parking lot. Supposedly I couldn't miss it.

I wasn't familiar with the Mecca-ness that is Cabela's. I mean, I'd heard of the chain, but I didn't know that people came from miles around on a Saturday afternoon to hang out there. The parking lot was flooded, but I eventually found my date and we took off for a hiking trail.

I asked Mr. Pennsylvania what he did and then sat in confused silence for quite some time. It had something to do with hydrogen. I tried to form an intelligent-sounding question before realizing there was nothing I could say on that subject that would sound anywhere close to intelligent. Instead I nodded my head and said, "Uh-huh," every once in a while, hoping he thought I was following, which I totally wasn't. On my website, I'd asked for smart guys, and today I'd definitely gotten a smart one. Too smart! I tried not to say anything stupid.

At the trailhead, a sign pointed out directions and mileages of different hikes; it said "Pinnacle – 4" which I hoped meant four miles *round trip*. I'd loved going hiking when I lived in Colorado, but since hitting the open road two months earlier, I'd spent most of my time sitting on my butt in my car. Translation? I was not in good shape.

The good news? We had a great time talking. Hydrogen didn't come up again and we stuck to topics I knew about, so I didn't spend any more time feeling stupid.

The bad news? I had to stop a few times to get my heart to stop racing. I didn't want to have a heart attack at thirty-five. I was sweating like a pig and he wasn't even breathing hard.

The overlook was fabulous and well worth the racing heart and heavy breathing (on my part – I swear he never even broke a sweat). Several hawks were circling, and standing there watching their graceful gliding, it was one of those moments when I felt really blessed and happy to be alive and there in that moment. There were a ton of people up there, which I found interesting since we'd hardly passed anyone on the trail. They must have been either just ahead of or just behind us. We sat up there for a long time, just talking.

We talked a long time about our mutual feeling of being kind of different from our families. We both loved our families, but we both kind of felt like the black sheep, too. Both of us had parents and siblings that all lived fairly close together while we had taken different paths, moving away, traveling, and not being part of every family gathering, save the major holidays.

Mr. Pennsylvania said he believed in something; he didn't necessarily think it was God, but "an energy." Sigh. So close. Smart, funny, and . . . not a Christian. It made me sad, because we really clicked, conversationally. He was easy to be around, and I love that in a person. Having to try really hard to connect with someone is so much less enjoyable than when it comes naturally.

We got back to his mini-van ("It's good for hauling my drum equipment around," he'd said.) in decent time. It was indeed four miles to the top, then four miles down. Overall I thought I'd hung in pretty well for an out-of-shape, aging woman, despite my full-body coating of dried-on sweat.

He'd planned for us to go to a vineyard after our hike, but it had taken longer than he'd expected (translation: my frequent "let's take a break so I don't have a heart attack" stops had set us back a bit, timewise), so we went to Cabela's instead. I don't think he really wanted to, but I said I wanted to see what was in there that drew so many people.

"I've heard it's full of stuffed animals," he said.

"Stuffed animals . . . as in teddy bears? Or taxidermy?"

"Taxidermy," he laughed. "I guess I should have clarified that."

And full of stuffed animals it was. I'd never seen so many dead things in one place. Mountain goats, deer, elk, wolves . . . a plethora of Plains animals rose above us in a crazy mountain-like display. We wandered around some more and found another display of African safari-type stuffed animals: water buffalo, lions, crocodiles, and even an elephant. It was crazy. There were a ton of people there with their kids; I guess you don't have to pay to take the family to a zoo if you can walk around Cabela's and check out the dead animal displays for free.

We were heading toward the doors when we saw a display of hunting DVD's for sale. One was playing as an example. A big male turkey appeared to be sneaking up on an unsuspecting female turkey.

"Are we about to see turkey sex?" I asked. Then BOOM. The turkey got his head blown off. An old man who'd heard my question looked at me, threw his head back, and laughed. Guess not.

We walked back out to the parking lot, and as I was about to leave, Mr. Pennsylvania handed me a CD.

"I saw your list of favorite bands on your website, and I thought you might like this," he said. Aw. Thoughtful as well as funny and smart and so, so attractive. Great combo. Just missing that one must-have. Sigh. He'd make some girl happy one day; unfortunately that girl was not me.

#20 – NEW JERSEY

Driving into New Jersey, I saw a sign for White Castle. I didn't really have plans for my New Jersey date, and I briefly considered the possibility of watching *Harold & Kumar Go To White Castle*, then going to get food at White Castle, and then watching the second Harold & Kumar White Castle movie. It seemed appropriate for the location. But then I rethought that plan because a) movies are a crummy date idea; you sit beside someone for two hours, but at the end of those two hours, you haven't spoken to each other and therefore don't know each other any better than you did before you met; b) watching DVD's would require a DVD player, and since I'd found my Mr. New Jersey on the internet, I wasn't about to go hang out at his house; and c) I'd never seen them, but I was pretty sure both movies were about stoners who got the munchies . . . not exactly my idea of great film. I just had to hope my date had some ideas.

With some time to kill before meeting my old friend Sara at her house, I found a Panera Bread, home of free Wi-Fi and good hot chocolate. I called to check in with my CSO.

"So are you meeting Mr. New Jersey tonight?" she asked.

"No, not 'til tomorrow night," I replied.

"Are you excited about this one?"

"Not really. I mean, I don't really know anything about him other than what's on his internet profile. He sounds fine. I'm just kind of sick of dating."

"You're only on date #20."

"I know. That's not good, is it?"

"Well, you can come on back to Colorado. All your stuff's in my basement anyway. We can grow old alone together and hire a home health aide to come take care of us once we start needing to be fed and changed."

"I don't think I'm quite ready to abandon all hope that I'll ever find a husband . . ." I hedged.

"Well, have you found anyone good lately?"

"Actually, I've found the most perfect man . . ."

"What? I didn't think any of the dates lately had been keepers?"

"Well, he wasn't one of the dates. He's this guy in Maryland who thinks I'm amazing but he didn't want to be in the book, so he wasn't my date . . . but we were emailing and IM'ing every night for a week . . . it sounds kind of lame, trying to explain it."

"What makes him so perfect?"

"Well, he's really smart, he's Christian, he wants to adopt kids, and, get this, he wants to do Doctors Without Borders. Is he my dream man or what?"

"But he didn't want to meet you?"

"He said he'd fly me back East once I finished all fifty dates."

"Have you talked on the phone?"

"He said he'd rather get to know each other over emails. We write these long messages back and forth. Alicia, he's read *Pride and Prejudice* and *Sense and Sensibility* and *liked* them! He's perfect for me!"

"He sounds too good to be true."

"I know."

"You know," she said as gently as she could, being a very straightforward person, "if he sounds too good to be true, he probably is."

"What do you mean?"

"Think about it, Tiffany. You listed on your website what you're interested in, what you're looking for in a guy, what your favorite books are — everything about you! Have you considered the possibility that he's just feeding you what he thinks you want to hear?"

Ouch. I couldn't believe one of my best friends was planting seeds of doubt about my future husband. He was perfect . . . wasn't he?

"Maybe he doesn't want to talk on the phone because he doesn't want his wife to see calls to your number on their phone bill."

"Oh, come on . . ."

"What time does he send his emails?"

"Um . . . really late. But he's used to weird hours because he didn't sleep much in med school . . ."

"Or maybe it's because that's when his wife and children are sleeping."

No way. This guy was perfect for me. He couldn't make that all up. Could he?

I had a gnawing feeling in the pit of my stomach as I opened my laptop. I know the internet wasn't created for stalking, but it sure makes it easy. He'd told me his first name and the internet dating website listed his city. I searched for doctors with his name within an hour of that city, and just that easily I had his last name. Searching with his full name, I found a bunch of articles he'd written for medical journals. I sifted through those until I found a picture of him; it wasn't the one he had used in his dating profile, but one of him holding a baby.

Maybe it's a friend's baby, I told myself, starting to feel a little sick. I checked Facebook, but no one with his name had a profile. A bit more digging turned up his address. A woman with the same last name lived at the same address.

Maybe I've got the wrong person, I thought. *Maybe there's another doctor with his first name in the same area. There's got to be some logical explanation.* I tried her name in Facebook and saw pictures of two beautiful kids; they were the same nationality of kids he'd told me he wanted to adopt. Last, I saw a picture of their beautiful, exotic mother. No wonder he'd said those kids were the cutest; that was what his kids and his wife looked like.

Mission trip? Liar! I thought. *He's probably on a fabulous Disney vacation, the jerk.*

I shut the laptop. I suddenly felt like I was going to throw up. Or cry. Very possibly cry. Not because I was crushed with disappointment over someone I'd had a one-week email relationship with, but because of the elaborate ruse. Who does that? What man thinks it's funny to lead a woman on, telling her everything she wants to hear, when he's got a wife and two kids? How many men in America thought that was high-quality entertainment? Was I ever going to find one good, decent man, or were guys like this all I was ever going to meet?

Mr. New Jersey should probably get a do-over. After my internet research, I was kind of in a man-hating mood. Dating sucked. I didn't want to do it anymore. I wanted to go crawl into my big, queen-sized bed in my quiet little townhouse back in Colorado. I didn't want to have to tell anyone who I was or what I was doing or answer or ask any get-to-know-you questions. I just wanted to be alone.

Instead, no longer having a home to go home to and having only one night to make New Jersey happen, I made plans to meet my date at a Cuban restaurant. Meeting for dinner wasn't my preferred dating plan; when planning out the trip, going out for dinner fifty times had seemed like an awfully dull prospect, so I'd tried to plan active dates where I could get to know a guy while doing something fun. Since I'd spent the night before internet stalking that jerk instead of looking for things to do around New Jersey, though, I didn't really have any ideas for a fun date that night. Mr. New Jersey suggested this restaurant, and since I'd never eaten Cuban food before, it sounded adventurous enough for me.

I was amazed by how, despite faithfully using my GPS, I still got lost on a semi-regular basis. I'll blame the New Jersey confusion on poor visibility, trying not to get hit in bumper-to-bumper traffic in a downpour. I finally got to the right place, be it a few minutes late, and there was Mr. New Jersey, waiting for me on the street corner. He held out his giant umbrella to shelter me from the pouring rain as I got out of my car.

A gentleman, I thought . . . and then the suddenly cynical part of me chimed in with, *or perhaps just another jerk trying to be impressive instead of showing me who he truly is?*

"The sign on the door says they're closed on Monday nights," he said. Great. Add a little more rain to today's parade. We walked down the street to an Irish pub instead. It wouldn't be adventurous, but it was open, and at this point, that was good enough.

The waitress greeted us as if we were an annoyance to her. We were the only people in the entire room when she seated us in a booth. She brought us some water and then ignored us for a good fifteen minutes. I looked around; it definitely wasn't busy, so what was the problem? Then I remembered where we were.

"Is this what eating out is like in New Jersey?" I asked. "I mean, is the stereotype true, that people here are really rude?"

"Yeah," he replied. "Pretty much."

Huh. This wasn't going to help my mood.

I asked about his work. Now two-fifths of the way into this adventure, I'd found work to be the one topic every man could talk extensively about. It had become my go-to question when I wanted to get a guy to come out of his shell. But as Mr. New Jersey began describing his job, I quickly became lost . . . again. He tested golf equipment or something. I generally thought of myself as a fairly smart woman, but other than that golf date I'd had with Mr. Delaware, I really knew nothing about golf. Mr. New Jersey's career was all about golf. Golf, golf, golf. My eyes glazed over.

After the waitress finally came back and took our order, we talked some about church, a conversational topic I could contribute to, and we searched the picture on our placemats for leprechauns. It said there were three hiding, but we could only find two. It was driving me crazy. I waved over a busboy.

"Is there really a third leprechaun in this picture, or are they just trying to keep us busy while we wait for our food?" I asked. He looked at me funny, then walked away without a word. Seriously?

It was another ten minutes or so before the waitress came around again.

"I asked the busboy if there are really three leprechauns on here and he ran away like I was a crazy woman," I said as she put our food in front of us.

"Who?" she asked.

"The busboy," I repeated.

"Huh," she grunted and walked away.

"So are there three leprechauns or not?" I yelled after her. She ignored me. Man, New Jersey. Have you ever heard of some stinking politeness?

After I finished eating, I excused myself to use the bathroom. I moved slowly and took a lot longer than was necessary, wondering how much time I needed to spend with Mr. New Jersey to make him feel he'd gotten his money's worth in exchange for the $8 burger he'd just bought me. It wasn't that he was a bad guy. He was a really nice guy, and pretty cute, too. I just wasn't really in the mood for a date that night. My friend Sara and her husband had recorded *The Amazing Race* the night before, and all I really wanted to do was go hang out and watch it with them back at their house.

Mr. New Jersey found the third leprechaun while I was in the bathroom, thank goodness, or we may never have known whether or not there really was a third one. As we left, the waitress was sitting at the hostess stand, reading a magazine.

"Thanks," I said, walking out the door.

"Yep," she replied, eyes never leaving the magazine.

"Shouldn't that have been the other way around?" I asked Mr. New Jersey. "I mean, shouldn't she have thanked us for coming in instead of us thanking her for . . . well . . . poor service and generally ignoring us?"

"That's just kind of how it is here," he said. He walked me to my car, keeping me dry under his umbrella the whole way. Good manners. I liked that. I was glad someone in New Jersey had manners, even if he'd been imported. What kind of night might it have been if I'd met a man born and raised in Jersey?

I drove away just an hour and a half after meeting him in the same spot. Back at Sarah's house, I reveled in my escapism, laying around and watching TV. I love *The Amazing Race*. I want to be on it. I wouldn't even have to win the million dollar grand prize, just enjoy the sights and experiences. And maybe come in first a couple of times and win fabulous vacations courtesy of Travelocity.

I felt a little bad that Mr. New Jersey didn't get a lot of my time, but I wasn't sure what to do about it. I wasn't really in the mood to try to be impressive. Maybe after twenty dates, I was getting burned out. This did not bode well for the thirty dates yet to come.

#21 – NEW YORK

I considered avoiding New York City. It's one of those places I'd always wanted to visit, but I definitely didn't want to drive there. Maneuvering through that traffic seemed like a nightmarish prospect. I also feared Cherry Cherry might get stripped if I parked her somewhere overnight. After consulting everyone I could think of who knew anything about the area, I left my car in New Jersey and took a train into the heart of Manhattan. I had only two days to see the Big Apple, so there was no time to waste. I'm sure I looked silly hauling around my overstuffed backpack, but I wouldn't be meeting my friend Erika until that night; I had to carry two days worth of clothes and my laptop around the city on my back until then.

I headed first for the Statue of Liberty, and on the way there, I discovered you can do some cultural anthropology in New York City. A Jamaican woman on the subway patiently helped a blind man off the train. I liked her. The Japanese tourists were so cute that I wanted to go visit Japan just to be surrounded by them. But the young German woman who made fun of a rural American teenage girl wearing a fuzzy fleece jacket patterned in wolves and evergreens? Well, I wanted to tell that particular tourist that we've got plenty of mean girls here already and she should go back to her own country.

Security at the ferry station for the Statue of Liberty was like airport security. I had to take out my laptop, which happened to be buried under my bras and underwear, so Mr. TSA got to see my skivvies. I was honestly beyond caring. Living in your car, showering at strangers houses, and squatting in the woods to pee will do that to you, I guess.

The Statue of Liberty was interesting, and Ellis Island was amazing. I couldn't imagine the relief people must have felt, coming into that harbor after enduring the open sea to get there. I spent the majority of the afternoon touring both, then took the ferry back to Manhattan. I hadn't been off the boat two minutes before I saw a man blow his nose in his hand, then wipe it on a tree. And that, my friends, is just one fine example of why I'm not married yet; there are so few quality choices left in the world.

I met my friend Erika that night at a fundraiser for an after-school program. It cost $25 to get in, which was a quarter of my New York budget, but I reasoned that I'd spent the last two months doing nothing for anyone but myself. In the long run, it was the equivalent of a tank of gas. I could spare one tank of gas to help kids, right? I bought a ticket. Lots of Broadway performers I'd never heard of each sang a song or two. Someone sang a song called "Beginnings" by Brett Kristofferson, and one particular line struck me: "You'll never know the ending if you never begin." I thought that was fitting for the adventure I was on. It was frustrating sometimes, not knowing if this trip was going to have a happy ending or not, but the uncertain ending was better than sitting at home on my couch craving adventure and wondering if I would ever find a good man. Yes, maybe I was a little sick of date after date after date, but at least I was out there seeing the country.

It was fun to catch up with Erika. We hadn't talked since college, and she'd had amazing adventures and cool jobs since then. I commented that it had to be hard to find a date in New York City; I hadn't heard many guys speaking English as I walked around the city or traveled on the subway, and those who did speak English were clearly gay. She agreed that it was tough, and even when you found a guy who wasn't gay and who spoke English, he often still had other issues. The last guy she'd gone out with had seemed normal the entire date, but when he kissed her good-night, he bit her. Yeah. Bit her. Hard enough to leave a bruise that people at work noticed the next morning. My previous dating disappointments suddenly didn't look quite so bad.

The next day I wandered around the city alone, keeping a

lookout for biters or other weirdoes. Walking along one quiet street, I heard someone yelling behind me. I looked over my shoulder and saw a lady walking up the sidewalk on the opposite side of the street. Alone. *Well, it's New York City*, I thought. *Maybe she's an actress and she's working through her lines. Or maybe she's on a Bluetooth.* But as she got closer, I realized, nope, just crazy.

I did the touristy things around the city. I bought a cheap limited-view ticket for that night's performance of *Wicked*, then rode the elevator to the top of Rockefeller Center and took my picture looking over at the Empire State Building. I went to a taping of Letterman, jumped on the giant piano at FAO Schwartz like Tom Hanks in *Big*, and window shopped at Tiffany's. You can squeeze a lot into a day if you don't have to consult anyone else and ask what they want to do. Sadly, all the money I'd saved by just hitting corners of some states flew out of my savings account. I only ate a hot dog and a slice of pizza from street vendors, trying hard to save my money, but all the tourist attractions in the city were really expensive.

I was strolling through Times Square when my phone rang.

"How's it going?" Sheri asked. "Met any keepers yet?"

"Let me put it this way: thirty dates to go and then I'm going to buy a farm and get a dog and be done with dating forever."

"That bad?"

I sighed. I tried to explain, over the honking horns and the sirens and the general noise of millions of people, how I was feeling. Tired. Disappointed. Frustrated.

"It sounds to me like you're driving all over the country, pursuing guys, when what you really want is for someone to pursue you," she reflected. I sighed again. She was so right.

My third and last morning in NYC, I made plans to meet an old friend from high school to stroll through Central Park. I was feeling rather woozy and was a little worried that maybe I was diabetic or hyperglycemic or hypoglycemic or whatever that illness is when your blood sugar plummets and you feel dizzy. And then I realized that I'd been staying awake 'til 2AM talking to Erika for the past two nights, so it was probably just sleep deprivation. And starvation.

Getting on the subway, I saw a guy sitting and playing guitar. I wished I had my guitar along. I could sit there for a while and play songs. I could put on the worst clothes I had and look sad. I mostly knew church camp songs, so I'd have to learn some new ones to appeal to a wider audience, but I figured it was kind of like how I wore the same few outfits on each of my dates because they were with different guys and they didn't know I'd worn the same outfit in several states. If I learned three songs, I could just repeat them over and over. It's not like people stop and listen. They just walk by in a hurry and throw money in the case. They'd never know I only knew three songs. And then I could go buy another slice of pizza.

I met Holly at the house where she was nannying; we loaded up the stroller and headed out for the park. We walked past the little boat pond where the proposal scene takes place in *I'm With Lucy*, a movie I'd watched over and over. In it, the main character goes on five blind dates, and you know from the beginning that she's going to marry one of the five, but you don't know 'til the end which one it will be. One of the guys makes a movie for her by splicing together home movies from his childhood and her childhood; it's the sweetest thing I've ever seen a guy do for a girl. It's horribly romantic, and for that reason alone I probably shouldn't have watched it repeatedly; maybe the reason my dating reality had been so disappointing sometimes was that I hoped for things from real men that are only done by fictional men (whose lines are probably written by women who want men to do things most men would never dream of doing).

Back in reality in the park, it wasn't so romantic when a bird pooped on me as we sat eating hot dogs from a street vendor.

"It seems like weird things happen to you more than other people," Holly commented as I tried not to puke (sensitive gag reflex!). I wasn't sure if that was true or if I just don't filter things enough. I mean, maybe everybody has strangeness in their lives and they just keep it to themselves instead of letting the whole world know.

It was fun to catch up with someone I hadn't seen in eighteen years, even if only for a short time, and she was sweet enough to lend me a washcloth to wipe off the bird crap before I left. I took the train back to New Jersey and prayed that Cherry Cherry would still be intact. I hated leaving her, not knowing if someone would break into her while I was gone or steal her hubcaps or something else. It was traumatic to be without her, even for the two short nights I'd been gone. More than just my car, she was my home. I didn't have stamps for the postcards I'd bought or snack food to fill my empty tummy or extra clothes to change into when a bird crapped on me. My life was in that little red car. I felt a rush of relief, getting back and finding her in one piece.

I drove over the bridge and headed for Long Island. My friend Nina back in Colorado had called her friend Kristin to see if she could help me find a date there. She'd emailed back that I could sleep on her couch and that she'd found me a date, too. Excellent.

"I need to warn you that he's picking you up in a town car," she said when I got to her house. "Not because he wants to impress you, but because he got picked up for drinking and driving, so he doesn't really have another option right now."

Oh boy.

He called her a few minutes before he was set to arrive and said the place he rented from was out of town cars and he'd be picking me up in something else.

Ohhh boy.

The doorbell rang and we opened it to see Mr. New York . . . and behind him, a white stretch limo.

Ohhhhh boy.

At first I wasn't so sure this was going to work. Kristin said he was a good guy, but I was a little worried. All of his stories were peppered with comments like "I was so hammered" and "I was so hung-over." I'm not opposed to having a drink once in while, but to be honest, I'd only been completely drunk one time in my life, and even that was an accident. (How was I supposed to know that two martinis and a box of Dots in one hour was a really, really bad idea?)

We had dinner at a seafood restaurant along the waterfront, and as we talked, I felt more comfortable. He was a decent guy. He was well known in the area for his work and he'd built up a good business. He had lots of great stories that kept me entertained. We strolled over to a little ice cream shop and he said he hoped his sister would have her baby soon so he'd stop craving such weird foods. I must have looked at him funny.

"She's my twin," he explained. "I went into a deli one day and ordered olive loaf and Munster on rye. The guy twisted up his face and said, 'Are you pregnant or something?' I said no, then dialed up my sister and asked her if she was. She was all crazy, like, 'How did you know? I just found out this morning!' I've been craving weird stuff ever since. But she's due next week."

I offered to pay for the ice cream since he'd paid for dinner (and the limo . . . how much must that cost for an entire evening?) but he wouldn't let me. He said that's not the way it works. Men pay. I felt kind of bad, because so far the night had been really expensive. He talked about hopping on planes and flying places on a moment's notice, though, so I figured he must make good money.

We drove to a bar that had a live band playing and went in and listened to the music for a while. He knew a guy there and we sat with him and his girlfriend. A few couples were out on the dance floor. Mr. New York and his friend got talking about how nothing was going on and we should take the limo into the city. As in New York City. How far was that from Long Island? An hour? I checked the time. Midnight.

"I'm not going to New York City tonight," I informed him. He shrugged. I was glad he didn't push it since the limo was my ride home. We danced instead. He was a good dancer, and he didn't try anything, which I appreciated. When the band announced they were done for the night, we walked up the street to another bar. I was trying hard to stay awake. His job kept him out 'til the wee hours of the morning, but I preferred a 10PM bedtime. I was already tired from staying up 'til nearly 2AM the two previous nights catching up with Erika. I was wiped out . . . but we walked down the street to yet another bar. I made a mental note to provide my own transportation on all future dates.

Mr. New York said he loved going places and seeing things and told me about booking a weekend in the Florida Keys through a website. It wasn't until later, when he was checking out the hotel's website, that he read some important info he'd missed before. Clientele: strictly gay men. He called the booking agency in a panic and was told the trip he'd booked was non-refundable. After explaining he was not gay to several people as he moved up the chain of command from operator to supervisor to manager, he was finally switched to another hotel.

"I'm not against gay people," he explained. "But I ain't going to the Keys to look at gay guys, you know?"

"Always read the fine print," I agreed.

As the night wore on, he got more serious and reflective, and I saw a depth I hadn't guessed was there when he'd first walked in the door. He opened up about his life and told me about his son. He said his ex-girlfriend had decided for him that he wasn't going to be involved in his son's life, but the boy would be turning eighteen soon and would hopefully come find him. I saw pain behind his eyes and felt bad for writing him off so easily earlier on. He had a heart. A big one. One that had been ripped apart and sewn up and scarred over. I ended up thinking he was a good guy, and I really hoped for good things for him. When he dropped me back at Kristin's house, I hugged him good-night and he kissed me on the cheek. He'd been the perfect gentleman.

The next day Kristin and I drove out to Montauk, as far as you can go on Long Island before you drive into the water. We drove around the Hamptons a bit and I marveled again at the amount of money people spend on houses. I could never live in a gigantic house knowing there are starving people in the world. The money you spend on a house that big could feed an entire village for years.

As we drove past a horse farm, I told Kristin how I used to ask for a horse every year for my birthday. Every year my mom would say, "It'll kick you in the head and you'll die." I never got a horse. These people had a whole herd of them. I was sad about their wasted wealth, but a little jealous, too.

Later that day, after I'd left Kristin at her house and headed north, I mentally composed a letter to my GPS. It needed a good talking to.

Dear GPS,

Oh, the fun times we've had together. You just crack me up sometimes. Like today, when I was heading from Long Island to upstate New York and had to go through NYC? And you said, "Heavy traffic ahead" and told me to exit at the next ramp rather than stay on the highway? And then took me through the back streets of Queens? And then into the Bronx? Oh yeah, fun stuff.

And then that street you were telling me to take through the Bronx was blocked off by ten police cars, so I had to turn onto a side street, and you kept trying to get me to turn around and go back to the blocked off street so I had to find my way myself while you kept barking "recalculating . . . recalculating . . . recalculating . . ." Yeah, that was a good time. And then I grabbed you off the dashboard and tucked you under my seat so I wouldn't look like an easy target there in the Bronx . . . not that my shiny red Corolla with Colorado plates wasn't probably a dead giveaway already . . . and people kept looking at me and I thanked God that at least it was still daylight . . . haha, yep, fun stuff.

You were happy when I finally got back on the route you wanted. I was a little concerned when that old rusted-out Bronco cut right in front of me and gave the old rusted-out hoopdie in front of him a little nudge on the corner of his back bumper and the one driver started screaming obscenities at the other. I thought, yep, this is where I see somebody get shot! But nope, the light changed and everyone drove away without a murder. Good times.

And then when you told me to turn left without warning me that I'd have to immediately turn right, so I had to cut off a delivery truck to get over to where you wanted me to be? Yep. Fun, fun, fun. But could we just avoid rough neighborhoods in the future? I mean, you've directed me through one in every major city I've been through so far. If we could just stop that, that'd be super. Thanks.

Love ya. Mean it.
Tiffany

#22 – VERMONT

Ah, Vermont. I'd had preconceived notions about many states, some of which I found to be true and some of which ended up being completely unverified. Vermont, however, pretty much lived up to my expectations of unshaven women and modern-day hippies. And I say that in a loving way. It quickly became evident to me that I would not fit in if I moved there. As foreign as it was for me, though, it turned out to be one of my favorite states.

I'd sent a couch surfing request to a young couple in Burlington.

"Oh, and I need a date, too, if you've got any single guy friends," I added.

Kellie Mae & Sam hooked me up with a couch to sleep on and a guy to go out with, too.

"We have a party to go to at 3PM," they told me. "You're welcome to come along."

People may be surprised to know how uncomfortable I am when I have to meet a group of new people. I think most everyone assumes that I wouldn't have taken on this massive project that requires meeting new people every day if I didn't enjoy meeting people. And I like people. I do. Mostly. It's just that by state twenty-two, I was getting low on energy. Large groups of people take energy.

This, though, I was looking forward to . . . because of my preconceived notions.

Mr. Vermont was going to be at the same party. It was incredibly hot, and I couldn't stop sweating. There wasn't time for a shower, so I changed my shirt, reapplied deodorant, and hoped for the best. Maybe he was one of those earthy types who liked his women a little stinky.

When we arrived, some people were in the process of digging a hole to plant the maypole in. I have to admit I'd never seen a maypole before. I mean, I'd heard about people dancing around a maypole, but I didn't actually know what it was. They stuck this giant log in the ground, put a bike tire rim on top of it, and started tying on ribbons.

The party was a potluck, which I was pretty excited about. Iowans are known for potlucks. Lutherans are known for potlucks. So being a Lutheran from Iowa, I liked potlucks. A lot. I hadn't had much time, so I had run to the local co-op, bought some fruit and yogurt, and thrown them together at Sam and Kellie Mae's apartment before driving over to their friends' house. I was so excited for a plethora of dishes.

This, however, was not an Iowa Lutheran potluck. There were no casseroles. There were no Jell-O salads. There was a pizza with some sort of green weed on top. It didn't look like spinach. I didn't think it was asparagus. They were kind of spirally, like those giant lollipops you can buy at amusement parks, except not nearly that big. I had no idea what they were. I was so hungry, though, that I took a piece; I could at least identify the dish as pizza, which was more than I could say for a lot of the offerings on the table.

"They're fiddleheads," I was told after asking about the unusual topping.

"What?"

"Fiddleheads. They're a fern that grows alongside the river."

"And they're edible?" I asked. I'd already eaten half my slice of pizza.

"Yeah."

"Never heard of 'em," I said. "Are they just in Vermont?"

"No, they grow in other places," I was told. "But they're only available for a few weeks each spring."

Hmmmm. Add one more odd food to my list of things I'd tried on this trip.

After the potluck (which really was yummy, despite the lack of casseroles and Jell-O), it was time for the maypole dancing. Kellie Mae instructed each of us to grab a ribbon, boy-girl-boy-girl around the circle. There weren't enough boys. We filled in where needed.

"Once a year, the god and goddess in the sky have sex," Kellie Mae explained. "We are going to capture that energy and bring it down to earth and into our gardens so the ground will be fertile. And if you have sex in your garden tonight, that will help, too."

Something like that. She made it sound prettier. I considered turning to Mr. Vermont and making it clear that we would not be having sex in his garden or anywhere else that evening, but I wasn't sure it was the time or place for that declaration.

The drumming began and we started circling. The men (and stand-in men) went one direction and the women went the other. You went under a ribbon, then held your ribbon over someone's head for them to go under. Under, over, under, over, around and around and around. People laughed and giggled and were having a fabulous time (despite the obvious fact that not everyone believed in deodorant . . . or in shaving their armpits). By the time we were through, the maypole had a beautiful weaving of ribbons around it. It was really quite pretty. And honestly, pretty fun.

We sat around talking, occasionally getting up to throw a Frisbee; some people churned a homemade ice cream maker. I was a little uncomfortable, not knowing anyone. Being so different, I wondered if any of these people would want to be friends with me if I lived here or if they were just tolerating me (in my non-earthy outfit purchased entirely at Target) because I was a guest.

Someone started singing a song I knew from church camp and I almost joined in . . . but then I realized that instead of singing, "Love the Lord your God with all your heart" they had changed the lyrics to, "Love the earth your home with all your heart." They'd revised a bunch of the other words, too, turning a camp song about Jesus into a love song for Mother Earth. I wondered if they'd bristle if I said I was a Christian who went to church almost every Sunday and prayed and read the Bible. Would they assume I was judgmental? Narrow-minded? They seemed to accept everyone, no matter how different they were, but I'd sometimes found that those who preach tolerance are intolerant of Christians. It was an odd feeling, being in the minority.

One thing I was sure of, though: they had a community I was jealous of. These people loved being together. I found out they had these potluck parties once a month and over a hundred people were on their mailing list. I missed my friends back home. I'd been a part of several different little circles of friends back in Colorado, and I'd driven away from all of them. Feeling alone in a group felt worse than actually being alone.

Someone declared it was time to watch the sunset, so off we went for Lake Champlain. As our herd meandered down the sidewalk, I was amazed again at their sense of community; people would come together in twos or threes, talk for a while, drift apart, then remerge into different configurations. I wanted this. I wanted to be part of a potluck party group once a month. I wanted some companionship other than Cherry Cherry and my GPS.

The sunset was beautiful, sometimes interrupted by laughter from some part of the group and sometimes quiet. We headed back as it started to get dark.

"Are you ready to take off?" Mr. Vermont asked after finding me in the group.

"Where are we going?" I replied.

"I could use some coffee to start with," he said, "then see what we feel like doing." He'd told me as we walked back from the lake that he'd gotten home around 5:30AM after he'd driven back home from visiting his family and friends in another state. I said we didn't really have to do anything if he was tired, but he said he was game.

We went to a cute little coffee shop where he got a latte with a double shot of espresso (that woke him up!) and I got a steamed maple milk. No one could accuse me of not trying new things here. When in Vermont, do as the Vermonters do, right?

The disappointments in dating I'd been feeling disappeared in that cute little coffee shop as he talked about his work with special needs kids. He told me about one of his blind students who could sense his mood the moment he walked in the door. He talked about one of his students who had cerebral palsy, and how incredibly smart this young person was but no one knew because they didn't take the time to find out. He was passionate about his work and I loved that. So many people work for a paycheck; he did something he truly loved.

I'm always attracted to the helper types. I wish I could fall in love with someone who brings home a big paycheck, because that would make my passion for helping kids in developing countries much more feasible; instead I always seem to be attracted to teachers and church workers and stinky Peace Corps volunteers.

When the topic shifted to dating, Mr. Vermont informed me that he'd decided not to have any expectations anymore because unrealistic expectations only led to disappointments. Instead of hoping someone would match a list of qualifications in his head, he wanted to let women be themselves and accept that. While he talked, I thought about how amazing it would be to be in a relationship with him. I knew that would never happen, because we were both upfront about our faith and beliefs and they didn't match up, but he was such a great communicator. I was mesmerized. I lost track of time, just sitting there soaking in the words and phrases flowing out of him.

We walked through the pedestrian street and down to the waterfront. I was kind of surprised that he didn't make a move of any kind . . . and a little disappointed, really. He didn't even try to hold my hand. We sat on some rocks for an hour, just talking. He told me about skydiving, one of his favorite things to do, and yoga, something he'd been introduced to since moving to Vermont. He made both sound appealing. I was amazed at how well this had turned out, considering it hadn't even been planned twenty-four hours in advance.

He drove me back to Kellie Mae and Sam's apartment. I grabbed my sleeping bag and pillow out of my car on the way to their door.

"So, how does this work?" he asked. "Is a goodnight kiss part of all your dates?"

I was caught totally off guard. He hadn't tried anything when we were alone beside the lake, and now I had a sleeping bag under one arm and a pillow under the other. One hand held my wallet while the other held my car keys. This would be awkward.

"Um . . . well . . ." I stammered, ". . . not usually." He gave me a confused look, then walked over, put one hand on either side of my face, and softly kissed me. I just stood there, full hands at my sides. His fingers were in my hair, slowly moving, making me feel protected and teased at the same time. It was amazing.

"You should have done that earlier," I said as he backed away.

"Why?"

"We could have done more."

The look on his face told me I'd said the wrong thing. I meant kiss him more throughout the night. He interpreted it differently.

"It's only 12:30 . . ." he said.

"Goodnight!" I tossed back at him as I ducked into the building.

"You can't just say that and walk away . . ." he said. I left him on the doorstep wanting more. Whoops.

Morning came way too early. I was on my laptop, trying to find a place to sleep in Canada that night when I realized I'd left my water bottle in Mr. Vermont's car the night before. Dang. It was my favorite. I asked Sam for Mr. Vermont's number and shot him a text message. I was hoping I could snag it before I left for Quebec.

Me: What are the chances I could grab my water bottle out of your car at some point, Mr. Vermont?
Him: Ah, the old leave-a-water-bottle trick. I saw it last night on my way home . . . went back and put it under your wiper blade. I hope it is still there.
Me: You rock. Thanks! And yeah, it was totally a ploy . . . :)
Him: If you're ever back around, look me up and I will take you on that jump. Good luck and safe travels.
Me: Definitely. Thanks for being part of my crazy little project!
Him: Thank you. You should go have breakfast at Magnolias.
Me: We already had breakfast here. Scrambled eggs with fiddleheads. You people are just crazy about these fiddleheads!
Him: U ppl? I was a fiddlehead virgin til last night.
Me: I thought maybe loving fiddleheads was a requirement to live in Vermont.
Him: It is a little crazy here.
Him: U should stick around today and then we could go on date 2 . . . I'll cook u dinner. What's one more day?
Me: Hmm . . . that would be a first . . . one of the fifty getting a second date . . .
Him: There u go. And I promise not to use fiddleheads.
Me: Would the offer still stand if I said I don't do one night stands? I'm not having sex in your garden or elsewhere despite the maypole mandate. :)
Him: Hahaha . . . absolutely! Who says I do? :)
Me: I just wouldn't want you to have unmet expectations. :)
Him: No expectations for more than continued good

conversation/company.

Me: I'll ask Sam if I can couch surf another night.
Him: No assumptions, but you can crash here if u want. Whole room open w/ a queen size bed.

Uh, no. That would not be a good idea. Nothing screams mixed message like saying, "I won't sleep with you" and then carrying in an overnight bag.

Me: Done deal. Got the okay from Sam. Just tell me where to be and when. :]

I had to stop using smiley faces in all of my texts. What was I, a seventh grader?

Him: Do you want to jump?

Holy crap. How did we go from dinner to skydiving all the sudden? Well, it was raining. The chances of going skydiving were slim. I could fake this . . .

Me: Do you promise I won't die?
Him: Yes, no dying but the weather looks iffy. Going to have to play it by ear. I will set it up just in case.
Me: Not a problem. Just let me know.
Him: U got it. If not how does 6:30 sound for dinner?
Me: That's fine with me. Want me to bring anything?
Him: Not unless you want. Do you like sweet potatoes, asparagus, and fish?

Um, no. Not really. But I didn't want to sound picky.

Me: I'm trying to expand on my meat and potatoes Iowa upbringing, so yeah. :]
Him: Good! At work, will give you a shout later and let you know how the jump's looking.

It poured rain all morning, so I figured I was off the hook for jumping out of a perfectly good airplane. Skydiving had been on my list of things to do before I died for years, but I always thought I'd check off everything else on the list first, just in case I actually died while skydiving. I was also a little afraid of peeing my pants.

I got a call from him a few hours later when I was at the local library. The jump was on.

I took some deep breaths. Did I really want to do this? I could still back out. Money could be my excuse. It was, after all, really expensive. He said it would normally be $225 but he could get me $50 off. I really didn't have the money. I started sending him a text message saying he should go without me and we could just have dinner later.

But then I thought, when would I ever get the chance to do this again? I mean, I guess I could do it anywhere I wanted, but I knew this guy. Well, knew in the sense that I'd spent a few hours with him the night before. That was more than I'd know any other guy I'd get strapped on to at any other skydiving place. He was a good guy. I was pretty sure he wouldn't let anything happen to me.

Driving to the skydiving place, I was surprisingly calm. Part of me still couldn't believe I was doing this. Part of me wondered if it was too late to back out. Part of me thought this was the most freaking amazing thing I'd ever done.

The people at the skydiving place were awesome. They gave me an incredible deal on the jump plus a video, too. After signing my life away, Mr. Vermont led me through what would happen in the air. He told me to arch my back and keep my feet back throughout the free-fall.

"When we land, you've got to keep your feet up, as high as you can," he explained. "If not, you could snap an ankle."

"Can you make sure it's my left ankle so I can still use my right foot for driving?" I asked. I probably shouldn't have joked about breaking an ankle, but I'm one of those people who rely on awkward humor to get through uncomfortable situations . . . like the fear of dropping 14,000 feet to my death.

I got suited up in a very unflattering jumpsuit, then got my harness on. Mr. Vermont tightened up the straps, and then we headed for the plane.

We took off, and as the little plane climbed higher and higher, I thought, wow, this is really, really high. Yikes. It was a very small plane. I worried about how high it could go without breaking apart in the atmosphere. I told myself that they do this every day and took deep breaths. Then Mr. Vermont was hooking my harness to his and tightening straps and nudging me to the door.

I thought maybe it would be kind of hot, being strapped to him, but it wasn't really. I mean, it was reassuring to have him with me, knowing that he'd know what to do if anything went wrong, but there wasn't one hot thing about it. As instructed, I sat on the edge and stuck my legs out the doorway; the wind immediately sucked them sideways and they banged against the side of the plane.

Holy crap, I was about to jump out of a plane.

Mr. Vermont waved at the camera; I tried to smile. It was probably more of a grimace. I couldn't believe I was doing this.

And then we were falling.

Screaming is my normal reaction to falling. I've been on the Tower of Terror at Disney World twice and everyone around me found my screaming and flailing rather humorous. I scream on roller coasters. I scream when I *dream* I'm falling. Falling through the sky, I naturally screamed. I quickly discovered that opening your mouth while falling through the sky is a very bad idea. I shut it and tried desperately to get some saliva going again.

Wow. This was crazy.

I arched my back like I was taught. I couldn't think about the fact that I was careening through the air because a guy with a camera was right beside me and I was trying hard not to look like an idiot. Every time I tried to smile, my mouth did funny things, partially because it was so dry and partially because of the effects of falling at a high speed; it looked like I was sticking my face in one of those high-powered air dryers in a public restroom. Here was the one movie I was ever going to be in during my lifetime, and it was not going well. I tried to look less "terrified," more "having an incredible time." I wasn't sure, though, how to achieve that look when falling from a great height.

The camera man motioned for me to take his hand and we started spinning. I puke on any amusement park ride that spins, so I shook my head and gave him a "cut it out" motion, slicing my free hand near my neck, and he let go. Puking as I careened through the sky would mean it would most likely hit Mr. Vermont, strapped onto my back as he was, and that would just be scarring for both of us. Unattached and just dropping again instead of spinning, I started to feel better. I waved at the camera and didn't think about dying once.

Pretty soon Mr. Vermont was waving his arms in front of me and pointing to his watch. That meant I was supposed to check my altimeter, and when we were at the right height in the sky, I pulled the chute. With a jerk, we were floating. I was struck again by how not hot this was. Yeah, we were touching, but not in any kind of sensual way. I was kind of hanging off him and the harness was digging into me, painfully close to my valuable girly parts.

We came in for the landing, and though he'd told me to keep my feet up, two and a half months of no exercise meant I had weak ab muscles and could barely get my legs up in the air. I kind of botched it and momentarily wondered what two broken ankles would feel like. They just kind of dragged underneath me, though, and then he said to stand up, so I did. Not graceful, but nothing was broken.

I was shaking. It was awesome. I couldn't believe I'd done it.

Mr. Vermont wanted to go up for another jump, so he and three other people who knew what they were doing took off and floated back down. I collapsed onto a lawn chair by Ole, the owner of Vermont Skydiving Adventures, along with his friend Mike and a random Brazilian guy who was there visiting. I tried to stop shaking.

"Want a beer?" Ole said, heading for the nearby trailer/office. "Or something stronger?"

"What have you got?" I asked.

"Oh, we've got some stuff that he brought up from Brazil," he said, pointing to the Brazilian guy swinging in a hammock.

"I'll take it," I said. I was really hungry. Pretty thirsty, too. I'd stopped eating and drinking hours earlier when I'd found out we were going skydiving. I didn't want to pee my pants or have anything in my stomach to puke up.

Ole brought out a little bottle of something Brazilian and a glass mug that had been in the freezer. We mixed it up with a little orange juice and it was kind of Screwdriver-like. I looked at the bottle: 39% proof. That was some strong stuff; I credited it in helping me calm down considerably by the time Mr. Vermont made it back to earth.

We picked up some Thai food and took it back to his place. While we ate (add Pad Thai and Curry Chicken to the list of new foods I tried on the trip!), he talked about eating organic foods and taking up yoga and what a difference those two things had made for him. It was kind of like listening to Mr. New Jersey talk about testing golf equipment or Mr. Pennsylvania talk about hydrogen. Some things I just didn't get. These I kind of wanted to try, though; my body was definitely hating me after three months of sitting in my car, eating horribly and never exercising.

We watched *LOST*, the one show we both sheepishly admitted

to being addicted to, and made out during the commercials. He was such a good kisser.

"You're my pretend boyfriend for the night," I said, leaning my head on his shoulder. I sighed. "You're fun."

"Is that all this is?" he asked.

"Yeah," I responded. "Is that okay?"

"Yeah," he said. "Just wanted to make sure."

Thinking about it later, I felt really sad. Here was a guy who completely respected my boundaries. I'd made it clear before I kissed him that it wouldn't go very far. He never pushed. And I'd dated several Christian guys who had pushed much harder. Be it the first date or several months into a relationship, most guys I'd dated had always wanted or expected more. One had even told me, "We're going to get married anyway, so what does it matter?" Mr. Vermont didn't share my beliefs but respected them more than those who did. It made me all the more confused.

When we'd sat and talked in that coffee shop the first night we met, we'd flipped through the local independent newspaper to see if there were any local bands playing that night. Mr. Vermont had come across the horoscopes and asked me my sign.

"Pisces," I replied, "but I don't believe in astrology." He read it to me anyway, and I only half listened. It was something about hearing an indie singer covering a David Bowie tune, and how duped he felt when he realized it was a car commercial. In retrospect, the writer said, he may have been too annoyed to appreciate what should have been a gift; rather than feeling appalled, the horoscope recommended looking past the bad and focusing on the good.

Mr. Vermont said it was very fitting. I couldn't agree or disagree, since I hadn't really been paying attention. I'd heard something about David Bowie but kind of missed the rest of it. Cleaning out my car a few days later, I read it again before I threw the newspaper out. He'd been right; it was fitting. Mr. Vermont wasn't the smart, funny Christian man I was looking for, but I'd had a ton of fun with him. After being sick of dating before getting to Vermont, he made me excited about it again. He made me want to find someone to spend my time with. I needed to enjoy that gift.

DETOUR – O, CANADA

I drove up to Canada the next day. I'd never been to Canada before, which I felt kind of bad about. You'd think that during my thirty-five years of life in the U.S., I would have made it up to see our neighbor to the north at least once, but I hadn't. Looking at the map, I decided to rectify that. It was so close! Unfortunately, I only had a day to do it. I'd planned on giving Quebec two days, which wasn't much better, but I'd spent an extra day in Vermont and was running short on time.

I breezed into the country with no problems but got a little worried when I realized all the road signs were in French. I once took a three-week summer course in French . . . in the seventh grade. I racked my brain, hoping for some sort of recall. I could count to three and ask, "Do you speak French?" That wouldn't get me far.

My trusty GPS guided me right to the home of a couple I'd found on couchsurfing.org. It looked like any suburb in any American city. A man and woman were sitting on the steps of the house; I approached and started babbling my hello's and thank you's and how happy I was to be there's . . . and then I realized I could be in trouble. The woman looked at me with a blank stare.

"Our English is not so good," the man said. This could be a long night.

His English turned out to be better than he admitted to. Hers wasn't as good, but she gave it her best effort. I was surprised – and a little freaked out – to learn she didn't live there. No woman did. His girlfriend, who was listed with him on his couch surfing profile, had broken up with him and moved out. The woman I met was not the woman in the profile but someone who had rented a bedroom from him for a couple of months. He had two other roommates, both male. The young woman was there picking up the last of her things to move to her new apartment. She had washed the bedding on her bed and carried it into her old room, showing me where I could sleep since she'd be sleeping at her new place tonight.

"I see you worry," she said in her thickly French-accented English, "but you, good. I have did the couch surfing, and once stayed with man who tried sex. But here, not like that man. These men good. All the time I live here, all three men good. No one of three men tried sex with me. You, good."

I caught her message, even if her English wasn't great, and thanked her for the reassurance as we made the bed. She left soon after and the guy and I went out to get some food before watching the big hockey game on TV that night. He'd first said we'd go to a bar and watch it, which sounded awesome. Montreal was still in the running for the Stanley Cup, and I thought watching hockey with Canadians would be entertaining for sure. Instead, the plan changed to watching the game in the basement with his roommate and one of their female friends. He and his roommate insisted I try poutine while in Quebec. I asked what it was, and they said it was basically French fries with cheese and gravy on top. Yikes. I grew even more skeptical when we went to a fast food drive-thru to purchase it, but it turned out to be okay.

Watching the game was quite entertaining, bar or no bar. There weren't a lot of Canadians to amuse me (three instead of a bar full), but his roommate was hilarious. He screamed at the players through the TV and didn't want to have any sort of conversation while the puck was in play. During the commercials, he was much more talkative. I told him I was an Avalanche fan, being from Colorado.

"Do not speak to me of these Avalanche," he said, dramatically turning his head away from me. "Before leaving us, they were our Quebec Nordiques. They break my heart, leaving here. And before they leave, no Cup. They move to you, they win the Cup. They break my heart."

After the game (Montreal lost, much to the roommate's chagrin), my host took me to see the stunning Montmorency Falls. It was a relief to have a little vacation from dating (according to my blissfully empty calendar, I had four nights off!), but this still felt rather date-like, being alone with a guy at a spectacular waterfall. It was probably a favorite make-out spot for locals. I considered changing the title of my book to *Fifty Dates in Fifty States (and One in a Canadian Province)*, but it just didn't have the same ring to it. The falls were beautiful, all lit up, and had viewing platforms at several different elevations; we started near the middle, then climbed a bunch of stairs to walk across the bridge that spanned the width of the waterfall. I realized the next time I'd be in Canada would be in a few months when I went to Niagara Falls. This one fall was amazing; I couldn't even fathom how huge Niagara Falls must be.

Back at the house, I got ready for bed and locked the bedroom door, just in case. The next morning I said good-bye to the guys (well, the two of them I'd met . . . roommate number three apparently only came home to sleep a few hours a night and was rarely seen). Trying to get to the downtown/old city area, I got horribly lost. I wondered again why I bothered going to major cities since I hated the nuisance of driving in them, and I wondered if my car insurance was even valid in Canada. I white-knuckled the steering wheel and prayed none of these crazy drivers would hit me.

Eventually I found the area where my host had instructed me to park, but then sadly realized I only had a few quarters. My time checking out the city would be limited to the one hour I had on the meter. I definitely got a workout, trekking up the hill, window shopping at tiny shops on narrow streets, snapping pictures of the famous Chateau Frontenac, and then power walking back. Quebec City looked like an amazing place to spend a weekend, and I marveled again at how different this road trip would have been if I'd won the lottery before setting out.

#23 – MAINE

The problem with pretending someone is your boyfriend is that you get this false sense of intimacy. Driving through the middle of nowhere in Maine, I started missing Mr. Vermont.

You don't really miss him, I told myself. *I mean, yeah, he was a fun guy, but what you're missing is* someone, *not necessarily him. You have to be able to differentiate the two.* I wanted *someone* beside me in the passenger seat, just there with me as I drove. I was tired of being alone.

I once broke up with a boyfriend a week before a blizzard blew through Colorado. I was stuck at home for two days, unable to drive anywhere on the closed roads, and I got so bored and so lonely that I almost called him. He'd made it clear, though, that unless I changed my mind about wanting to be with him, I shouldn't call. I was smart enough to realize I didn't want to get back together but was just a little hungry for company. That's what I was feeling about Mr. Vermont.

Maine was incredible. Ten minutes after crossing the border back into the U.S. from Canada, I saw two moose. I took it as a good sign. I couch surfed in Bar Harbor with a cool older woman who gave me a walking tour of the town at night. I tried lobster-flavored ice cream (gross) and caught up on writing in the local library (the most beautiful library of any I saw on the trip). Best of all, I spent two days exploring Acadia National Park. I hiked and prayed and often just sat looking out at the water. It was peaceful and pristine and my favorite place I'd seen on the trip thus far.

In finding dates for this little adventure, my first choice was always a personal reference; say, for example, my friend Jill worked with a decent guy and she set us up. My second choice was stretching that one degree; say my friend Jill *had a friend* who worked with a decent guy and then that friend set us up. Unfortunately, there were some states where I didn't have any personal contacts or even that second degree of contact. Then I had to take my chances, using internet dating websites or referrals from people who somehow happened upon my website.

Mr. Maine was referred by a stranger. A girl sent me an email saying she knew a good guy in Maine for me to go out with. She said he was a lobsterman, so dating him sounded to me like an authentic Maine experience. (And I didn't have any other offers.)

I drove south for a few hours, then met Mr. Maine at a dock. A pier? I don't know what they call it. Anyway, he was just finishing up a day on the boat. He was even wearing the lobsterman overalls. Awesome.

"We're gonna have a beer," he hollered. "Wanna come?"

"Sure," I yelled back.

He and two of his buddies came off the boat (minus the overalls), and I immediately realized I'd have to breathe through my mouth. Wow. "Fishy" isn't a strong enough word to describe it. Oh. Oh, oh, oh.

We walked back toward the parking lot where he'd told me to leave my car before coming down to find his boat. Well, the boat he worked on.

"I'm over here," I said, pointing to Cherry Cherry. "Should I follow you?"

"Nah, we got the beer right here," he said. Oh. I thought we were going somewhere. Nope. We were drinking in the parking lot.

A cooler was produced from the back of a truck, and each of the guys started downing a Bud Light.

"I'm good," I said when they offered me one.

"You don't drink?" one of the guys asked.

"I don't really like beer," I explained. They gave me a look like, *Who doesn't like beer?* but didn't say anything.

They were pretty entertaining. They told me how they baited

the traps and brought traps back up and how seagulls followed the boat when they hosed it down. It was foreign to me, but at least I could understand what they were talking about, unlike some of the guys I'd dated during this adventure whose jobs were totally beyond my comprehension. And I loved their accents!

"So what did ya wanna do on our big date?" Mr. Maine asked.

"Well, I don't have a lot of time, because I'm camping tonight," I replied. "I'd like to find the campground and get the tent pitched before dark."

"You're sleeping outside? Tonight?" one of the guys asked. I looked around. It was a beautiful day. The sun was shining. There was a bit of a breeze, but I was comfortable in my fleece jacket. I shrugged. He shook his head.

"I was kind of hoping to try lobster, being in Maine," I said, "but you're probably really sick of lobster . . ."

"Nah, I know a great place," Mr. Maine said, pushing himself off the tailgate. He threw his empty can back in the cooler. "See you guys tomorrow."

I'm pretty low maintenance. I mean, I was pretty much living in my car at that point. I never spent too much time doing my hair or my make-up, but I did try to at least shower before my dates. I generally assumed that the men would shower before dates, too. Not so this day. Mr. Maine was leading me along the waterfront and I was trying hard to keep up a conversation while breathing solely through my mouth.

We stopped at a little restaurant that was totally dead.

"How about we sit out here?" I suggested, pointing to the outdoor patio. I couldn't imagine sitting across the table from someone stinky in a small, confined place.

"Sure. You're the outdoorsy type, huh?"

"Yep, that's me," I replied. Outdoorsy with a sensitive gag reflex.

I'd planned to get lobster in Maine for a long time. It seemed like the thing to do, being right there by the ocean. The waitress suggested I order the "Lazy Man's Lobster" which was lobster meat that had already been taken out of the shell. I wouldn't have to crack it open and wrestle out the meat, she said, or look at the poor little creature as I ate it. I found it odd that a person who felt sorry for lobsters worked in a place where she served 'em up every day. I took her advice and it was good, but I felt a little cheated afterward. Cracking the thing open would have been the real experience.

While we ate, we talked about life and love, like I'd done on most of my dates. Mr. Maine explained that his friend had told him he should do this because he hadn't dated anyone since his girlfriend moved out. Hmmm.

"So . . . you were living with someone?" I asked.

"Yeah. For seven years," he said. "And then she just left. Said she couldn't do it anymore. So I guess it's time to get back out there and get my moon juice back."

I tilted my head in that confused way, wondering where to begin. Maybe guessing why she left? (Tired of waiting for him to marry her? Tired of him smelling like lobster bait?) But I went a different direction.

"Your moon juice?" I asked.

"Yeah, you know. Getting back in the game."

Another confused look from me.

"Do you mean, 'get your mojo back'?" I clarified.

Now it was his turn to look at me confused. He pondered it for a while before speaking.

"Is that, like, a shortened way of saying it?" he asked. "Like slow motion is slo-mo?"

"Hmmm . . ." I debated being gentle or being straightforward. "If that were the case, it would be moo-joo."

"Moo-joo," he snorted. "That would just sound stupid."

Uh-huh.

Sometime after I'd gone to sleep, it started raining. It rained and rained and rained some more. The temperature dropped fifteen degrees overnight. I was cozy in my sleeping bag while I slept, but my fingers were frozen by the time I got my tent taken down and packed up the next morning. Stupid rain. And stupid friend of Mr. Maine, being right and silently judging me.

#24 – NEW HAMPSHIRE

New Hampshire was another state where I didn't know anyone, so I had to go shopping for a Mr. New Hampshire on a dating website. The man I found met me at a local pizza place on Mother's Day. It was packed.

Mother's Day sometimes sucks when you're not a mother. This Mother's Day wasn't too bad for me, probably because I was on this crazy journey that I wouldn't be on if I'd had kids. There had been other Mother's Days in the past, though, when I'd sat in church, trying not to cry, as women beamed at their children, glowing on their big day. When I'm hanging out with kids at the orphanage in Africa, or cuddling up reading books with one of my three nephews, there's something in me that tells me I was made to mother. I don't think God would put that desire in my heart if marriage and motherhood weren't part of the plan for my life, but when I have dates like the one with Mr. New Hampshire, I wonder if I'll never find a man who I want to father my children.

I'd chosen Mr. New Hampshire because a) he said he loved to travel and b) he didn't look like an ax murderer. He also said he was a good listener, which is usually a good quality. When we met, though, I feared "good listener" meant "non-talker." I wasn't sure if he was shy, reserved, or totally uninterested in me, but he wasn't saying much. I tried not to be insecure, but I had a fresh zit on my chin and I suspected he was disappointed I wasn't hotter. Once I got him talking, I found out that he grew up in New Hampshire, so unlike a lot of guys who had represented their adopted states, he was actually a native. We talked a bit about the area and our work; he had one of those helping careers I'm always attracted to.

"So do you ask all the guys questions about dating, or how does this work?" he said. Fair question. Several of the guys had voiced surprise that I didn't take notes during our dates.

"No, I just kind of let conversations go where they go," I said. He nodded his head but didn't say anything, like it would have been easier to just answer my questions instead of trying to think of something to say.

"I've heard lots of dating horror stories, if you want to tell me one of those," I suggested. I could tell he was trying to think of something bad, but then he smiled.

"I dated a girl about a year ago," he began. "I met her through a dating website. She contacted me, and I couldn't believe it. She was gorgeous. On our third date, she said she had to tell me a secret. She said she wasn't really an office administrator, like she'd told me, but that she was actually a stripper."

My eyebrows shot up. "Wow . . . how'd you feel about that?"

"Are you kidding me? It was awesome."

Huh. Guess I could scratch Mr. New Hampshire off the list.

"So what happened? I mean, if you're out with me today, it must not have worked out."

"Well, she was a little bit crazy. I mean, clinically. Like, bi-polar, I think. And she didn't want to take her medicine, so that was kind of a problem. And then one day she called me and said she had moved to Florida, so that was it."

"Bummer."

"Yeah, but it was okay. She had this gigantic pet rat that really bothered me. She would let it run around her place, and when she cooked, she had a special little plate and bowl for it. She would put him right up there on the table and serve him first before she sat down and ate with him. It was kind of weird."

I shuddered. "That's disgusting. Why didn't you break it off with her when you first saw that?"

He looked at me like I was an idiot. "She was a stripper," he reiterated.

Ah, men.

He asked what my ten-year plan was, and I said I had no idea. Over the years I had considered getting a Masters, but getting a Masters seemed to point toward a career direction or goal, and I never really had a career direction or goal. I was always happy doing what I was doing, working at the church, so I hadn't worked toward anything else.

We wandered around the little town, taking in the tiny patch of New Hampshire waterfront and the cute tourist shops. We sat outside a little corner coffee house, sipping hot chocolate, before eventually heading back to my car. I asked him one parting question.

"If you could make a dream list, what qualities would you hope for in a woman you could see yourself spending the rest of your life with?"

"Someone who's healthy, emotionally and physically," he began, then listed several traits that were pretty typical. He also mentioned "has goals," which felt like a bit of a dig after my earlier explanation of how I had no plans for my life. I figured that made us even, though. He didn't want me and my no-goal life, and I didn't want him and his stripper love. Fair enough.

#25 – MASSACHUSETTS

I'd been to Boston before, so I thought I'd go somewhere different when I went to Massachusetts. Salem sounded interesting and historical, so I searched couchsurfing.org for someone to stay with there. I came across a former Peace Corps volunteer, and I figured she had to be decent and sane to pass all the tests people have to go through to get into that. Sarah turned out to be pretty much the sweetest girl I'd ever met. She'd moved to Massachusetts from Idaho and had that down-home goodness I associate with people from the Midwest. Idaho's not exactly the Midwest, but the goodness must have stretched a little further west to include her.

We went to a local hangout and met up with one of her friends. He had ridden his bike through Iowa and Sarah had driven through Iowa on her way east, so they were both familiar with the flat landscapes I loved so much. A guy they knew, sitting one table over, asked what my address was. I found that rather odd, but weighing my options, I decided he probably wasn't going to drive all the way to Iowa and kill my parents or anything, so I told him. A minute later, he was showing me his computer screen; there, via the magic of GoogleEarth, was my parents' farm. Technology is awesome.

"What was it like to grow up in the middle of nowhere?" her friend asked.

"You make it sound like *Little House on the Prairie*," I responded defensively.

"Well, were your parents really old fashioned?" he persisted.

"How old were you when they let you start dating?"

"Fifteen."

"And was he from a neighboring farm or what?"

"Well . . ." I hesitated. People who didn't grow up in rural Iowa were not going to understand this. "I met him in the hog barn at the Buena Vista County Fair."

Disbelieving stares, then laughs.

"Did you make out right there, surrounded by pigs?" he continued.

"No! That would be gross," I said. "That's just where I met him. I didn't kiss him 'til a week or two after that."

"And not surrounded by pigs?" they asked.

"Definitely not," I reassured them, then shared the story of my first kiss. I hadn't wanted this guy I'd met in the hog barn at the fair to know it was my first kiss; I thought I'd look baby-ish. But as he walked me to my front door, I got really nervous. When he leaned in, I giggled.

"Have you ever done this before?" he asked.

"Yeah," I lied. I had kissed a boy on the cheek at a junior high dance, so it wasn't a complete lie. It was only stretching the truth.

He leaned in a second time, and again I started giggling. He leaned back, getting a little annoyed, I think. I was blowing my first kiss!

"Um . . . I can't see your lips," I said. Duh. Okay, I wasn't the quickest thinker. I was trying to keep him from walking away, though, and that was the best I could come up with.

"Just a second," I said, opening the front door. I reached inside and turned on the light above the door, closed the door again, and turned to face him.

I took a step closer, took a deep breath, and told myself not to screw this up. I smiled at him, took a step closer, and rrrrRRRRRR RRREEEEEEEEEErrrrrrrrrrrrr.

I stepped on a cat.

I was definitely not going to get kissed after that.

"How about we try this again tomorrow?" he'd asked.

"Okay," I replied, disappointed.

The next night we did indeed try again, this time with no unfortunate cat incidents.

Before meeting Mr. Massachusetts, I flew home to Iowa to hang out with my family for a week. Physically, I needed to catch up on my sleep. Emotionally, I needed a week of being surrounded by people who already knew and loved me, who I didn't have to impress or tell about my cross country adventure. Then I packed up my backpack and flew back to Boston. When I climbed into Cherry Cherry, who'd spent the week in a parking lot, I actually hugged her steering wheel. After nearly three solid months of driving, I had missed her. She was my Wilson.

I had a minor meltdown the next day. I was so sick of this dating disaster. I had really liked Mr. Virginia and Mr. Texas, but I hadn't heard from either of them since leaving their states. I'd made out with Mr. Florida and Mr. Vermont, two men I had no chance of a future with. I was frustrated with myself and couldn't understand why it was so hard to find someone to share what I so deeply, deeply wanted. Would I ever find someone I could really be myself around and have honest conversations with? Someone who didn't judge me, who I didn't have to strive to impress? I wanted someone to share lazy weekends. Someone to goof around with in the kitchen while making dinner. Someone to think out loud with, to work through what I dreamed and thought and believed. Someone who would promise to be faithful to me for the rest of our lives. Someone to fall asleep next to at night. Someone to grow old with. I was starting to wonder if I was ever going to find that someone.

The other thing that sent me into my sad state was the realization that I had left behind my community, taking off for a solitary life on the road. I was seriously hurting without the support of my friends. I had sensed that when I was in Vermont, feeling a sense of longing at the hippie potluck. As much as I loved my little car, she was not filling the void. Driving down a highway in Massachusetts, I cried and cried and cried. I knew I was living every single girl's dream, but I missed being surrounded by people who knew me and loved me. I was tired of not really being known.

I'd made plans to stay the night in Cambridge with an old friend I had worked at a camp with twelve years before. I was done crying by the time I got there, and I got to meet Seth, Tracy's new husband. He was a very cool guy, and I was happy that little Tracy (as I remembered her . . . she'd been a high school student when I was in college) had found someone so fabulous. I parked myself at their kitchen table, not super excited to go on a date that night, being as down as I was. Eventually I dragged myself to my backpack to see what my fashion options were.

Mr. Massachusetts had said to meet him at the Paul Revere statue on Hanover Street in Boston. Seth walked me to the subway station in their neighborhood, made sure I got on the right train, and wished me luck with my hot date . . . and hot it was. I started sweating the moment I emerged from the subway. I looked awesome. (Just in case sarcasm doesn't translate well into print, by "awesome" I mean wet-faced, limp-haired, and poorly dressed.)

At this point, I would have completely embraced that TV makeover my friends had been pushing for years. In the past, they used to get the same old same old from me: "What's wrong with what I wear now?" It was becoming more and more clear to me. Mr. Massachusetts said to wear good walking shoes. For me, the only option was my hiking boots. That meant I should put on jeans, because my legs are so short that when I wear capris with shoes and socks, you can only see about an inch of leg skin and it just looks ridiculous. My jeans were hot and heavy and sticky. Unfortunately, the cute shirt covering my top half didn't match the hiking boots gracing my bottom half. I honestly just didn't know how to put these things together. I knew it wasn't good, but I could tell by the looks I was getting from fashionable females on the subway that it was bad. Really bad. But it was too late now.

Emerging from the subway, I asked a group of strangers how to get to Hanover Street. I wasn't embarrassed about asking for directions, being halfway through the states by this point. I figured I'd rather look stupid for a few moments than wander in the wrong direction for half an hour. And did I mention I was already sweating? I didn't want to walk any further than I had to.

Mr. Massachusetts, after a long string of non-Christian dates in the Northeast, advertised himself on his internet dating profile as a conservative Christian fundamentalist extremist. I thought he'd be an interesting switch-up. When I eventually found him, I had one of those moments where what I'm thinking just slips out before I edit it.

"Wow. You're tall, huh?" I said in a tone that implied circus freakishness. He was at least a foot and a half taller than me. We're talking really, really tall.

We wandered around, looking at the Old North End and the church where Paul Revere hung the "one if by land, two if by sea" lanterns. Mr. Massachusetts had made a reservation at a fancy little Italian restaurant, and I drooled over my menu. Everything looked good. After placing our orders, Mr. Massachusetts surprised me with a little nugget of information.

"I'm writing a book, too," he said.

"Oh! What's yours about?"

"It's a Biblical end-times thriller," he said.

"Huh," I responded. I was pretty sure someone had already done that . . . and Kirk Cameron had starred in the movie version.

"I already wrote the beginning a few years back," he continued, "and when I let a friend read it, he said it was crazy, because he'd just seen a movie that was exactly like it."

Here it comes, I thought.

"The Bourne Identity."

I mustered another, "Huh."

Dinner was delicious. I had the chicken marsala and I could only eat half of it, the portion was so huge. Mr. Massachusetts cleaned his plate. Maybe your stomach is larger when you're freakishly tall. Excuse me, *very* tall. (Must work on that filter!) I asked if he'd like to box up my leftovers and take them home, since I wasn't going to be anywhere the next day where I would be able to warm them up. He agreed.

"You shouldn't pay as much as me," he said when the bill came, "since I'm taking home part of yours."

I looked at the bill. $50. I probably shouldn't have been annoyed, but I was. My budget was minuscule, a fact clearly stated on my website. That he'd made a reservation at a restaurant where entrees started at $20, then expected me to pony up? Frustrating. I'd paid my own way (and sometimes paid for both of us) during other dates, so it wasn't like I went into these fifty dates presuming the men should pay for everything. Had I known, though, that I was going to be paying my own way that night, I would have chosen something more in my price range, like a burger at a pub where the Celtics game was playing on the big screen TV, not an expensive Italian restaurant. When I handed over a twenty dollar bill, I no longer thought my chicken marsala was all that great.

We meandered down the street to what Mr. Massachusetts declared to be the best pastry shop around. There were lots of yummy-looking treats behind the display cases, but I was still full from eating half my entree back at the restaurant. When you're existing primarily on fruit and granola bars, your stomach must start to shrink.

"I'm not going to get anything," he said.

"Oh. Well, I don't want anything either," I said, turning to go.

"But you have to," he replied, blocking my path to the exit. "It's the best pastry shop in Boston."

"I'm full," I said shortly.

"Then get something as a gift for your hosts for breakfast tomorrow," he suggested.

I got the feeling he wasn't going to let me leave without a purchase. At this point I was getting pretty annoyed. I bought a fruit tart, and yes, when I ate part of it for breakfast the next morning, it was delicious, but seriously? Was he purposely trying to kill my budget?

We wandered around the area some more, now with me carting along a little pastry shop box in one hand and the chicken marsala leftovers in the other. We sat on a bench overlooking the waterfront, watching planes take off from the airport and fly over the water. He talked about moving from Arizona to Boston, and about his work in a Ph.D. program. He was smart but still pretty personable, not one of those crazy, over-the-top mad scientist types. We got up after a while and walked along the water, and I asked where he planned to go after he was done with school.

"Maybe back to Arizona, or somewhere near Texas," he said. "When Texas secedes, it would be nice to be nearby so I could move over there."

I had to think for a moment about what he was saying.

"Don't you think some people in Texas would object to suddenly no longer being U.S. citizens?" I asked.

"They can leave if they don't like it," he responded.

"I don't think it's that easy," I said. I mean really, what would you do if you didn't want your state to secede and you'd lived in the same place all your life? Just pick up and leave? Doubtful.

He was a decent guy, even with his very strong political views. He didn't come off as angry, which I honestly had kind of expected. I guess the word "extremist" has a certain connotation in my mind, like, "I live in a shack deep in the woods and plan attacks on federal buildings." But he was just a regular guy. He was taking the train home to the same stop that I was, so we went together, parting unceremoniously on the street corner above the subway stairs.

The next day Tracy and I walked around Harvard. She told me about how she and Seth had met, how they'd Skyped and fallen in love long-distance, and how much she loved her new husband. It was so good for me to hear. She literally glowed from the inside out, and that gave me such hope. Massachusetts was the halfway point. Twenty-five states down, twenty-five to go. Maybe I hadn't met the man of my dreams yet, but hearing Tracy talk about Seth, I felt like it was still possible.

#26 – RHODE ISLAND

The drive to my Rhode Island date took no time at all. That is one small state . . . the smallest of our fifty states, to be exact. I found it kind of funny that the smallest state had the longest name. It's official moniker is, "The State of Rhode Island and the Providence Plantations." That's a mouthful.

My date with Mr. Rhode Island had been hastily arranged over the internet, but I was excited. He was a Midwestern boy, and I'm a big fan of wholesome. After the guy who wanted to secede from the U.S., the guy who loved dating a stripper, and the lobsterman who hadn't showered before dinner, I was ready for someone a little more . . . well . . . just . . . Midwestern. We met on a side street in Newport and took off on the cliff walk. Nora and Steve back in Maryland had showed me a book they'd bought when they'd visited Newport, and I was interested in seeing the gigantic mansions I'd seen pictures of.

I'd put on my hiking boots, North Face pants, and a t-shirt for what I thought was going to be a serious hike. I quickly realized, walking along the paved sidewalk, that this was not going to be the challenging hike I'd been led to believe it was. Women were walking in flip flops, sundresses, and, in a couple of cases, even bikinis. I mentally apologized to Mr. Rhode Island for being so completely covered up.

We made small talk as we strolled and I found out he'd grown up and gone to college in Indiana, then moved to Rhode Island for a job. He said his mom had liked this cliff walk when his parents came out to visit, so he thought I might be interested in seeing it. I wasn't sure if that was thoughtful or insulting. Yes, I was a few years older than him, but not as old as his mother.

The mansions along the water were really pretty amazing. The fact that they had only been summer homes blew my mind. I can't imagine how much money these people must have had back in the day, and what they could have done if they'd used that money to build schools or libraries instead of gigantic homes. The path ended after a while and became a scramble over rocks.

"Should we turn around?" he asked me.

"I think we should keep going. Don't you? I mean, it doesn't look that bad." And I was wearing hiking boots, for Pete's sake. I wanted to do something more difficult than sidewalk ambling.

"Okay. Well, don't twist an ankle or anything," he advised. I assured him that I have strong bones and teeth from drinking lots of milk. I didn't mention that, because I'd cut back my health insurance so much, I couldn't afford to snap an ankle, but I was careful where I set my feet. Still, it wasn't that tough of a trail. I probably could have done it in flip flops if I'd been going for the pretty girl look like other women (who had, ahem, turned around when the sidewalk ended . . . pansies).

We sat down on some big rocks for a bit, looking out over the ocean.

"Do you miss the Midwest?" I asked. "Rolling fields of grain instead of endless water?" He was quiet for a bit.

"Yeah, I do," he said. "But I didn't think I could pass up the job offer when I got it."

We started heading back. Even though he was a bit younger than me, there was something about him that made him seem older. I wasn't sure what it was, but I got my answer when I asked what the dating scene was like in Rhode Island.

"I haven't dated much here," he said. "You're only the fourth person I've gone out with since I moved here."

"I thought you said you moved here two years ago?" I clarified.

"Well, yeah. But I was dating someone when I moved here."

"Someone from back home in Indiana?" I asked.

"Yeah. I met her my last year of college. She was a freshman. But I got a job close to the college, so it was easy to keep dating. And then, after a couple of years, I got this job offer out here. We talked about it, and she said she'd move out here after she graduated."

"But she didn't?"

"She came out to visit once, and then a month later I got a text message saying she wanted to see other people."

Ouch. The text message break-up. I'd heard it happened, but I'd never actually met someone it had happened to.

"I paid a ton of money to get a plane ticket home that weekend. I thought I'd persuade her to stay with me. Maybe plan more weekend visits or something. But when I got there, I found out she'd already moved on to another guy. I was gone for less than two months, and she cheated on me."

"That's hard to forgive," I commiserated. He shook his head.

"That's the thing. It didn't matter to me. I was ready to take her back," he said, shooting me a glance out of the corner of his eye. "I suppose that doesn't make me sound very manly."

I shrugged. "You were in love."

"Yeah . . . I really thought we were going to get married."

"And you're just starting to date again now?"

"Well, one of my co-workers set me up with his girlfriend's friend six months or so later, but I was miserable the whole night. I just kept thinking about her. Dates we'd been on. Stuff we'd said to each other. How we'd made plans . . . and then she just moved on."

"And you couldn't," I interpreted.

"Nope," he sighed. "I didn't want to date anyone. So I didn't. But after a year of sitting home alone, you realize you've got to get out and start doing stuff again or you're just gonna shrivel up and die, you know?"

"Yeah," I said, though I didn't really know. I'd never had my heart broken. "So you joined a dating website?"

"Yep. I went out with a couple of women. And it was good. I mean, I didn't want to see either of them again, but I was at least able to talk and eat and laugh and not think about my old girlfriend the whole time, you know?"

"That's good."

"You're a really good listener," he said. "Do you get told that a lot?"

I looked out over the water, smiling. How to answer that . . .

I'm so sick of talking about myself that I'm happy to listen to you? I'm still half a mile from my car and don't have any choice but to listen to you? You're wounded and I want to make that better by taking the time to listen to you?

"Yeah," I simply replied.

I took some pictures of the mansions as we walked back. We talked about my trip, and he asked when I'd be going through his home state. He said he could help me find a date or a place to stay, and that his mom would just love me.

"Most moms seem to," I replied.

He asked if I wanted to go get something to eat, but I said I needed to get going. I wanted to find my next campground and get my tent set up before it got dark. And honestly, as sweet and good as he was, I didn't want to hear any more sad stories when I was trying so hard to be hopeful.

I had to cross a toll bridge leaving Newport, and I was annoyed at the $4 charge. Iowa doesn't have toll roads. Colorado has one that I know of. But I'd been nickeled and dimed to death on this trip. I was mad at all the states who'd taken my money as I handed over a twenty. The toll booth lady handed me back a wad of cash in a rubber band and I drove off.

A few miles down the road, I thought I probably should have counted out the change before I drove away from the toll booth. I undid the rubber band to find two fives and a wad of ones. I counted them. Then counted again. $21. I'd *made* a dollar, crossing that bridge.

Rhode Island, I thought, *you are excluded from my wrath . . . and I will pray for your educational system.*

I found my campsite easily, and after pitching my tent, I sat at the little picnic table in my campsite, trying to catch up on some writing. A guy walked by and asked if I got an internet connection. I said no, I was working, not using the internet. Half an hour later, he walked by again and started chatting about my Colorado plates. He sauntered over and sat down at my picnic table.

Ah, crap.

I'm not very good at being mean. I had really been looking forward to a few hours of uninterrupted writing time, but I figured maybe he was lonely. Since I'd been feeling lonely earlier, it seemed wrong to tell him to get lost. I was sick of meeting strangers, but I didn't want to be unkind. Besides, he was already well into his life story. I found out he was from Vermont and had driven down to Rhode Island for the surfing.

"You must have a good job," I said, "if you can just take off in the middle of the week to go surfing."

"I'm a journalist," he said. "I can write from anywhere."

"And an understanding wife," I said, pointing to his wedding band, "who's okay with you leaving home to go surf."

"Yeah, she's great," he agreed.

He told me about his farmer wife, which I thought was an interesting gender role reversal. She ran an organic CSA farm, which stood for Community Supported Agriculture. I'd heard about them when I was in Vermont; basically a bunch of people get together and buy "shares" of farm produce. You get to see where your food is coming from and know that it wasn't sprayed with anything harmful to your body. The farmer gets to grow their crops without worrying whether or not anyone will buy them. It's a good situation for everyone.

He asked what I was doing, so far from Colorado. He was intrigued by the story and had a hundred questions. It came up that I was a Christian, and he was completely flabbergasted that a Christian was adventurous. He said he pictured Christians sitting around their TV's in some Southern state, not really interested in doing much other than going to church and sending money to TV evangelists.

I asked how he'd met his wife, since I'd been so encouraged by Tracy & Seth's story earlier in the day. He didn't take much time to tell me their story, though; he was more interested in asking questions and spouting advice.

"So, are you one of those Christians who think sex is for marriage?" he bluntly asked.

"Yep."

"Well, that's probably why you can't get dates," he said. "Sex is an important part of a relationship."

"Who said I can't get dates?" I shot back, suddenly defensive. Who invited this guy? He'd come into *my* space, sat at *my* picnic table, and somehow thought it was okay to tell me how to live *my* life?

"Well, you're driving around the country looking for a man. Sounds kind of desperate to me."

"It's an *adventure*," I stressed. "I'm not desperate."

"Well, either way, I don't know anyone who would go out with you if you wouldn't have sex with them," he continued.

I had to get out of the Northeast.

I stood up and made myself busy, but he didn't take the hint. He sat around talking while I got out my little Coleman stove and made myself something to eat. He asked if I'd been to the overlook and if I wanted to go before it got dark. I agreed to it, thinking it might be pretty and he might never leave my campsite if I didn't.

He'd talked earlier about being diagnosed with dry eye syndrome after his wife's soap-making experiment had given him a chemical burn that destroyed his tear ducts. As we walked past a campfire, he put a hand over his eyes.

"I can't open my eyes," he said. "It hurts. Can you guide me 'til we get past the smoke?"

I took him by the elbow and dragged him along the path. He moved his arm so that he was holding my hand, which creeped me out, but he let go after about three seconds, when we'd gotten past the smoke, so I didn't have to knife him. The overlook was nothing fabulous. I was hoping the view would look out over Narragansett Bay, but instead we only saw a marsh. Lame. I was ready to be done with this guy. We headed back. We walked past the campfire again, but I walked around the back of it, opposite of the direction the smoke was blowing, so I wouldn't have to guide him again. He noticed.

"We could hold hands anyway," he said.

"Uhh, no," I said. "You're married."

"Sometimes human touch just feels good," he said. I shot daggers at him with my eyes.

"What would your wife think of that?"

"Holding hands? That's nothing."

"I wouldn't want my husband holding hands with some random woman in a campground."

"Before we got married, we agreed that we would always have an open relationship. We've never acted on it, but we could if we wanted to."

"You wouldn't be bothered by the fact that your wife had sex with someone else?" I asked, incredulous.

"Well, I probably wouldn't want to know," he admitted.

"Didn't you pledge faithfulness in your wedding vows?" I asked.

"No, we wrote our own. We didn't include that."

I shook my head, disgusted. Were there no men left who wanted to be with just one woman? Was it really that hard to find a guy with the same morals and values I had?

I made it clear when we walked by his tent that he was staying there and I was going back to my tent alone.

I called my friend Sheri, and before even saying hello, I begged her to reassure me that there were good men out there who believed in God and believed in monogamy, and that one day I would find one who was a great match for me. She listened to me as I tried to describe all I was feeling: loneliness, disappointment, disillusionment.

"It's not like marriage is all weekend canoe rides and romantic nights in front of a fire," she said. "Most days it's not very exciting."

"I know . . . and I'm not expecting it to be."

"You just need to get out of the Northeast," she advised.

"I know . . ."

"There's someone out there for you."

"I know . . . it's just hard for me to remember sometimes." It was good to have someone who knew me talk me down.

"I'm so sick of myself," I said. "I meet new people every day. Dates, couch surfing hosts, random strangers who approach me in campgrounds . . . and everyone wants to talk about what I'm doing. I'm so sick of talking about myself and spending every waking minute focusing on me and what I'm doing and planning where I'm going next."

"That's not who you are," she agreed.

"I'm just so grateful I have a job to go to for three months," I said. Just two more nights and I'd be at the summer camp I'd signed on to work at for the summer. "I'll be able to focus on making sick kids happy instead of myself all the time."

"I'm so happy you're doing that," Sheri replied. "I don't know if you've been reading my Facebook updates, but my sister's friend is about to lose her four-year-old to cancer. You feel so helpless . . ."

She went on to tell me about this little girl and her family. It was a rare form of cancer, and little was known about it or how to treat it. Sheri said they thought she had a couple of weeks left. Even worse, her mom was 30 weeks pregnant. She'd been pregnant before and miscarried when they got the diagnosis. People who loved her feared she'd miscarry again when her beautiful four-year-old died. Losing three children? I couldn't imagine it.

"Hearing that makes me feel like my issues are so petty," I said. "My problems are nothing . . ."

"Don't minimize what you feel," Sheri advised. "We each have a story. We each have problems. This is your reality right now. This is what's hurting you. We all have pain."

True. Still, it was hard not to compare. I fell asleep praying for that mother.

I woke up early the next morning and got ready in the campground shower house. I thought about my teen years and how I'd spent hours in front of a mirror, teasing and spraying my permed hair. Now my head was under a hand dryer in a public restroom in a campground. My, how things change. I also got ready for dates in high school by seeing how tall I could get my bangs; twenty years later I got ready for dates by seeing how short I could get my mustache. Didn't see that one coming.

I packed up my stuff and drove to Narragansett Bay. I'd been told it was a beautiful, must-see spot, and it was. I must have beaten the crowds in the early morning light that May morning; I had the beach completely to myself.

I sat on a rock, looking out over the water. I talked to God a little and counted my blessings. It wasn't like me to get down; I'd been described more than once as "overly optimistic." I was ready to ditch my dumpy attitude and move on.

—

#27 – CONNECTICUT

"I'm worried about you," my friend Stephanie said over the phone.

"You should be," I sighed. "I'm lonely . . . and I'm tired of meeting guys who aren't right for me . . . and I generally just want to go home, but I don't have a home to go to anymore."

"You have lots of people back here who would gladly take you in."

"I know, but I miss *my* house."

"I read your Vermont blog," she said. I sighed, knowing what was coming next. "What happened to the woman who wanted her kisses to mean something?"

"You don't know what it's like," I said, trying to defend myself, even though I knew she was right. "You have no idea how depressing it gets, thinking there's not a single man in the entire country who's right for you."

"So you make yourself feel better by making out with one who isn't? What if there is a guy who's perfect for you and you just haven't met him yet?"

"I know . . ."

"Do you really want your future husband to read about you making out with different guys all over the country?"

"No . . ."

"How do you think that will make him feel? And what if you have kids? Would you want them reading that someday?"

"No . . ." I said again. I agreed with her in theory, but I was conflicted as to whether or not I really regretted it. No, I didn't want my future husband to be hurt, but at the same time, I was seriously questioning whether or not there was such a thing as my future husband. What if I was holding out for someone who didn't exist?

I distinctly remember one question from the interview that would land me my first job after college. I'd been through the wringer with a six-person interview team, then had to meet one-on-one with the principal. He'd asked a series of expected questions about educational theories and my student teaching experience, but then caught me off guard with his last question.

"What's your favorite movie?" he asked.

"Hmm . . ." I appeared to give it great thought, but in reality I was smartly filtering what was about to come out of my mouth. "I'd say it's a tie between *Braveheart* and *The Shawshank Redemption*."

Now don't get me wrong – I really did love both those movies. *The Shawshank Redemption* is even one my top five movies of all time. But had this been a girlfriend asking and not a forty-something-year-old male who, I was hoping, might possibly give me a job, I would have answered differently. As it was, I kept my love of 80's chick flicks in the closet.

I think it all started with *Pretty in Pink*. When I'm scanning through radio stations, driving down the highway, and "If You Leave" by Orchestral Maneuvers in the Dark suddenly fills my car, I am instantly transported back in time to prom night. No, not *my* prom night (and I went to three different proms, so you'd think one romantic thing would have happened to me at one of them, but no), but prom night in that spectacular ballroom at the end of the movie, escorted in by my BFF Duckie. And then Blane approaches me and says, "I love you . . . always . . ." and I fall in love all over again and run out to the parking lot to stop him with a kiss before he drives out of my life forever.

It was even worse when I saw *Dirty Dancing* (on VHS a couple of years after it came out in theaters, because with that title, my mom gave it the big N-O). I spent the following summer wanting to *be* Baby Houseman. I had a frizzy-permed bob that kind of looked like her hair. I cut off my jeans and rolled the hems, just above the knees.

I religiously wore Keds (okay, fine, they were the $3 knock-offs from K-Mart, but really, unless you asked a person to turn around so you could check for the authenticating blue rectangle on the heel, who could tell?). I secretly practiced her dance moves. And more than anything, I wanted romance, bad boy and all.

Unfortunately, I grew up in rural Iowa and my family didn't spend summer vacations at ritzy resorts in the Catskills. Neither were there hot older men just waiting to fall in love with a quiet girl and her Peace-Corps-future-planning dreams (not that I actually had them . . . that movie was the first time I'd ever heard of the Peace Corps and I didn't even really know what that meant). What we did have in rural Iowa were farm boys at the county fair.

The Buena Vista County Fair was pretty much the highlight of the summer when I was in junior high. Being out of school for the summer was awesome . . . for about a week. Then reality set in. Our farm was six miles out of town, and my mom forbade me walking or biking in to see my friends (the need to cross a major highway may have had something to do with it). So by mid-July, after a month and a half of being bored, I'd be itching for a week of frivolity at the fair. And I had recently acquired an interest in boys.

I'm sure it's hard for city dwellers to understand, but my best friend Carrie and I could spend hours strolling through the sheep barn, the John Deere exhibit, and the midway, trying to look casual while secretly following whatever cute boys we'd set our sights on that summer. I think today we'd call it stalking, but back then it was just our summer tradition.

That particular year, the summer I idolized Baby, I was about to enter the eighth grade. I was drooling over an older man (a soon-to-be tenth grader) who was not only gorgeous but mysterious as well (he went to school in the next town over from mine, and that qualified him as mysterious . . . oh, gimme a break, I was in eighth grade!). And – get this – he drove a black car. It didn't look anything like Johnny's car in *Dirty Dancing*, but it was black. Close enough.

One afternoon, after having lunch at the Presbyterian Church food stand with my parents, I set out in search of Carrie. The hog barn seemed a logical place to find her, so I headed there first. At the far end of the barn, I could see a group of teenagers. Figuring she was among them, I started in that direction. About halfway there, though, I realized it wasn't our group of friends. It was the guy I'd been drooling over, his younger brother (whom Carrie had been drooling over), their very popular friend (whom I would meet two years later in that very hog barn and later step on a cat in front of while trying to claim my first kiss), and a gaggle of their equally intimidating, way-cooler-than-me friends.

Did I mention that I was horrifically shy at this point? That "popular" was not a word that had ever been used to describe me? That I had a frizzy perm that my own father once told me gave me the appearance of a Cocker Spaniel? My confidence level, despite my desire to be Baby, up on stage in my pretty pink dress, dancing the last dance of the summer with Johnny Castle, every girl's dream . . . well, it was already pretty low. Little did I know it was about to plummet even further.

I tried to look casual. I avoided eye contact with anyone in the group. What kind of loser walks around the fair alone? It was a social event, and I was all by myself. I figured my best bet was to attempt invisibility while walking past them, then continue on to the cow barn in search of Carrie. At the end of the barn, though, just feet away from the cool crowd, a fence blocked my exit.

I did some quick thinking. The way I climbed fences at home was the universal way of climbing fences: one leg over, half turn, other leg over. But this was also how my dad climbed fences. On the off chance that the guy I had a crush on might actually be looking at me, I opted for a more feminine-looking plan. I would climb the fence like a ladder, then gracefully hop back down to the ground on the other side. My bob would bounce a little upon landing, the guy would think I was cute, and next thing you know, he'd be asking me out.

Unfortunately, someone two steps behind me needed to get over that fence, too. As I stepped onto the top of the fence, ready to do my prance-jump off, a fat little girl yanked the fence toward her. My feet went with the fence. The rest of me propelled forward. I belly-flopped onto the dirt below.

There's a chance that if the group of cool kids had been deep in conversation, they might not have seen it. However, in my shock, I screamed as I careened to the ground. Nothing like drawing attention to yourself mid-humiliation. (Oh, and FYI, if you think belly flopping hurts in the pool, try it on solid ground.)

I got up, not daring to glance at the boy, and gingerly walked to the cow barn. I found Carrie, put my head on her shoulder, and cried . . . partly from the pain but mostly from embarrassment.

And Baby in *Dirty Dancing* thought that whole "I carried a watermelon" thing was mortifying.

Mystic Pizza, another of my favorite chick flicks from the 80's, had no painful memories attached to it. I'd been wanting to go to Mystic, Connecticut, ever since I'd first seen it. People loved Julia Roberts in one of her earliest roles and remember Matt Damon in his movie debut, but Annabeth Gish's character was the one who always drew me in, falling for (and then being crushed by) the older man. I wanted to go to their little seaside town, ride a moped up and down its salty streets, and eat that pizza, chockfull of secret ingredients.

Mr. Connecticut humored me and met me there. Sadly, the real Mystic Pizza isn't where they filmed the movie. It looked nothing like it. The pizza was good, though, and they had movie memorabilia all over the place, so that was kind of cool, even if I was disappointed.

Mr. Connecticut was really friendly. He had come to the U.S. to get an Ivy League education, so he definitely got the check mark for being smart. He was even a Christian. Unfortunately, I just wasn't attracted to him. It could have been that I was emotionally drained by date number twenty-seven. Maybe it was the fact that a TV right above his head was showing *Mystic Pizza,* so I was distracted and had a hard time focusing on what he was saying. Or perhaps it was that he never stopped smiling, and in my negative state, I wanted to smack that constant grin right off his face.

You are a horrible person, I told myself. *You're becoming bitter and it's making you mean. You don't deserve a good man if you're going to rip him to shreds just for being happy!*

We left the pizza place and went to the Mystic Seaport, but I almost left again when I saw the entrance fee. I felt bad when guys offered to pay for things that were really expensive, and especially bad when I already knew it wasn't going to go anywhere. I might have been turning into a mean and horrible person after three long months of traveling and dating, but I was not and never would be a gold-digger. Mr. Connecticut said he'd never been before, though, and he really wanted to see it. He didn't mind paying, he said. Really.

I reluctantly agreed.

I had no idea Connecticut would be so humid. When I had made plans to stay in Connecticut for the summer, I pictured cool ocean breezes. I was sadly mistaken. It was hot. I wasn't just perspiring, I was dripping. I thought about all those cold and rainy dates I'd had in the spring in the South and was glad I wasn't there in the summer. How did those Southern belles do it?

We wandered around, looking at a rebuilt version of the Amistad and touring an old shipping vessel. There were all kinds of displays in the old town, like a printing press and a blacksmith shop. It was so hot inside the buildings, though, that I couldn't bring myself to stay and watch their demonstrations. At the very end of the property, right beside the bathrooms and the service entrance, a Dasani sign glowed like a light from heaven. I flew over to the pop machine like a moth to a flame. Up close, I saw that Gatorade was a choice, too. I gladly forked over two dollars for a bottle of grape Gatorade, then repeated the process for Mr. Connecticut. We sat on a bench, enjoying our beverages, looking out over the water, and making typical first date small talk.

He was such a nice guy. He reminded me of a friend of mine who is also a very nice guy and who more than once I had tried to talk myself into feeling something more than friendship for. You can't force what's not there, though; I didn't feel it for my friend, and I didn't feel it for Mr. Connecticut. I had to get going and was honestly relieved to climb back into my air-conditioned car, but I drove away wishing again that I could somehow match up nice girls with nice guys like Mr. Connecticut.

That night I couch surfed with Dave and Sue in their million-dollar mansion right on the water. When I'd made a profile on the couchsurfing.org website and planned to occasionally stay with strangers, I'd pictured free but semi-sketchy nights on dirty couches in seedy apartments. I couldn't have been more wrong. Up and down the East Coast, I'd stayed with incredible people in their very non-sketchy homes. I'd been fed steak, received sightseeing advice, and been welcomed as a member of the family. It was one of the best decisions I'd made, looking into it as an alternative to hotels or camping. And this, my last couch surf before a three-month break for the summer, was the granddaddy of all my couch surfing experiences. They showed me to a private guest room with an en-suite full bath and a view of the water. Amazing.

The sleeping arrangements were just the tip of the iceberg, though. Dave and Sue were part of a sailboat racing team and they invited me to join their crew for a race that night. It sounded awesome. It turned out to *be* awesome. And a little bit holy-crap-I'm-gonna-pee-my-pants terrifying.

There were lots of people on a not-very-big boat, and everyone was busy pulling ropes and hollering at each other. My job was to stay out of the way. Literally. I basically scrambled from one side of the boat to the other whenever they turned around, doing all I could not to get hit in the head with the boom. The adrenaline rush was good, though, because I barely noticed all the bruises I was accumulating, accidentally sitting on cleats in my rush to park it before I got clotheslined or worse. At one point, my hand slipped as I was scrambling on all fours and I did a full-body belly flop, much like I'd done twenty years earlier at the county fair. (The next day, though not reeling with embarrassment, I was in a fair amount of pain; a path of bruises marched up the entire right side of my body: knee, hip, breast, and shoulder.) During the entire race, I kept praying that I wouldn't fall overboard. I mean, it was a race, for Pete's sake. I wasn't sure, if I went sliding into the Sound, that they'd stop to pick me up; there was a strong possibility they'd leave me treading water 'til they'd crossed the finish line and then come back for me. I wasn't the only person in the world who was competitive.

DETOUR #2 – O, CANADA. AGAIN. BRIEFLY.

There was a time in my life when I was modest . . . and then one day I took off my pants in the Niagara Falls parking lot.

I'd spent three blissful months working at a summer camp. I didn't tell any of my coworkers about the dating aspect of my adventure until the very end of the summer, so instead of having to answer questions about dating, I just got to be my regular old not-that-interesting self again. And instead of focusing on me, me, me – where I was driving next, where I would sleep, who I would date, and what fun activity we'd do – I'd spent three months hanging out with very ill but nevertheless beautiful children. It had been an amazing three months, and emotionally I left in a much better place than I had been in when I'd arrived.

I headed out of camp at 6:45AM. I'd only gone to bed at 1AM; besides saying good-bye to everyone I'd worked with for three months, I also had to pack up everything I had spread out in a dorm room for three months. Cherry Cherry was once again filled to the brim when I fell asleep, long past my preferred bedtime. I was awake at six, though, an hour before my alarm was set to go off. Obviously the lure and excitement of the open road was back! My little red car and I took off for Niagara Falls.

It was refreshing to be back out on the open road again; it reminded me how much I love road trips. Yes, I'd gotten discouraged in dating and grown tired of constantly being on the move, but now I was headed west, back to the area where I'd grown up and spent all of my adult life. I had friends scattered all over the Midwest and the West, so I had a feeling the second half of the trip was going to be vastly different from the first half.

I had a new eight-hour audio book loaded on my iPod, so I plugged that in. After about twenty minutes, I thought maybe I should turn it off. It wasn't making sense. Emotionally, I was driving away from an incredible experience; was I still thinking about camp and not focusing on the book? Was that why I was so confused? I was completely lost; it was the most discombobulated audiobook ever. From what I could tell, the woman fell in love with someone while her husband was away at war. But then she was an old lady. Three minutes later, she was a young woman again. What? I didn't get it. Maybe it was one of those books that was better when you read it instead of listened to it. I focused harder and tried to figure out the plot between the jumping back and forth, present and past. And then, two hours into what was supposed to be an eight-hour story, it ended. Only then did I realize I'd had the iPod on shuffle. Whoops. My bad. At that point I'd already heard which guy she chose, so I didn't figure there was any point in going back and listening to the whole book in the correct order. I unplugged the iPod, cranked the radio, and had a little sing-along.

Sometime that day, I had a brilliant realization: if I'd just buckle the passenger side seatbelt – even if no one was sitting there – then I could pile up my laptop, my purse, and pretty much anything else I wanted without that incessant dinging going off every time the little sensors thought I had a passenger along. I felt like an idiot, having gone through twenty-seven previous states before making that realization.

After eight hours of driving, I stepped out of my car at Niagara Falls and was hit by a wall of humidity. Yikes. I was wearing pants and figured maybe I'd be more comfortable if I put on some shorts. I dug around in my laundry bag until I found the one pair I owned. They were wrinkled as all get out but not noticeably filthy, so I wriggled off the pants and wriggled on the shorts. I was pretty sure no one was looking.

I bought my ticket for the Maid of the Mist and got on board with fifty families. We all wore matching blue plastic rain ponchos that made us look like we were going to a Smurf convention. I tried to take some pictures but was getting sprayed by the water off the falls so much that I put my camera away for fear it would be ruined. Pocketing it under my poncho, I reminded myself that sometimes just soaking in the moment instead of trying to capture it on camera makes for a better memory. I turned my face to the sun and smiled as it got soaked. The sunshine, the blue sky, the water . . . it was beautiful. If the little girl who was pitching a fit and screaming her bloody lungs out would have just fallen overboard, it would have been perfect.

Getting off the boat, I noticed a bride and groom having their picture taken overlooking the falls. I thought of that episode of *The Office* when Jim and Pam got married at Niagara Falls. I loved Jim even more than usual in that episode. When he said getting married on the boat was Plan C, and getting married at the church was Plan B, but marrying Pam much, much earlier – pretty much the day he met her – was Plan A, I had nearly cried. I wanted a Jim.

I left the falls and went to get checked in at the local hostel. Some friends had bought me a hosteling membership as a going away present, telling me hostels were a good alternative to camping or couch surfing, so I thought I'd give it a try. This one was in a lovely neighborhood where several houses' windows were boarded up. I felt a familiar fear for Cherry Cherry's windows that night. The hostel itself was sturdy and clean. I put my backpack in the room I was assigned to upstairs with three other women, then came back down to the common room to send out some emails.

I joined a guy who was watching TV while eating directly from a pot. The TV show was about dinosaurs and how they became extinct, and perhaps my brain made an unfair connection between that ancient era on TV and the guy watching, but I'm pretty sure I would have thought he looked like a cave man even if I'd met him at the mall. When he spoke, I couldn't quite place his accent, mainly because he grunted more than he enunciated. When the dinosaur show ended, some survivalist show came on. A man was showing how to use a dead sheep to drag yourself out of a mucky bog. I wondered what the likelihood was that he'd actually found a dead sheep just conveniently lying there for him to use for the segment; more likely, some poor, perfectly alive sheep had been sacrificed and thrown out there to be "found." It got worse though. After successfully crawling out of the muck, with the dead sheep's help, he showed how to cut off and use the fleece to keep warm, then how to cut up its innards for food. I thought I might puke. Cro-Magnon man just kept eating out of his pot.

I packed up my computer and headed back out, this time to the Canadian side of the falls. I'd heard there was a better view on that side and that they lit up the falls at night. It felt a little strange, wandering around by myself. I had gotten used to being alone during the first three months of my trip, but after three months of being surrounded by my camp friends, it felt wrong to not have anyone to turn to and make sarcastic comments like, *Wow, that cover band singing "Every Rose Has It's Thorn" is pretty awesome . . . and the international tourists must think they're famous, the way they're zooming in with their high-power lenses and taking fifty photos.*

It was after ten when I got back to the hostel, but even in my tired state, I instantly broke into a smile as I walked in. I could hear a dog eating in the common room, and I rounded the corner excitedly anticipating a Golden Retriever or something cute and cuddly to pet. Instead, there sat the cave man, shoveling more food into his trough. At least he was using a plate this time. I sighed and continued on to my shared room, observing that if I had to choose a lifelong companion, I'd definitely pick a dog over that guy.

People wonder why I'm still single. Limited options, friends. Limited options.

#28 – OHIO

Imagine a place – a magical place! – that holds within its boundaries not one roller coaster, not two roller coasters, but FIFTEEN freaking awesome, lose-your-lunch-it's-such-a-steep-drop roller coasters. I had long heard legendary accounts of the roller coasters at Cedar Point Amusement Park, and heading for Ohio, there was no other place I wanted to go on the first date of the second half of the trip. After a three-month hiatus, I would be starting off with a bang.

There was one small problem: I didn't know anyone in Ohio. A few guys from dating websites had emailed me, offering to be my Ohio date, but none of them lived close to Cedar Point, and I was determined that this would be the setting to meet Mr. Ohio. Besides, I had to knock out four dates in four days – Ohio, Michigan, Indiana, & Illinois – to get to Iowa by Labor Day Weekend for a little family time. If I wanted three days with them, I didn't have time to swoop down to Columbus or Cincinnati . . . and even if I did have the time, I'd still prefer to visit the alleged roller coaster capital of the world.

I tried a new approach to date-finding: I contacted a radio station. After a little internet research, I found a morning show DJ named Randy and sent him an email asking if he could help me find a date. We taped an interview, he played it at his station in Sandusky, and then he screened callers to find me the perfect date. He even used his connections at Cedar Point to snag us free admission to the park. Why hadn't I tried this long ago?

I got an email the day after the interview from a listener named Roseann. She'd gone to my website, read about my adventure, and wanted to offer me a free haircut when I got to town. Her timing was perfect: I was about to start round two of the dates, and I hadn't had a haircut since April, back in Virginia. Oh, and she also had some friends who ran a bed & breakfast if I was looking for a place to stay. She'd call and get me a free room for the night if I was interested.

Was I interested? Are you kidding me? I'd never spent a night at a B & B in my whole life! I hadn't even gotten there yet, and already Ohio was my new favorite state.

The five hour drive from Niagara Falls to Sandusky was surprisingly scenic. Besides the occasional glimpses of Lake Erie, there were several vineyards, which pretty much shocked me. I mean, Napa Valley, Bordeaux, Tuscany, and . . . Ohio? I had no idea. The ride was smooth until I hit Cleveland. I'd left with plenty of time to spare, hoping to get a pedicure somewhere along the way. I think we've established that I'm not really a girly-girl, but after three months of working at camp, my toes needed some prettying up before I started the autumn round of dating. I poked around on my GPS, looking for a salon. It found one called Lena's Nails, so I selected it as my new destination and headed that way.

When I drove into a residential neighborhood, I suspected something wasn't right. When I continued into worse and worse neighborhoods, I started to get a little worried. I figured maybe in a bad part of town, though, pedicures were cheaper (the glass is almost always half full in my world!). I followed my GPS's every command until it told me I had arrived at my destination. I was in front of an empty lot with run-down, boarded-up houses on either side. Either Lena used to do nails inside her recently-bulldozed crackhouse or my GPS had, once again, thought it would be fun to detour me through the ghetto.

Eventually my GPS led me to a good location: Our Sunset Place Bed and Breakfast in a little town called Catawba Island. I might have drooled a little as Bart led me around the place, showing me the three rooms I could choose from . . . but how could I choose? One room had that fancy shower set-up where you get hit with water from several angles, and one had a Jacuzzi tub. They all had big, comfy-looking beds and incredible views of Lake Erie. Bart showed me the deck, where I'd have breakfast the next morning, and I suddenly wasn't so anxious to get to those roller coasters. I wanted to pull up a lounge chair and just sit, reading a book, looking out over the water.

I was late for my date, of course, after getting sidetracked by the fabulous place where I would get to sleep that night. I thought again about how different this trip would have been had that dating component not been thrown in. It would undoubtedly have been much more relaxed, with more time for just sitting and reading and relaxing . . . but then again, if it weren't for the dating, there would have been no radio interview and no free hook up at this fabulous B&B. I'd be in a tent somewhere instead of looking forward to that soft bed and Jacuzzi tub at the end of the night.

Mr. Ohio was running a little late, too, so it turned out not to be a problem. We'd arranged to meet at 4PM to try to squeeze in as many roller coaster rides as we could before the 9PM closing time. He was leaving work early to get there, and although I had no idea what he did for a living, I feared he might be more dressed up than I was. I sent him a text.

Me: I just want to warn you that I'm very casual. As in, I'm wearing a t-shirt. And it's wrinkled. So don't show up all dressed up and make me look bad.

I considered adding "sweaty" to the description since the humidity made the air thick enough to cut, I swear, but I feared he might change his mind and be a no-show, so I abstained.

Him: Dang now I have to take my tux back. Can you pay for my deposit? :]
Me: Hilarious! I would crack up watching you ride roller coasters in a tux...you'd probably pass out since Ohio is hotter than any state I've visited so far!
Him: The weather is hotter and so are the guys. You probably won't want to leave.
Me: Ha ha . . . we'll see about that.
Him: I knew you were going to say that. If you didn't know I have a lip ring. Just to for warn you.

Lip ring? That was a new one. I racked my brain and couldn't think of anyone I'd ever dated who had rings in any location. I didn't really care; the former English major in me was, however, a little

bothered by his spelling of *forewarn*.
>**Me:** Not an issue! Now if you're bringing along your four kids, that might shock me . . .
>**Him:** Dropping all 6 of them off now at the sitters.
>**Me:** Awesome.

I like a sense of humor. At least I hoped he was joking.

When Randy, the DJ, had sent me an email with the name and number of the guy he'd chosen for me, he'd said my Mr. Ohio was 22. I had hoped that Randy was not an excellent typist and had meant 32 . . . but as Mr. Ohio walked toward me, there at the front gate of Cedar Point Amusement Park, it was very apparent that, no, he actually was 22, the youngest guy I'd dated so far on this adventure. Some quick math brought me to a thirteen year age difference . . . let the awkwardness begin!

I'd dated quite a few guys who were younger than me – not thirteen years younger, but as many as six. If you look around at older people, you see many more women than men. Men always seem to die first, so maybe if you marry a younger man, you'll die around the same time; marry an older man and you're almost certain to spend your golden years alone.

My Mr. Ohio turned out to be a good man for the activity, really. I mean, an older man might have had a heart attack. We rode every roller coaster in the park, except for one. (When I saw that it went backward, I explained to him my theory of men not finding you attractive if you puke on them . . . and going backward would definitely have made me puke.) The only one I didn't like was the roller coaster you rode standing up. My head got bounced and jiggled all over the place, and as I stumbled away, I thought, *You know, maybe I'm too old for this kind of thing anymore.* Geesh. Thirty-five and my best years were already behind me?

I sheepishly admitted I needed a break after that one, so we sat and ate frozen lemonades while my brain resettled. Based on my initial impressions, he seemed like a good guy and a hard worker. He told me he had a little girl, which shocked me. He wasn't the first of my fifty dates to be a dad, but for Pete's sake, Mr. New York could have been Mr. Ohio's dad. I couldn't imagine being a parent at 22. He seemed like a good kid, but too young to have his own kid. We had plenty of time to talk while we waited in lines, and I wondered again why so many people fall into that dinner-and-a-movie rut when dating. I was getting to know someone while having a blast. And going from 0 to 120 miles per hour in four seconds? That ain't on the menu at Applebee's.

Toward the end of the night, I was getting hungry. Maybe my stomach had gotten stretched during the three months I was at camp. After a steady diet of kid-friendly foods, I was honestly happy to be back in my granola-bar-and-fruit routine instead of eating pizza, hot dogs, and fries all the time, but after getting used to three meals a day, I'd been hungry for two straight days since leaving camp. We went into a diner and ordered milkshakes.

"My treat," I said. "You bought the frozen lemonades." But then I realized, to my horror, that my money was gone.

I'd chosen not to carry my purse in. There's never a good place to put one when you're on a roller coaster. You can't take it with you, because it might fall out if you go upside-down. Most amusement parks provide bins to put your personal items in, but I'm always afraid some klepto girl will snag my purse and walk away. Instead I'd brought along a small bag that just fit the essentials: my camera, my ID, chapstick, and $40. Everything else I'd locked in my trunk. I knew I'd put in $40 because I'd sat in my car, cash in hand, trying to figure out how much I should take in. The tickets were going to be free, but I'd probably get hungry, and amusement park food was always expensive. I'd decided on $20, but then I thought, *you never know what might happen, and it's better to be prepared*, so I stuck in another $20. Now, here at the cash register in the diner, the little bag held my camera, my chapstick, and my ID . . . but no twenty dollar bills.

"Do you think someone took it while we were on a ride?" Mr. Ohio asked. I had put it in the bins a few times when the rides went upside down. Crap. Crap, crap, crap. $40 might not seem like a lot of money to some people, but when you've got very limited funds, every dollar counts.

"Maybe I dropped it in my car . . ." I ventured. I doubted it, but I had been in a hurry, being late. "I'm pretty sure I had two twenties. Someone must have taken them, unless . . ."

Oh crap. How could I have been so careless? I'd pulled out the camera to take a picture with Mr. Ohio earlier. The money must have fallen out then. Some redneck probably found it and was now eating all the funnel cakes and cotton candy he could stomach with *my* money!! I was so mad at myself. And I felt really bad when Mr. Ohio had to pay for our shakes. We downed them while walking to the next roller coaster.

"Um, are you limping?" I asked. We'd been cruising around the park for several hours by that point.

"It's nothing," he said.

"No, no, let's hear it," I egged him on, thinking it was probably some high school football injury.

"Well, I was fighting with my ex. She was driving and our kid was in the backseat, and I just wanted to end the conversation, so I got out."

I processed that for a second.

"While the car was moving?" I clarified.

"Yeah," he said, sounding a little embarrassed. But then he came to his own defense. "It wouldn't have been a big deal if she wouldn't have slammed on the brakes, but then the door hit me."

"Oh," I said. I couldn't really think of another response that wouldn't come out sounding like a lecture. I suddenly felt more motherly than I had on any other date. I tried not to treat him like a kid, but I definitely held back. I mean, sometimes I do those flirtatious things like touching a guy's arm while I'm talking to him or batting my eyelashes or whatever. I didn't give this poor guy anything. Instead I told him how I wanted to start a matchmaking service to set up all the guys I'd dated on the trip. Mr. Ohio said I should pitch it as a new reality TV show. After I was done with the trip and the book had been published, I could revisit all fifty guys I had dated, but this time I'd set them up with a woman who had read the book and written me about the guy she liked best. I could pick which reader I thought best matched each guy and then send them on a fabulous date together in his state. How fun would that be? Mr. Ohio requested a Megan Fox look-alike for his date. I laughed, not surprised; at 22, what's more important than looks?

Leaving the park, we both realized that we'd been hurrying so much, being late, that neither of us had taken note of where we'd parked. We wandered around the parking lot, him limping slightly and me thankful I'd worn comfortable if not attractive Keens. You never realize how huge amusement park parking lots are until your car is lost in one. We found my car first and he gingerly wedged himself onto the small bit of upholstery not taken up by the atlas, the briefcase-sized CD case, and the plethora of other objects filling the generally-unused-by-humans passenger seat. Then we cruised around the parking lot, looking for his car. When we finally found it, he said he had a present for me. I pulled an Ohio State t-shirt out of the gift bag and was touched by his thoughtfulness, even if the shirt was made for someone quite a bit larger than I was. (Did I look fat in my online profile pictures? I made a mental note to check that in the morning.) We ended the night with a hug and I said I'd do my best to keep an eye out for a Megan Fox lookalike to set him up with. I tried not to speed on my way back to the bed & breakfast. That Jacuzzi tub was calling my name.

The next morning, I fell in love with the people of Ohio. Bart & Sandy served dish after delicious dish on the deck. (French toast with caramelized peaches on top? Seriously? I'd never been treated like a queen before, but I could definitely get used to it.) I'd also never had such a beautiful setting in which to eat my breakfast. I didn't want to leave. I promised to come back for a week if I ever won the lottery, but for now, I had my haircut appointment to get to, then three more dates that week. Go, go, go.

Roseann was waiting for me at her salon in nearby Port Clinton. She greeted me with a bottle of wine from one of the wineries along Lake Erie and some road trip popcorn from the business next door. I couldn't believe it. As she was cutting my hair, two guys from the local paper came in to interview me and take some pictures, and a lady came in with a basket of fresh local produce – grapes, apples, and peaches – for me to snack on as I drove. Before I left, Roseann gave me big bottles of shampoo & conditioner, enough to last me the rest of my trip. These people were amazing. I was so happy to be back in the Midwest. The second half of the journey was off to an encouraging start.

#29 – MICHIGAN

I love surprises. I mean the good surprises, not surprises like those whack-job internet pranks where they tell you to look really closely at the screen to try to find what's wrong with the picture and then this gruesome face jumps out screaming at you. That's just wrong and could give a person a heart attack. Anyone who sends me one of those automatically gets removed from my Christmas card list. But I like the pleasant surprises, like when you find money in your coat pocket when you put it on for the first time in the fall. Or when you open up your mailbox and find a real letter instead of just bills and junk mail. Or when you have low expectations for a guy you're meeting and he turns out to be really, really great.

I was feeling more hopeful, starting out the second half of the trip. I'd been so discouraged by the end of round one and all those not-right-for-me guys on the East Coast, but I'd met a sweet guy at camp who'd given me hope that there were still good guys out there. He was one of the college kids working at the camp for the summer, and he lamented that girls his age didn't appreciate good guys. They wanted bad boys, he said. I assured him that in time, those women would realize how rare it was to find a mature, good-hearted, fun loving guy who would remain faithful. I, for example, would never pick a bad boy over a good guy. (Well, unless you throw Rhett Butler into the mix. But seriously, if Ashley Wilkes wasn't such a pansy . . .)

But then I had to turn to the internet again for a date in Michigan, and after some not-so-great set ups via internet dating sites in round one, I didn't have high hopes for this one either. Plus he called as I was driving in from Ohio and said he'd been called in to work that night. I thought he was going to bail, but he said we had enough time to go kayaking if I could get there fairly soon. I headed his direction but wondered where I was going to change. I was wearing the big t-shirt Mr. Ohio had given me the night before, and while it was perfect for comfy driving, it wasn't exactly flattering.

I hit road construction coming into Ann Arbor and couldn't do anything but sit there and watch the minutes tick away on the dashboard clock. Then my gas light came on. Ugh. I pulled over at a gas station, and while the tank was filling, I pulled a smaller t-shirt out of the trunk. My plan had been to shower and change before meeting him, but I guessed I'd probably get sweaty and smelly kayaking anyway, so it didn't really matter. If I wanted a date in Michigan, this was as good as I was going to look. I didn't even bother worrying about modesty. I was wearing a sports bra, which I figured covered more than most bikinis, so I just switched shirts right there in my car and got back on the road.

He was waiting for me when I arrived, and we were on the river shortly after that. It was a perfect day: blue skies, sunshine, and surprisingly good conversation. He was a traveler, too. He'd taken five months off between his current job and his previous one to travel through Europe, the Middle East, and Africa. There were still several places he wanted to see.

"I'd like to travel the world for a year for my honeymoon," he said. I started mentally counting out the number of months it would be proper to date before getting engaged, calculating how soon we could be on the road.

"I have a friend who once told me you should take a trip with the person you're dating before you decide to get married," I said. "He thinks that people can show you what they want you to see in your normal day-to-day dating, but the curveballs that come with international travel show you who the person really is."

He nodded. "I think you should date someone through all four seasons. It's kind of the same idea, I guess." He mentioned dating someone for two years, and I expressed my shock.

"I don't get that," I confessed. "I hear about couples who've dated for a year or two or even longer, and then they break up. I don't get it. How can you date someone that long and not realize they're not the person you want to marry? Why does it take so long to figure it out?"

"How long was your longest relationship?" he asked. I hate when people answer a question with another question. Especially that one.

"Um . . . about five months," I said.

"So you've never been in a long-term relationship?"

"That was a long-term relationship," I argued. When he gave me a look that said, *I disagree*, I pled my case. "Why bother continuing to date someone when you know it's not going anywhere? I mean, I don't see the point of dating just to date. I've got plenty of friends who I don't have time to see; why waste the time I could be hanging out with my friends by dating someone I'm not going to want to be with a year from now, let alone twenty years from now?"

"How can you know in such a short time that you can't work through things?"

"Okay, here's an example: finances. It's not like I'm looking for someone rich, because I live pretty simply, but I am looking for someone who's financially responsible. When I got out of college, I paid off my ten-year loan in four years. When I bought the car I'm currently driving, I paid for it outright. I don't owe anyone money – no bank, no credit card company, nothing. So when I found out that my last boyfriend was nearly $100,000 in debt, that was a deal breaker. Some things are minor, and you can work through them, but some things aren't. Struggling for the next fifty years to get out of debt *he* racked up before he ever met me? I'm sorry, I'm not going to do it. To me, if you know what qualities you're looking for and what you just can't deal with, there's no point in trying to 'make it work.' It's a waste of time."

He nodded. I wasn't sure if he was agreeing with me or if he just wanted to switch topics so I'd shut up. We pulled over at a dam and strolled alongside the water for a bit before getting back in our boats. I didn't get on my soapbox any more, but I asked a lot of questions and liked the answers I got. He was outdoorsy and smart and funny and Christian. His priorities weren't messed up and he had plans for the future. Simply put, he was a good guy.

He suggested getting smoothies after I returned my rental

kayak, and since his meeting was going to be downtown, near where we were headed, he changed clothes. I don't know if I'd been so frazzled by being late that I didn't even look at him when I first met him, or if his sunglasses were hiding his eyes, or if he became cuter as I got to know him a little or what, but when he reappeared in a polo, all I could think was, *Wow!* Team the looks and the personality, and we might have ourselves a winner here in Michigan. I declared him nearly perfect.

We sipped our smoothies as we wandered around downtown Ann Arbor. I was kicking myself for scheduling four dates in four states in four days. I suddenly wanted to stay in Michigan and see this guy again. I got this sad feeling as we walked back to our cars. He had asked, while we were kayaking, what I'd do if I found someone I was interested in. Would I keep going, or would I stay with the person I was interested in? I'd told him the original plan had been to travel and dating had been an add-on, so I'd keep going. I reminded myself that I was the problem here. It's hard to date someone who's not around. And really, I didn't even know if he was as interested in me as I was in him.

I got in my car and was fiddling with my GPS when Mr. Michigan pulled up alongside Cherry Cherry and gave that "roll your window down" motion. When I did, he said, "I just wanted to tell you that it's too bad you don't live in Michigan, 'cause I'd like to see you again." (Insert girlish scream! He liked me, too!) He said maybe we could meet up when he went to visit a friend in Colorado in November and my face fell a little; I had no idea where I was going to be in November.

I wondered which was worse, having a bad date you couldn't get away from fast enough, or having a good date you had to leave behind?

I spent the night with my Chief Safety Officer Alicia's friend Chickie in Grosse Point. I'd noticed the VW Eurovan parked in her driveway when I'd arrived, and after commenting on how jealous I was, she promised to give me the brief tour the next morning. I probably should have just said no and saved myself the major envy, but instead I spent fifteen minutes drooling over the little kitchen and the comfy bed and the pop-out shower. I was pretty well set for the next two weeks, staying with family and old friends as I crossed the Midwest, but I thought of that raccoon that had freaked me out . . . and how I'd been scared that a rapist was creeping around outside my tent one night . . . and how annoying it was to have to take down a wet tent with numb fingers . . . and how all those problems could have been avoided if I'd had my own freakin' Eurovan.

#30 – INDIANA

As I drove around the country, people kept asking me what I was going to do after my little adventure was over. Truthfully, I had no idea. Before leaving, I'd been a little frightened by the prospect of being unemployed, but once I was out on the road, not tied down with any responsibilities or commitments, I didn't really want to think about having to get a job. Ever. I knew I'd have to find work sooner than later, though; the bank account dipped lower and lower every day. I had some possibilities in mind. I liked working with teenagers, so I could probably do that again. I also liked old people, but I didn't want to watch them die, and I wasn't sure what market there was for work with active retirees. I loved traveling, obviously, but I wasn't sure anyone would pay me to do that. So, in all honesty, I really had no idea what I'd be doing when the fifty-state journey ended. After Indiana, though, I had some options I'd never considered: police officer, Olympic biathlon competitor, or mall security guard. Turned out I was pretty good with a gun.

My old college friend Kristen found me my Mr. Indiana. They were both medical school residents and worked eighty hours a week. They didn't really have much time for social lives. (Her husband joked later that med school was a good time to swoop in on a person because they're so darn happy to be dating someone that they easily fall for you.)

Mr. Indiana & I arranged to meet up at a shooting range – definitely a new date location for me. He'd read one of my initial blog posts where I'd written about safety concerns, quoted Jennifer Grey in *Ferris Bueller's Day Off* ("I am very cute, very alone, and very protective of my body. I don't want it violated or killed, all right?"), and declared that I may or may not be packing heat. I had to admit to him that I had just posted that to keep the creepers away and had never even held a gun, let alone owned one. He had a gun, though, so we made plans to go shoot it.

The shooting range was in a store with lots of display cases full of guns and ammo. We donned protective hardware for our eyes and ears, then entered the actual room where people were firing away. Even though logically I was aware that we were in a shooting range, I still started like a spooked horse the first few times a gun went off near me. (Luckily, despite my GPS's tendency to take me through the ghetto of every major city I'd been through, I'd never actually heard a gun go off at close range.)

I'm gonna let you in on a little secret: loading .38 Specials into a revolver feels totally badass. As I was sliding each one into its little round hole, I thought, "This is like being in a movie!" I clicked the barrel shut, pointed at the target, and fired away. I was amazed at how much kick that little gun had. I mean, I'd heard that when you fired shotguns or rifles or whatever those big ones are, you generally ended up with bruises on your shoulder from the kickback, but this little thing was just in my hand. It wasn't teeny-tiny, but comparatively, it seemed fairly small; still, when I pulled the trigger, the whole gun jerked up. Yikes.

We took turns shooting. He'd fire off six shots, then I'd reload and fire six shots. We put up a fresh target and I got to shoot first. Six shots left six bullet holes in that body-shaped piece of paper. I took a picture. I'm not trying to brag, but I was pretty proud of myself, especially when another couple came in and the woman was obviously also shooting for the first time. Whereas I had gotten used to the sound of shots pretty quickly, she was still jumping every five or six seconds when someone in the room fired. She also didn't appear to be a quick learner. Or maybe she just had poor aim. Or maybe she was afraid of the gun. I don't really know. But I do know that although it wasn't officially a competition, I won. (I can't help it.)

When we'd used up all of our bullets, Mr. Indiana asked if I wanted to go get something to eat. I sheepishly asked if we could go to Culver's. I'd seen a billboard on the way into town and instantly started drooling since I hadn't eaten at one since I'd left Colorado in February. No, it was not a romantic date location, but dang it, I wanted a Butter Burger. We hadn't really gotten to talk much during the bullet-fest, so it was nice to chat while we were eating. I learned that while I was gallivanting around the country, he was working his tail off. It seemed to me that med school and all that came after it was a huge pain. Getting up at 4:45AM every day? No, thank you. Getting home after 8PM every night? Seriously? You must really, really want to be a doctor to put up with those hours. Kristen & I had been out of college for thirteen years. Thirteen years is a really long time to be sleep deprived. I couldn't even imagine it. I was glad Mr. Indiana had gotten out of the hospital to spend a couple hours with me. I should have asked when his last date was. My guess was that he was probably too tired to pursue anyone.

I found Kristen's house pretty easily and envied the big lawns and elegant houses in her neighborhood. I'd met her husband at their wedding a few years back, but I had yet to meet their almost two-year-old. He was adorable. I melted. I sometimes think, nah, I don't need to be a mom. Then I hang out with an adorable kid who is the perfect mash-up of his mom and dad, and I can't help but wonder what my child would look like. Would he take after his dad or me? Would he be quick to laugh or so tenderhearted that he more often cried? I caught up with Kristen and Kevin while cartoons played in the background. Ah, domestic family life. When I woke up the next morning and hopped in the shower, I noticed a plastic frog full of bath toys in the tub and a squishy whale covering the water spout so Zachary would never bump his head during bath time. I didn't envy the long hours and sacrifices Kristen had made for her career, but I envied this.

I grabbed coffee before I left town with a guy I'd met at camp over the summer. He had said then that he'd help me find a date in Indianapolis or that he'd be the back-up if it didn't work out. I got the feeling that he wasn't going to try very hard to find me a date so that he could be my Mr. Indiana. When Kristen set me up with her friend, I'd let the camp guy know he didn't have to ask his friend, but then he asked if I wanted to meet up the next morning at a coffee shop anyway. I didn't want to be a jerk, so I did. But as I drove away after our hour of hanging out, I got a text message that verified what I'd guessed.

Him: I have a little bit of a crush on you.

Ugh. Why is it that the ones you're not interested in are always the ones who like you? I tried to think of something that would let him down easy. I guessed he probably wasn't a Christian, so I went with that, trying to keep it light so I wouldn't hurt his feelings.

Me: You'd get over it once you got to know me better. Jesus talk sends the men running. :]
Him: I'm a Buddhist. Guess that's like oil and water isn't it.
Me: Not as bad as it could be but not workable either... sorry.
Him: I bet your a good kisser..sigh. You've got great looking lips.

Oh geez. I needed to wrap this up.

Me: Um...thanks? I've never been complimented on my lips before.
Him: Well, you've never met me before ;]

That seemed like a nice comment to end on. I didn't text back, and I never heard from him again.

#31 – ILLINOIS

I've never been good at picking up guys. I'm fairly shy, really. The only time I attract men is on the dance floor. I used to think I must be a pretty awesome dancer, but then some friends pointed out that no, I'm a really *funny* dancer. But anyway, I was worried about finding a Mr. Illinois since I'd never met a guy in a coffee shop. Well, not without previously arranging it.

The guy I had hoped would be my Mr. Illinois cancelled the day I planned to meet him. In his defense, he had said it might not work out, but since he hadn't definitively said it wouldn't, I thought that meant he was in unless I heard differently. Nope. And I couldn't find a replacement date on such short notice, so I went to a coffee shop to try to find a new Mr. Illinois. This was my first attempt at picking up a date on the spot. My first thirty dates had all been arranged in advance.

There are a couple of techniques I've learned over the years that are supposed to help you attract men, but I've had mixed results. One is the "Bend & Snap." If you've seen *Legally Blonde*, you know this one. You "drop" something on the floor, bend at the waist rather than the knees to pick it up, and then snap perkily upright, flipping your hair for good measure. It looked better when Reese Witherspoon did it than when I tried it. When I saw *Wicked* in New York City, I learned another move from Glenda. It basically involves tossing back your hair and shaking it out a little. It didn't really look right with chin-length hair like mine, though. My favorite go-to attention-getting method was "The Look." You catch a man's eye, then look away. You look at him again with your head tilted down, kind of through your eye lashes, all flirty and demure, then look away again. And then, the third time you look at him, you hold eye contact. I've been told by friends I've shown it to that it's more creepy than attractive, but I tried it on the meat counter guy at Safeway once and it totally worked . . . or maybe he was just hoping I'd buy some expensive steaks. I'm not sure.

So there I was, in a coffee shop in Illinois, waiting for an attractive man to come in so I could pounce. Walking down the street, looking for a coffee shop, I'd seen mostly white-haired old men, so I was a little bit worried about my chances of finding a guy in the right age range in this town. I ordered a hot chocolate (I sometimes think I'm the only grown-up in the world who doesn't like coffee or tea) and found a place to sit. There was a really comfy looking couch in the back with a strange John Lennon-posing-as-a-saint picture lurking over it, but I figured my chances would be better if I placed myself closer to the flow of traffic.

After half an hour, a guy finally came in. He was wearing a yellow Fedora, which normally would have disqualified him on the spot, but he was the first man to enter the place, so I overlooked it. Unfortunately, he never looked my way. He ordered his coffee, looked at the pastries while he waited, got his drink, and walked out.

Um, excuse me? How can I give you "The Look" if you won't even make eye contact?

It took nearly an hour for another guy to come in. Geez. Dating here had to suck. This one was wearing a huge basketball jersey with equally huge shorts. Every visible bit of skin was covered by tattoos. He had five earrings in the one ear I could see. Not the norm for me, but it was no time to be choosy. Hello, Mr. Illinois.

I smiled at him as he walked to the counter. It hurt a little. After he ordered a drink, he looked at the artwork on the walls, then pronounced the art to be "awesome." I turned around and looked . . . a series of drawings of women were on the wall behind me. Most of them were naked. Some had long hair partially covering them, but yeah, mostly naked. I nodded back at him.

"I'm an artist, too," he said.

"That's great," I said, trying to feign interest in someone I was completely uninterested in.

"A professional tattoo artist," he elaborated.

"Oh," I said, motioning toward his arms. "Nice."

"Illinois just passed a law that you can't discriminate against people because of their tattoos."

I nodded again. Man, I sucked at this. "That's great."

His name was called and he got his drink. I had to try to keep him there. Who knew when another guy was going to come in?

"Do you want to join me?" I asked.

He looked at me kind of funny. I'm sure it was pretty obvious that I wasn't his type. And I may have been about ten years older than him.

"I've got to get back to the shop," he said.

"Okay," I said. Man, getting shot down sucked, even if you weren't actually interested in the guy. "Have a good day."

And a nice life.

Ah, Illinois.

I tried.

It counts.

#32 – WISCONSIN

As I crossed yet another state line, I bit into my last peach from that generous lady who worked at the greenhouse in Ohio. I savored it. I'd never eaten a peach so juicy. I wondered if they got sick of them, though. I mean, if you grow peaches, you probably get tired of peaches and want a mango or an apple or a banana instead. It reminded me of a conversation I'd once had with a friend who is a massage therapist. I'd said it would be great to marry a massage therapist, because you'd never have to pay for a massage again. She'd countered that after a long day of giving massages, the last thing she'd want to do when she got home was work on her husband's back. Scratch massage therapists off the list of potential husbands. And gynecologists.

After my not-so-successful attempt to pick up a guy in Illinois, I was excited to move on to Wisconsin. I'd emailed a guy I'd met online a few years before. He'd sounded pretty close to perfect back then, and we'd emailed back and forth three or four times, but he was in Wisconsin and I was in Colorado, and it understandably petered out (says the girl who once ditched a guy from Denver because she wasn't interested in a long-distance relationship . . . that hour drive was too much of an effort). Mr. Wisconsin, from what I could tell via email, was cute and outdoorsy and smart and Lutheran. What more could a girl ask for? I was really excited that he remembered me and said yes, he'd be my date for his state.

I'd bought a bunch of cute clothes over the summer. (Okay,

fine, maybe two shirts and one sundress don't qualify as "a lot" in your world, but I was making an effort, okay? Give me some credit.) I planned to wear the cute little sundress, because I'd learned over the summer that guys dig sundresses. I was also informed by one of the guys I worked with that this particular dress showed my figure nicely without looking skanky, so I plucked it out of my trunk tub and relocated it to my backpack.

Once I got to Wisconsin, though, I quickly realized impressing Mr. Wisconsin with the sundress was not going to happen. The flags on the flagpoles were completely horizontal. When I opened up my car door, the fierce, chilling wind almost blew it off. Mr. Wisconsin wasn't going to get cute, summery Tiffany. Nope. He was going to get the jeans and jacket girl who had toured the South through the rainy Spring.

At the gas pump, I got really annoyed with its little game of Twenty Questions. Do you want a carwash? No. Credit or debit? Credit. What is your zip code? 80917. Denied. Crap. My bills were going to my parents' address now. I tried punching it in but the screen went blank, then back to the first question. What do you mean I have to start over? Do you have any idea how cold it is out here? Do you want a carwash? No. Credit or debit? Credit. What is your zip code? 50510. Success! Would you like a receipt?

You know what I'd like, Mr. Gas Pump? I'd like to pump my freaking gas! I'm in capris and flip flops and it feels like Santa's about to visit! Would you let me get my gas already?

Unfortunately, arguing with a gas pump gets you nowhere. (Much like screaming at the GPS . . . but I didn't foresee that stopping anytime soon.)

My sister-in-law had recommended I stop at a house along the way that she had toured before. I called the place to find out if they were a museum or what. Jenni had said each room seemed to be full of different varieties of one item; one room was full of dolls and another was full of teapots and so forth. I wasn't quite sure what the point of it was.

"Is it a museum?" I asked the man who answered my call.

"It's more 'a collection of collections,'" the guy said. What did that mean? I didn't get it.

"How much does it cost for the tour?"

"$28.50 for the basic tour," he began, then named off higher prices for additional tours of more buildings and more collections.

"Great," I lied. "Thanks so much!"

That made the decision easier.

I'd once scared the living daylights out of my youth group kids by taking them to a place in Colorado that seemed interesting. Signs along the interstate said you could see seven states from the top of the tower. Every time I went by, there were cars in the parking lot and people up on top of it. It had to be good. So, at the end of a week-long trip, I pulled the van off the interstate and into the parking lot. There were three other cars there. They were all on blocks. I should have kept driving, but instead the ten of us piled out and approached the door.

"It'll cost you a dollar each to get in," the old man who opened the door said. Not a problem. But then he informed us that if we broke anything, we'd have to buy it.

The place was strange. There were "collections" everywhere. I'd label most of it "junk." In one room there was a two-headed goat.

"Um, you can see the stitches where someone sewed two goat heads together," one of the kids pointed out.

"That's disgusting," another said.

"But for $300, it could be yours," another chimed in. *Everything* had a price tag on it. Ridiculously-priced price tags.

"Don't touch anything!" I hissed at the kids. We entered the stairwell to the tower, and as we wound higher and higher, the passages got more and more narrow. All kinds of crap lined the walls, and the prices on the price tags got higher as the stairwells got narrower. Old pop bottles were priced at $7. Plates were $22. I cringed and waited to hear breaking glass.

At the top, we found that the "people," much like the cars in the parking lot, were a crock. Mannequins looked out over the landscape. Seven states? We highly doubted it. We carefully made our way back down with no breakage, thankfully.

"You can't leave yet," the old man cackled as we reached the bottom. "There are three more rooms to explore."

We dutifully wandered around, looking at the dust-covered "collections" that seemed to have accumulated over the last seventy or eighty years. Newspaper articles were framed on the wall, showing this as a top tourist attraction in Colorado in the 70's. There were letters and postcards telling the owners that the tower had been a highlight of their vacation. We stared, flabbergasted.

"Everybody ready?" I asked after five minutes of moseying around. Everyone made it clear they were ready to get out. The old man, though, was blocking the door.

"I've got a hunnerd items in this here case," he said. "If you can tell me what ten of 'em are, you kin getcher dollar back."

He held up the first item. Several people made polite guesses. No one got it right. He held up the second mystery item and got the same results. After about five, the kids looked at me with the same eyes the gorillas at the zoo do and sent the same telepathic message: please, please get me out of here!

"You know what, sir, you can keep our dollars," I said as kindly as possible, grabbing the door and hustling the kids out. On the way home, they crafted the plot of what might be a major motion picture someday; the story centered on a group of teenagers who have car problems late at night and take shelter in a scary tower . . .

I guessed that the "collections" in Wisconsin were probably a bit nicer, if people paid $28.50 to see them, but I wasn't taking any chances.

Before meeting Mr. Wisconsin, I went to meet the people I was couch surfing with that night. I saw two little faces peering out a window as I drove up – a welcoming committee! This was the first time I'd couch surfed at a home with small children, and I wasn't sure what to expect. They were adorable and seemed genuinely excited to have me staying with them. They even had cute names: Emmalea and Lucy. I got the feeling that if I didn't have to run off for my date, we could have a fun night playing board games.

Mr. Wisconsin and I had planned to stroll through the gardens of a local museum. We'd even gotten special permission to be there after hours. Unfortunately, spitting rain joined the biting wind. Awesome. Forget about being bummed that I couldn't wear the sundress; now the weather was ruining our plans for the night, too. Instead we met by a restaurant along the river.

You might not believe me, but I would say that at least half the Misters had been above average in the attractiveness department. Some were downright hotties. But when I walked into the restaurant, turned the corner, and came face to face with Mr. Wisconsin, I felt a literal physical jolt I don't even know how to describe. It was strange – something I'd never felt before in my entire life – but in a good, good way.

We sat and ate and talked and talked. We had some things in common, like our families being really important to us, and some complete differences, like him being a marathon runner and me not being able to run a marathon if you gave me a million dollars to do it.

The conversation kept on flowing. When he excused himself to go to the restroom and I checked the time, I couldn't believe it; we'd been there for two and a half hours! I was torn – go "home" and hang out with that super sweet family who was letting me sleep at their house tonight, or go find a bar to sit in for a few more hours with this fabulous man? He was a teacher, though, and it was a school night. I would have felt bad, keeping him out late. Oh fine, who are we kidding? I turn into a pumpkin after 10PM.

I gave him a hug in the parking lot and told him I was happy I'd finally gotten to meet him. As I drove away, I wondered what he thought of me. He was so nice. Maybe too nice for me. I mean, I'm generally nice, too, but sometimes I think I'm a little too loud for nice, quiet people. He was probably looking for someone who didn't talk so much or slap her knee when she laughed really hard. Sometimes I worry that I'm just too much for those good guys who I so want to like me. But then I remembered that I shouldn't assume I knew what any guy wanted. Maybe Mr. Wisconsin thought I was awesome. Maybe, as he was driving home, he was thinking about how happy he'd be to have me to come home to every night. Maybe.

The girls were already in bed when I got back, but Shannon and Jean stayed up a while and talked to me. I love couples who still seem to be in love, even after they've been together for years and years. These two had met in grad school. One of my friends was currently dating a guy she'd met in grad school. Maybe I should go to grad school if I couldn't find a husband through the fifty dates method.

In the morning there were eggs and toast and giggles and a brief piano recital. The girls read me a story they'd both written and illustrated. They were adorable, and I felt this sense of longing. Yes, the baby years seemed absolutely hellish with the crying and the diapers and the crying and the teething and the crying and the sleep deprivation and the *why are you still crying?!* But this? Elementary school? It seemed to be delightful. They showed me their backyard and introduced me to their friend next door and ran parallel to my car as I drove away, waving and shouting good-bye. I loved it. I wanted little Emmalea's and Lucy's of my own.

#33 – MINNESOTA

Mr. Minnesota agreed to take me out as a favor to his Aunt Sylvia, a good friend of mine. We'd set the date but not the date activity. When I called to find out where to meet him, he said he'd just gotten his pilot's license that morning, and if I was brave enough, I could be his first-ever passenger as a licensed pilot.

If I was brave enough? The last time I went up in a small plane, I'd had to jump out of it. This would be cake.

The airport was really close to Valley Fair, a place where I'd been brave years before and had, for the first time in my young life, ridden an upside-down roller coaster. That was the same family vacation when we'd gotten horribly lost after visiting an apple orchard ("I think we've been through this section of road construction before, Dad," my brother said.) and then got lost again leaving the Twins game ("The interstate is right on the other side of this retaining wall! I can see it! Why can't I get to it?" my dad growled.) and eventually ended up in a not-so-great neighborhood ("Lock the doors, kids," my mom commanded.). It wasn't a Malcom family vacation unless we were lost at least once.

As Mr. Minnesota went through his preflight checklist, I got a little worried. When I'd gone up in the plane with Mr. Alabama, I'd reasoned that I couldn't die that day because it was my mom's birthday and surely God wouldn't be that cruel, letting me die and making my mom live with that reminder every birthday for the rest of her life. But with Mr. Minnesota, it was just a regular old Thursday. I sighed and looked over at Valley Fair. I reasoned that I couldn't die so close to where I'd first ridden an upside-down roller coaster.

Victory and defeat couldn't reside so close together! (That was the best I could come up with.)

Mr. Minnesota was awesome at keeping me in the loop. He explained every gadget and what it did and what was going to happen next. It took away a lot of my nervousness because it showed me he knew what he was doing. Yeah, he'd just gotten his license that day, but he'd spent hours and hours in training flights. He wasn't going to kill me. Hopefully.

As we flew over a ritzy suburb of Minneapolis, I was rather shocked to see huge houses with backyard pools and tennis courts. I'm a big fan of Garrison Keillor, so I thought all Minnesotans were simple, humble people like the ones in his Lake Wobegon stories. It seemed, though, that he lied; a bunch of people in Minnesota spent ridiculous amounts of money on houses and toys.

His take off and landing were like butter. I never felt the need for an airsick bag once. It was probably the fastest date of the bunch, though, because Mr. Minnesota had to go back to work. I was really glad I didn't live in the corporate world. I'm not a big fan of stress, long hours, meetings, deadlines, or pretty much anything that went along with a job like that.

I headed back over to my friend Monica's house. I was staying with her for my two nights in the Twin Cities. We had gone to preschool together but lost touch somewhere, only to be reunited via the magic of Facebook as adults. As we talked, I was amazed at how someone I was friends with in preschool was someone I still wanted to be friends with thirty years later. International travel was one of the perks of her job, and I was jealous. She said she'd chosen her college because of their highly-regarded study abroad program; I sheepishly admitted that I'd chosen my college in hopes of meeting a good Lutheran boy. Sigh.

It's kind of true. I mean, there were other factors involved in making that decision, but that was one of them. Being Lutheran, I could get a scholarship if I went to a Lutheran college. I narrowed it down to two. My brother went to the other, and I thought going to the same school he did wouldn't be as adventurous as going somewhere else. Plus, Sioux Falls was a metropolis to this farm girl. I mean, they had a mall. I prayed two specific prayers during my senior year of high school: please let me get along with my roommate when

I get to college, and please let me find my husband there.

Batting .500 ain't bad.

The next day, I set out in the rain for North Dakota. Rain makes me want to sleep; I wanted to lie in bed and read a book until I couldn't keep my eyes open, then sleep some more. I missed sleep.

Minnesota drivers, I realized, had never heard of the "drive right, pass left" concept. (Just in case you haven't either, here it is in uber-simple terms. You drive in the right lane. Should you come upon a vehicle not moving as fast as you would like to, you signal, slide over into the left lane, pass them, then slide back over into the right lane and continue on your merry way. You do not – I repeat – DO NOT hang out in the left lane, because someone, likely me, wants to pass your slow sorry self if you'd just move it back into the right lane where you belong! Get out of my freaking way!!)

I almost got hit by a crappy Minnesota driver. He decided to change lanes and veered right in front of me. I hit the brakes, then looked in my rearview mirror to see if the guy behind me was paying attention or would keep cruising and rear-end me. Honestly, I thought Cherry Cherry was about to get crunched and I felt a wave of sadness for her. I braced myself for impact, but just in time, he slammed on his brakes, too. I could see him yelling and waving his arms around and hoped it was directed at the truck driver, not me.

I popped a Jube Jel Cherry Heart in my mouth and tried to enjoy it. I'd hidden a bag in my trunk back in February when I'd left Colorado, thinking it would be a nice surprise to find later, spreading out my enjoyment of them. Unfortunately, Jube Jel Cherry Hearts that have been in a hot trunk from February through September are not great. Kinda crusty. I was eating them anyway because a) it would be February before Brach's would put them out on store shelves again, and b) I eat when I'm bored, and I was bored.

It was a dull drive. The GPS showed blue blobs everywhere – some of those famed 10,000 lakes, I suppose – but I couldn't see much of anything thanks to the rain. Lightning and thunder struck a little too close for comfort and I wondered if I should be on the lookout for funnel clouds. I reassured myself that tornadoes hit in the spring, not the fall. At least I hoped that was true. I kept driving.

#34 – NORTH DAKOTA

I think it's safe to say I'd never looked worse on a date. I'd had problems with acne, bad wardrobe choices, and dark circles under my eyes, but looking in the mirror at that moment, all I could do was laugh.

I was late for my date. Someone told me it took three hours to drive from the Twin Cities to Fargo; that person was a big, fat liar. I knew I was never going to make it on time. I called Amanda and she said not to worry. She'd make a few calls and we'd do the date at six instead of five.

Who's Amanda? She's a morning show DJ in Fargo. After a great experience via the radio route in Ohio, I'd emailed her, explained what I was doing, and asked if she could help me find a Mr. North Dakota. She'd sifted through the applicants and found me a good one. Her coworker Tonya in the sales department had lined up a place for the date, too. The two of them met me at a truck stop so I could follow them out to where the date was going to be.

When we turned onto a gravel road, I admit I had a brief moment of "I hope this isn't some cruel trick where they take me out to the middle of nowhere, steal my car, and leave me to be eaten by prairie dogs" panic. They seemed safe enough, though, so I kept following them until we turned again at a sign that read "Adventure Shooting Sports."

I tried not to get a complex, shaking hands and saying hello. Amanda and Tonya were both prettier and more stylishly dressed than I was, and neither of them had a blossoming zit on her chin. I made small talk and hoped they'd skedaddle before Mr. North Dakota got there so he couldn't compare us. He joined us a minute later, though. As he walked in the door, I thought, *Nice job, Amanda!* He was cute. Very cute. And he came bearing gifts. He gave me an NDSU t-shirt (his alma mater) and a pretty peach rose wrapped up in paper and ribbons. (Yeah, yeah, I shouldn't allow myself to be bought, but let's be honest: presents help!)

John, the owner of the place, gave us a few options for shooting before dinner. I'd just shot pistols in Indiana, so I said I wanted to shoot something big. He handed me a shotgun. Sweet! We headed out to the clay pigeon range. Mr. North Dakota was an experienced shooter, so he went first. When he said, "Pull!" I pushed a little button that launched the clay pigeon. He was a really good shot. When it was my turn, I lined up the shot like John had showed me when he'd handed me the gun. I pulled the trigger and felt the jolt. Yikes! I missed. At least I knew now what it felt like, so I wasn't as scared as I was before. I wasn't a natural, but I hit a few. Not nearly as many as my date did, but a respectable amount for my first time, I'd say. I still needed a few tips, though.

"I don't think your leg is supposed to come up off the ground like that," he advised at one point. The kickback had knocked me off balance a little. I was still upright, though, thank you very much. He showed me how to lean my weight forward so I wouldn't get knocked back again.

My favorite parts were snapping the barrel back in place after loading the shells (a totally badass sound) and popping it open again to let the plastic casings fly out with a poof of smoke. It felt like a movie. *My life rocks*, I thought.

When we ran out of shells, we headed inside. I went to use the bathroom, and that's when I caught sight of myself. My hair was the most noticeable disaster. It had been a little drizzly outside while we were shooting, and I had that ever-so-attractive look I can only compare to a nearly-drowned dog. I tried to finger-comb it back into some style. I sighed. Fairly hopeless. I had that lovely zit on my chin, and it also appeared that half my mascara had been washed away from my left eye. All I could do was laugh. I went back out to Mr. North Dakota, lucky devil, and sat down for dinner.

Yep, a shooting range and a restaurant in one. Laugh if you want to, but their surf and turf dinner was incredible. Savannah, my pick for North Dakota Waitress of the Year, placed a beautiful plate in front of me: a huge steak on top of mashed potatoes, with grilled shrimp on top and asparagus on the side. I was in heaven. I tried to keep up the conversation while shoveling it in. All I'd eaten that day was an orange and a granola bar. When Savannah asked if we wanted dessert, I was already stuffed, but we split a piece of cheesecake with raspberry sauce. Wow. Bliss.

After talking for a long time, I noticed that the kitchen had gone dark and we were the only ones left in the place. Whoops. I guess Mr. North Dakota and I had been too busy talking about his daughter and his home remodeling project to notice how late it had gotten. I said we should go so John could go home, then found him to say thanks for a great night. He gave us both t-shirts as we left – was there no end to his generosity? I love Midwesterners.

I followed Mr. North Dakota back into the city. We walked from North Dakota to Minnesota, which sounds major, but it really just involved crossing a bridge. He was fun to talk to because he had such a positive attitude. He'd decided he wanted to take more risks in life, like going on this random date with me, because, as he said, what was the worst that could happen? I completely agreed.

#35 – SOUTH DAKOTA

South Dakota: home of more suicidal bugs per capita than any other state in the union. At least that was my guess, looking at my windshield. Gross.

I was flying down the interstate, desperately looking for an exit with a gas station. I needed to wash my windshield – the wipers couldn't wash away all the dead bugs – but even worse, I needed to pee. Really, really bad. I fiddled around with my iPod until I found a song I could sing along with to distract myself. I was already halfway past it when I saw a rest area fly by. *Dang it, woman, would you pay attention?*

I eventually came to an exit, went to the bathroom, cleared off the bug carcasses, and filled my gas tank. I'm not sure there's a hard and fast rule about this, but I feel it's good etiquette to buy something if you pee in a place. I mean, yeah, I suppose the cost of the water for that one flush probably isn't equivalent to the $30 I paid to fill my tank, or even $5 for a fast food meal, but I just feel bad if I use a bathroom somewhere without buying anything . . . like the people who work there give me the stink-eye as I walk out the door. I hate having people mad at me, even if I don't know them.

I stopped in Sioux Falls and wandered around my alma mater, Augustana College. Lots of changes had been made since I'd been a student there – some buildings had been torn down and replaced with newer ones, and some were nearly unrecognizable inside due to major remodels – but in the Humanities building, I teared up, walking down the hallways. I felt so . . . grateful. Those four years hadn't necessarily gone as I'd planned, but those four years had definitely shaped me. Maybe I hadn't found the husband I'd prayed for, but I'd left four years later with so much more than I'd expected. Stronger faith. Increased confidence. Deep relationships. Incredible memories. Grateful indeed.

I kept driving, not wanting to be late for yet another date. I was excited for this one. My old friend Trisha had set it up and Mr. South Dakota and I would be double dating with her and her husband. I racked my brain, trying to remember if I'd been on a double date yet. My memories were all starting to jumble together after thirty-four previous dates around the country, but I was pretty sure this was a first for the trip.

Mr. South Dakota arrived and the four of us set out for downtown Vermillion's annual Ribs, Rods, and Rock'n'Roll Festival. Everyone in the tri-state area seemed to be there. We strolled down the street, checking out all the food booths, each proudly displaying the awards they'd won. You didn't know they gave out trophies for the best ribs? And that there were intense rivalries among the BBQ rib grillers? Yeah, me neither. But these people were serious. They had trophies taller than me on display.

I took a picture of the multiple trophies at one food stand, then turned for a shot of the guy at the giant grill. Beautiful racks of ribs slathered in sauce were cooking to perfection.

"Come get a picture of you behind the grill," the guy said. You didn't have to ask me twice. I love goofy shots. I handed my camera to Trisha and started walking around to the other side.

"Ow! Ohahaow!" I wailed. I'd rammed my shins right into something blocking the general public from getting to the goodies. Luckily I'd been smart enough not to try to break my fall by steadying myself on the grill. It would have been hard to drive with third-degree burns on both hands. But why, why, why was I so clumsy? Especially when on a date? I could feel the bruises forming, and I was sure Mr. South Dakota was shaking his head, thinking, "Seriously? This woman is dating her way around the country?"

After assuring everyone I was fine (I mean, really, who needs shins?), we finally decided on a food stand. We chose the locals, not the out-of-towners with the biggest trophies, and ordered our meat and side dishes. We sat and ate, listening to a cover band play 70's and 80's hits. They sounded surprisingly good for a bunch of old guys from South Dakota. I wanted to get up and dance, but no one else did, so I just did some hardcore seat dancing. It's a good thing I don't embarrass easily. (Again, I'm pretty sure Mr. South Dakota was pretending not to know me.)

Trisha and her husband suggested we ditch the noise and go up the street to a local bar where we might actually be able to have a conversation. On the way, we walked past a coffee shop that was for sale. You could buy the entire building – the shop on the main level plus two apartments upstairs – for only $65,000. I'd paid nearly twice as much for my townhome in Colorado.

"After your trip, you could live here and have your own coffee shop," Trisha suggested. "Maybe knock out a wall upstairs and have a giant apartment."

"But I don't even drink coffee," I countered. "How could I run a coffee shop?"

"You'd just have to hire someone who knows about coffee," she suggested.

I'll admit that I'd toyed with the idea of running a little shop like that before. I love small towns, and I could picture my own little place on some Main Street somewhere. I could bake cookies. I make a mean peach pie. It would be a cute little place for people to get a homemade goodie and talk with their friends. My friend Naveen, whom I'd stayed with back in Florida, is an idea man. He's always dreaming up stuff like his idea for a specialty ice cream shop. People would pick a flavor of ice cream, then put it between their choice of cookies. They'd get to choose what sprinkles to roll the sides in, and voila! A custom-made ice cream sandwich. Strawberry ice cream between chocolate cookies with rainbow sprinkles, or vanilla ice cream between oatmeal cookies rolled in mini-chocolate chips. The possibilities were endless. It was brilliant!

The logistics terrified me, though. What licenses does a person need for a place like that? What happens if no customers come in and you can't pay the mortgage? What's the perfect temperature for storing ice cream so that it's soft enough to squish between two cookies but not so soft that it runs all over your hand while you're trying to eat it?

I wasn't sure entrepreneurship was for me.

Upon arrival at our destination, we each ordered a drink at the bar and moved to a table. Soon after we sat down, and identical quartet of drinks was delivered.

"I can't drink two," I protested, still full from the big dinner, then realized the others looked equally confused and dismayed. The bartender cocked his head to a couple sitting at the end of the bar. Trisha knew them from work. They held their drinks up to us and we all put on fake smiles and air toasted back. Dang friendly Midwestern folks, buying us another round of drinks. We tried, but none of us succeeded. Three of the four of us had to work in the morning, and one of us was pulling out before sunrise for a twelve-hour drive. We knew when to say when.

I don't know whether to feel bad that Mr. South Dakota didn't get my full attention or to think he got off lucky, not having to answer my usual round of questions about dating. Trisha and I did most of the talking and the guys chimed in occasionally. I thought it was a fun evening; I'm not sure what Mr. South Dakota thought of the night. When we got back to their house, Trisha and her husband quickly said goodnight and made themselves scarce. I don't know if they thought we'd want privacy for a goodnight smooch session or what, but I just told Mr. South Dakota goodnight and thanked him for being part of my crazy adventure.

I set my cell phone alarm for 5:45AM (ouch!) and fell into a coma-like sleep. "Dancing Queen" rang through the room after an indeterminable amount of time and I inwardly cringed as I dragged myself out of bed, lamenting the fact that morning had come way too quickly. The digital alarm clock, though, read 2:47AM. It wasn't the alarm. Someone was calling me at two-freaking-forty-seven in the morning. I looked at the caller ID: Mr. Michigan.

He is no longer perfect, I thought, hitting the ignore button.

In the morning, I noticed several splotches of BBQ sauce on the sleeve of my light blue fleece jacket. I was annoyed by the stains but strangely fascinated by their location. The same spot had been a target for a bird in Seattle several years before. I wiped it off as best I could, hugged and thanked Trisha, then took off. Another adventure was about to begin: my mom and dad were joining me for the next six days.

#36 – MONTANA

"We have to be in the hotel by seven o'clock tonight," my mom declared. We'd been in the car for about an hour. I'd been trying since I left Colorado in February to persuade my parents to meet me somewhere along my route; now, in September, they were riding along on the Montana leg of the trip.

"I didn't think you'd reserved a room yet," I replied. I was kind of excited about sleeping in a hotel room. I hadn't been in one since May. Don't get me wrong; I loved catching up with friends and meeting new people as I couch surfed, but I thought it would be refreshing to not have to talk about my travels every night with someone new. I definitely wouldn't be talking to my parents about one part of my adventure that week: they hadn't been on board with the solo-travel plan in the first place, so I had decided not to mention the dating part of the trip until I was done and safely back in one piece. I was pretty sure they would be worried sick if they knew I was meeting fifty men across the country. That's fifty potential rapists and murderers, you know. They watch *20/20*.

"Well, no, I haven't reserved anything yet," she verified, "but we'll have to find one by then. *Big Brother* starts at seven."

It was going to be an interesting week.

I love going places. I like camping and hiking and pulling over to read those historic information signs along the side of the road. My parents don't like any of those things. Their idea of relaxation is a night in front of the TV.

It hadn't been easy, coordinating travel plans, but I wanted to make this happen so we could spend some quality time together. Since I wouldn't be driving back to Iowa, my parents needed one-way flights home after seeing Glacier National Park. The best flight I'd found was from Spokane, Washington, to Omaha, Nebraska. And by "best" I mean "most direct." My parents had flown a few times but never had to change planes. Almost every flight I found would have had them changing planes, either in Minneapolis/St. Paul or Denver. Both were pretty big airports. I didn't want my parents wandering around, frustrated and cursing the day I was born.

The flight from Spokane to Omaha had a stop but not a plane change, so I jumped on it. Unfortunately, that meant I had to wake up at 5:45am the day after my date with Mr. South Dakota to get on the road so we could squeeze everything into six days. I met my parents in a McDonalds parking lot north of Omaha and they followed me to an airport parking lot. Trisha had recommended a place where they left their car when they flew out of Omaha, so I set the GPS and away we went. Within half an hour we were lost. Already it was a Malcom family vacation!

We got their car parked and they squeezed into Cherry Cherry. My dad is not a little man. His knees were touching the dashboard. It wasn't much better for my mom, squished into the backseat along with their two suitcases and my food crate. Everything else I had crammed into the trunk. It may not have been too comfortable for them, but after hours and hours alone on the road, I was thrilled to have company while driving.

We all unfolded ourselves a few hours into South Dakota to get some lunch, then continued on our way. A few hours later, the discussion turned to knee replacement surgery and they debated which one of them needed it more.

"You could barely get out of the car back there," my dad informed my mom.

"You're no Spring chicken yourself," she shot back.

Things started going south, attitude-wise, about a third of the way through South Dakota.

"Never in my life have I seen such boring scenery!" Mom declared before settling in for a nap. Dad and I looked at each other and shrugged. A farmer to the core, he was content to look at the fields.

"I think they call that 'milo,'" he said, pointing at one field. He happily pointed out sorghum, sunflowers, and wheat as we passed various plots of land.

"Is Mom asleep?" I asked.

"I don't know. Is her mouth hanging open?" he replied.

She woke up after about an hour and looked out the window.

"Well, it doesn't look any different than it did before I went to sleep," she complained, then added a sarcastic, "lovely, lovely, lovely."

We stopped at the famous Wall Drug and got some fun family photos: Mom by a big stuffed buffalo ("Yuck. It probably has fleas."), Dad by a saloon girl statue ("Hurry up and take it already!"), and me avoiding pictures due to unfortunate acne outbreaks on both my chin and my forehead. Filling up the gas tank on the way out of town, I saw someone who made me feel better about myself; a haggard-looking older woman was having a cigarette, leaning up against the gas station in cutoff overalls with no shirt underneath.

"Wow!" was all my dad could say.

"Well, her red, white, and blue bra matches her star-spangled visor," I said, pointing out the American flag theme. "At least she's got that going for her." Yikes.

Eight hours after we left Omaha, we made it to our destination of the day: Mount Rushmore. It was there that I discovered my dad didn't know how to use a digital camera. I asked him to take a picture of me, and I was definitely in it, but only three of the four presidents also made the shot. But really, how important is George Washington?

The next morning we went out to explore Custer State Park. I'd been there a couple of times before and knew it wasn't flat like the drive across the majority of the state had been. I hoped Mom would appreciate the new scenery, but not so much.

"I've about had my fill of trees," she said after half an hour of winding through the forest. Sigh.

Suddenly we were part of a traffic jam. What the heck? In a state park? I was considering passing when we saw them: bison. Lots and lots of bison. And they were close. Very, very close.

I'd had some close encounters with bison before. In Yellowstone National Park a few years before, I'd been in the backseat during a family vacation. Dad was driving and Mom was beside him. As we'd crossed a bridge, a huge, old bison decided to cross, too. He stayed in his lane, but we all kind of held our breath. I mean, it was amazing to be so close that we could see his battle scars and hear him breathing, but we got the feeling that if we made one wrong move, he could easily buck our Chevy Impala right off the bridge. (That didn't stop Mom from thrusting her camera at my sister, demanding she hang halfway out the window for a good shot of the beast.)

A few years after that, also in Yellowstone, I was in a rented suburban with a bunch of youth group girls. When we'd paid to get in, we'd been handed flyers that said bison are extremely dangerous, can run very fast, and can even kill you. And yet, there beside the road, three Asian tourists were approaching one for a close-up shot. One of the girls had taken Chinese classes at her high school, but they hadn't taught her how to scream, "Stay away! Bison are fast and lethal!" Instead she tried, "Stop! Danger!" but they kept right on approaching. They probably weren't even Chinese. We'd made our attempt to intervene, so I drove away. I thought it might be traumatic, subjecting teenage girls to the gruesome scene of death by bison goring.

So anyway, back in Custer State Park with my mom and dad, we were smack dab in the middle of a gigantic herd of bison, up close and personal. Some of them were bigger than Cherry Cherry, causing my dad to urge, "Drive! Drive!" when one got a little too close for his comfort. It was pretty amazing.

Unfortunately, the amazingness didn't last all day. After crossing the border into Montana, the GPS directed us to a road we soon found to be under construction. As in, sixteen-miles-of-gravel-instead-of-pavement construction. While not necessarily lost, I think this counted as a traditional Malcom family vacation experience. Mom did a bit more complaining. I tried my best to distract her.

"They call this "Big Sky Country," I said.

"Look at that sky, Jude," Dad enthused.

"What's different about it?" Mom exclaimed, exasperated. She asked to see the map. "Where are we going, anyway?"

"Right under your thumb," I said. We were only miles away

from the ranch where we were stopping to see relatives. "Baker."

"I know where Baker is," she snapped. "I mean where is this Glacier thing we're driving to tomorrow?"

"Flip the map over. Glacier National Park is on the other side of the state . . . up by Canada."

"You have *got* to be kidding me," she said. Then, after locating it, added, "You couldn't pay me enough to go on this trip again."

There was silence in the car as my dad and I tried not to laugh.

"Um . . . I'm dropping you off at the airport in Spokane, Washington, so . . . you knew you had to cross the entire state of Montana, right?"

She ignored me.

We got to my dad's cousin's ranch and were greeted by his wife, Patty. I hope in another twenty years I'll have the same spunk and energy she does. She loaded us up in the truck and bounced us around their ranch, pointing out where the cattle spend the winter and where they stack the hay. We ended up several miles away where her son was combining wheat. Dad and I got out for a closer look. He showed me how to pick it and roll it in your hands, then pick out the edible parts. The sky was indeed big and seemed to go on forever. It was beautiful. It was easy to imagine America a hundred years ago, out here where there were so few buildings and people. My dad talked to his cousin for a while and would have been happy to stay for a week and help with the harvest, I think, but we were still a long way from a hotel.

We stopped in Baker to grab a bite to eat before hitting the open road. There appeared to be two choices on Main Street, both with signs declaring "Bar/Restaurant/Casino." Neither appeared to be significantly better than the other, so we just picked one and went in. We had to wait a while for the waiter (and I use that term very loosely) to come around. When he finally did, he looked at the menu he was about to hand to me, paused, wiped it on his shirt, checked it out again, and decided it was good enough to hand to me. I tried not to vomit. Sensitive gag reflex!

It was a Monday night; the bar/restaurant/casino was full of guys drinking beer and watching football. As we waited for our food (and were later pleasantly surprised by how good it was), I lost count of how many loud belches I heard from the table behind me. Gross.

"I've heard there are a lot more single men than women in Montana," my mom said, keeping her voice low. "Your chances of finding a husband would be good here. Your choices, maybe not so good. But your chances . . ."

"I just can't believe it," my dad added quietly, not wanting to be overheard. "They're drinking beer like I drink water. I'd be on the floor if I drank that much beer."

We finished up and headed for Miles City, an hour away. Looking at the map, that seemed to be the closest town that would have a hotel. Out on the deserted highway, it was dark – really, really dark – as in, absolutely no street lights and very few other cars out on the road. And then – oh no, oh no, oh no – something big and dead was in the middle of the road and I didn't have time to swerve. Instead Cherry Cherry straddled it, and I heard a sickening scrape as we went over. A few miles down the road, we heard a rattle. Crap.

"Is your gas gauge dropping?" my dad asked.

"No."

"Oil light coming on?"

"No."

"Heat gauge going up?"

"No."

"It's probably okay, then," he reassured me. Thank God he was along, or I would have been freaking out. I knew it was too late to take it anywhere, plus we were in the middle of nowhere. I didn't really have much of a choice but to keep driving.

When we got to Miles City (after much silent praying that the car would make it), we started walking into hotels and getting a chorus of no's. I felt like the town was conspiring against us. Had they somehow heard me calling this the middle of nowhere? One woman finally advised me to keep driving since every room in Miles City was taken. Are you kidding me? It was a Monday night. IN THE MIDDLE OF NOWHERE! How could every room in town be booked? We called every hotel in the next town and found one room still available. It was first come, first served, the proprietress said, so we needed to hustle. I said another silent prayer that Cherry Cherry would be okay, then headed back out onto the highway.

Half an hour later, we found the hotel with the one available room . . . but seeing the place launched us into a debate as to whether or not we should keep driving, despite Cherry Cherry's ominous rattle. In the end, we decided to keep going; Mom was convinced we wouldn't make it out alive the next day if we stayed. I had to agree that there was a bit of Bates Motel/Hotel California flavor to it. We started calling hotels in the next city, Billings, and found plenty of open rooms. Unfortunately, Billings was another hour and a half down the highway.

It was now after ten, my preferred bedtime. Desperately needing something to help me stay awake, I got out the iPod to look for some songs I could sing along to. It was also a move of necessity, since there were no radio stations IN THE MIDDLE OF NOWHERE. Dad fell asleep, and I felt bad listening to songs Mom didn't know since she was valiantly trying to stay awake to keep me awake. The last time I'd put new music on my iPod, I'd hit that "fill empty space" button, and good thing. The only songs I could find that my mom would know and be able to enjoy, too, were holiday classics. We sped down the highway on the dark September night singing Christmas carols with James Taylor and Kenny Rogers, trying to ignore the menacing rattle.

The next day we found a Toyota dealership where we entertained the mechanics.

"Looks like you've got some meat cookin' under here," one called up from under the car.

"It's done!" a second guy added. They both laughed. I was so glad they were amused. I waited for the diagnosis.

"She's got a bent bracket," one of them explained. "See here? This is the exhaust pipe. It naturally vibrates. And with your bracket bent like that, the pipe is just knocking against it."

Sounded like an easy fix.

"Unfortunately . . ." he continued. Oh, no. ". . .we don't have any of this particular bracket in stock. How long you folks in town?"

"We're just passing through," I clarified.

"Couldn't you just bang it back into place with a hammer?" my dad suggested.

"Well . . . I suppose we could do that," the guy said reluctantly. I could tell he was disappointed he wasn't going to be making the big sale he'd hoped for.

Fifty-one dollars and two hours in the waiting room later ("I could have banged it out myself twenty times by now," Dad grumbled), we were on our way.

We fell into an easy pattern, traveling together. It was different, traveling together as adults as opposed to the family vacations of my childhood. Now, while they insisted on paying for gas, I was an adult who got to drive and control the radio. That was a big step up. When we pulled into gas stations, Mom would whip out the credit card, Dad would pump the gas, and I would wash the windows. It was fun to have travel buddies. Sometimes we talked and sometimes we didn't, but overall, after seeing so many states alone, I was just happy to be sharing the experience. As much as I like doing what I want to do and not having to answer to anyone, I also appreciate good company. And with my parents getting older, I wondered how many more experiences like this we'd have left. I wanted to enjoy my time with them as much as I could.

Later that day, I checked in with my Chief Safety Officer.

"How are you going to have a date in Montana with your parents along?"

"I told them I'm hiking one day with a friend of a friend."

"Why don't you just tell them what you're doing?"

I looked over at my parents, standing near the counter at Dairy Queen, waiting for their number to be called.

"They worry so much already," I told her. "They worry I'm not sleeping enough or eating enough. They worry about me driving at night. They worry that I'm driving around the country alone. I feel like if I throw in, 'Oh, and I'm meeting fifty strangers for dates,' it might just put them over the edge. I don't want them to worry any more than they already do."

Western Montana was beautiful. From the college town of Missoula to the clear, quiet waters of Flathead Lake, I pulled Cherry Cherry over again and again, making my parents pose for pictures. It was fun to have someone to take pictures of. And in return, they kept me laughing and shaking my head. At one point, Dad said the scenery reminded him of that movie with John Wayne and Fabian.

"Which one?" Mom asked from the backseat.

"I can't remember the name of it," Dad admitted.

"Was it the one with that singer?"

"Yeah."

"Ricky Nelson?"

"No, I just said Fabian!" Dad exclaimed.

"Oh, that's right. Fabian," Mom conceded.

I didn't know who Fabian was. I was picturing Fabio riding a horse alongside John Wayne. I was pretty sure that wasn't right.

When we stopped for lunch at a fast food restaurant, Mom took out a handful of pills.

"What are all those for?" I asked.

"Well, this one is for high blood pressure, and this one is for cholesterol. This one is for arthritis, and this one . . . well, I don't remember." She added that after what we'd just ate, she'd probably be needing some Imodium sooner rather than later. I couldn't say I disagreed. I was glad fast food wasn't part of my regular diet. Mom and Dad had lacked enthusiasm in copying my steady diet of fruit and granola bars, though, so we'd tried this place. Now we were all feeling a little bit queasy.

I froze when she reached into my bag of chips, pulled one out, and ate it. I recovered, feigned a casual attitude, and pushed the bag toward her.

"You can have the rest," I said, but she saw through my act.

"Oh, for Pete's sake. I'm your mother."

I shook my head. I couldn't explain it. I do not share food. Even with my mother. I realize it's irrational. Maybe even a little psychotic. My brother still made fun of me years later for the time I almost threw up when he reached into my bowl of popcorn. I felt even queasier just thinking about it.

Half an hour later, I found myself in the wrong lane, trying to get to Glacier National Park. As I did some quick maneuvering, shifting from the wrong lane to the right one, I noticed an old man in a big Buick just sitting in the turn lane, waiting for all the traffic to go by so he could do some maneuvering of his own.

"Looks like Grandpa's confused, too," I commented.

"Yeah," my dad said apologetically, "I'm not helping you navigate very well, am I?"

"No, Dad!" I laughed. "I meant that eighty-year-old guy back there!"

We drove the scenic Going to the Sun Road through Glacier National Park. Well, I drove, and Mom and Dad held on for dear life, trying not to look down. At the highest point in the park, looking down, down, down the steep drop-off right next to the shoulder-less road, my mom's voice, through gritted teeth, broke the silence: "I repeat: you couldn't pay me to go on this trip again."

We had noticed little white crosses alongside the roads all through Montana. They showed where someone had died in an accident and encouraged drivers to be careful. Dad noticed there weren't any alongside this road, weaving up through the mountains.

"They're probably about a mile straight down, where they recovered the bodies," I joked. I got an audible huff from the backseat for that one.

After settling in at the hotel that night, I walked down the hall to the laundry room for a little privacy. I called Mr. Montana, a friend of a friend of a friend, to set up our date. It quickly became apparent, though, that it wasn't going to be easy. I was free the next day, but he had to work. Crap.

"Are you busy right now?" I asked.

"Um . . . well . . ." Crap, crap, double crap. I had a sinking feeling in the pit of my stomach, thinking I was going to have to go out yet tonight to find some random cowboy drinking at the local watering hole. I could not endure another attempt at picking someone up like Mr. Illinois.

"We could just have a phone date," I tried, thinking, *Please don't hang up!*

"Oh. Okay."

"Awesome!" I replied enthusiastically. It wasn't really awesome, but it was better than a random pick-up at a bar. We talked about the area around Glacier and how the population exploded in the summer with all the tourists. We talked about the oil rigs I'd seen in the eastern part of the state, and how most of the state's money came from that, logging, and tourism. The friend whose friend set us up said Mr. Montana worked on a ranch, so I asked what he did there.

"I specialize in cutting," he said. "Do you know what that is?"

Cutting? I pictured castration. What else do you cut off an

animal? I'd never heard of anyone specializing in castration, but maybe on a ranch, lots of boy cows needed to be castrated?

"Um . . ." I started, trying to decide whether or not to venture a guess. "Not really."

"It's a competition," he explained. "We go around to shows and compete against other cutters."

Okay, if this was what I was thinking it was, that was just wrong. Sick and wrong. And possibly really bloody? I didn't know.

"Basically you get two and a half minutes to ride your horse into a herd of cattle, single out one cow, and then get it away and keep it away from the herd," he continued.

"Ohhhh . . ." I said. That sounded a lot less grotesque than de-sexing entire herds of beef. "So, is that part of a rodeo?"

"No, they have separate competitions. We go all over: Idaho, Oregon, California, Canada . . ."

"And you get paid to do that?"

"Well, I get paid to do a lot of things on the ranch," he explained. "The competition cutting, training horses, taking care of the cows, and lots of haying."

"So you get to ride horses and drive tractors every day?"

"Yep."

"So you're pretty much living every little boy's dream?" I phone flirted.

"Yeah, I guess so," he laughed.

He seemed like a great guy, and I was disappointed we weren't having the conversation in person. Cowboys are hot, and I was missing out on my chance to go out with a real one! Instead I asked about what he did for fun, and he talked about camping and fishing and hunting with his buddies. He had a boat and liked to go wakeboarding in the summer. He sounded cute, and I couldn't believe I was *thisclose* to meeting a cute cowboy but was sitting in a laundry room in a Super 8 instead of next to him. On the plus side, though, I wasn't having that "Do I kiss him at the end of the night or not?" debate going on in my head.

I wrapped up the conversation after my mom poked her head into the laundry room a second time. It had only been forty-five minutes. I felt bad, thinking they must be feeling sad and neglected, but I found out otherwise when I got back into the room.

"Tiffany Ann, I don't even want to think of the things you do when you're not with us. If you sit in a laundry room talking on the phone when we're here, who knows what kind of crazy things you do when you're alone?"

As I heard the words coming out of my mom's mouth, I visualized the room where I'd just spent the last forty-five minutes: a washer, a dryer, two pop machines, and a candy machine. Where, exactly, was the danger?

"Some insane sex maniac could have grabbed you!" she continued. I held up one finger in that "just a sec" gesture as I rummaged in my purse for the little notebook I took notes on.

"Are you going to write this down?" she huffed. "Write this down!" I turned to look, waiting for a finger to rise, but not from my good Lutheran mother. She pursed her lips, shook her head, and went back to her magazine.

I decided, yeah, maybe it was best not to tell them about the fifty dates just yet. Mom would be convinced they were fifty sex maniacs just waiting to grab me.

The next day, we explored the cute little town of Whitefish and ate extremely expensive pie. For souvenirs, Dad bought a little jar of huckleberry jam and Mom bought little toy buffalos for the grandsons. We took a scenic drive into Idaho and strolled along the lakes in Sandpoint and Coeur d'Alene. After the desperate Christmas caroling the night of the deer incident, I'd reloaded the iPod with a playlist of songs I thought my parents might know.

"Turn it up," Mom said when "Danny's Song" came on. "That's one of Dad's favorite singers. He just loves her."

"Kenny Loggins?" I verified.

"Oh . . . it's a man? I thought a woman sang that song."

"Yeah," my dad agreed from the backseat.

"She's Canadian," my mom offered helpfully. This was news to me. I had no idea my dad was a big fan of some Canadian singer.

"Celine Dion?" I tried.

"No."

"Shania Twain?" Strike two. I was out of guesses. The only other Canadian singer that came to mind was Alanis Morissette, and I was pretty sure my parents weren't familiar with her work.

"Mmmmm . . ." I could hear from the backseat. "Mmmm . . . mmmmm . . . Murphy!" There was a long pause.

"Anne Murray?" I guessed.

"Yep. Yeah. That's it," they both agreed. It was like being on a low-budget game show.

That night in the hotel, Dad asked me how to turn off his cell phone when he got on the plane the next morning.

"You don't know how to turn it off?" I verified. I'd added them to my plan a few months before I left Colorado and gotten them both the simplest, frills-free phones I could find. Dad struggled to get down on his knees next to the hotel bed, preparing for a long tutorial.

"If it rings, I can answer it," he said. "That's about as far as I can go." I showed him how to hold down the red button until it turned off.

"Now how do I get it back on once we're back on the ground?" he asked.

"Hold down the same button again until it turns on," I explained.

"Well, that's easy enough," he said confidently.

"Want me to teach you how to text?" I asked. I felt bad that he'd gotten down on his knees for nothing.

"Nope," he declared quickly and dropped his phone back into its place in his shirt pocket. Baby steps.

I was bummed the next day when I had to drop them off at the airport in Spokane. They worried too much, but they cracked me up, too. It had been a fun week. We pulled into the parking garage at the airport and Dad climbed out of the backseat. Mom, in the passenger seat, leaned toward me and spoke quickly and quietly.

"If anything happens, our important papers are in the lockbox in the closet," she said.

I bit my lip, shook my head, and said, "Mom, how about we think positive thoughts, like, the plane is NOT going to crash today?"

Gotta love 'em.

#37 – IDAHO

I went back to sleep. After driving my parents to the airport and waving to them as they wound through the security line, I went back to the hotel and crawled back into bed. I couldn't seem to get enough sleep. I stayed in bed a little too long before backtracking half an hour back to Idaho. I had to send the guy a text and let him know I'd be late. He responded back with, "No worries. It'll give me a chance to shower the hay off me and pick you a beautiful bouquet of potatoes." Awesome.

I'd told someone back east that summer that I had grown up on a farm in Iowa. She'd responded with, "Oh wow. So did you grow potatoes then?" I'm not sure how people get Iowa and Idaho confused. I mean, yeah, they both start with an "I" and both names have three syllables, but they're not even that close on the map. They also have very different terrains. And while Iowans take pride in things like the State Fair and helping their neighbors and feeding the world with the corn they grow, Idahoans grow potatoes and hole themselves up in cabins, stockpiling food and guns in survivalist camps. Really? You can't tell the difference?

I met Mr. Idaho in a parking lot between Coeur d'Alene's big resort hotel and the trailhead of a path that meanders beside the lake. I normally wouldn't meet a stranger for a hike, but this guy had been referred to me by Sarah, the sweet girl I'd couch surfed with back in Salem, Mass. She said he was a good guy and definitely wouldn't kill me. Plus I'd seen a ton of people hiking this trail the day before when

I'd walked the boardwalk with my parents. I didn't figure he could drag me kicking and screaming into the woods to kill me without attracting some attention from fellow hikers.

We had to stop before we even started, because there was a statue of a moose with a mouse sitting on his antlers, and I just couldn't walk by a statue like that without taking a picture. Mr. Idaho informed me that there were several identical statues along the trail. A local artist wrote a children's book about this moose/mouse pair, and if you followed the trail on the sign beside the statues, you could read the whole story about their adventure in Coeur d'Alene. It was really cute.

It was a cloudy day but the views were still amazing. I was just kidding about the survivalists. I mean, yeah, they're there, but Idaho is a really beautiful state, and everyone I met was great. Mr. Idaho, I quickly found, was a fabulous guy. We stopped and stood on big rocks looking out over the lake, and he pointed out which ones you can jump off of. It was easy to picture him as a teenager, spending lazy days there with his buddies. It was hard to picture him laying in a hospital bed, immobile, but that's right where he'd been a few years before.

After a rappelling accident that dropped him the equivalent of two and a half stories, his mom got a phone call saying that if he ever woke up from the coma, he'd never walk again. The fact that he was back to normal today was nothing short of a miracle. And here he was, helping me scramble over boulders and fallen trees.

We talked about everything. He guessed I was an only child instead of the middle of three; he was the oldest of his siblings. We talked about family dynamics and our roles in our own families. We talked about our childhoods and our churches and our hopes for the future. We had a lot in common. He took my water bottle and tucked it away in his vest so I wouldn't have to carry it. I thought that was gentlemanly. But then he took my now-empty hand. Smooth.

I thought it was a little weird, since I'd just met him, and, let's be honest, I am not the touchy-feely type. But then I remembered how just that morning as I'd driven to the date, I'd been thinking about how no one does that anymore. Guys jump straight to making out without the preliminary hand holding or hugging. I had dated a guy several years before who'd made me melt the first time he held my hand; his thumb traced small circles around my palm as his fingers lay entwined with mine. I wondered if guys knew how sensual hand holding could be, or if they even cared. Call me old fashioned, but I like the baby steps.

I had a harder time getting over the fact that he kept calling me "sweetie" and sometimes "sweetheart." I can't stand it when people I don't know give me little pet names, like waitresses calling me "hon" or old men calling me "dear." Coming from someone I'd just met? Grating. And of all the pet names in the world, for some reason "sweetheart" drives me absolutely insane. I can't stand it. If we'd been in a relationship, I would have flat-out told this guy to call me by my given name, not "sweetie" and definitely not "sweetheart," but at this point I thought I'd just come off as mental if I freaked out about it. I asked about his past dating experience to distract him.

"I'm done dating beautiful girls," he said. Did I mention he was a hottie? I had no trouble picturing gorgeous girls fawning over him, but it kind of felt like an insult. I mean, if he was done dating beautiful girls but was on a date with me, then that meant I must not be beautiful, right? And yeah, I fully understood I was not a model and guys didn't turn their heads as I walked down the street, but the romantic side of me wanted to be with someone who thought I was beautiful. I didn't have much time to mull it over though, because he went on to present one of the cutest theories I'd ever heard.

"Beautiful girls are like the chocolate bunnies you get in your Easter basket," he said. "They look great on the outside, but they're hollow on the inside. You know what I mean? You get all excited, 'cause they look so great, but then you find out there's nothing to them but that initial beauty. I want to be with someone who has substance. The total package, you know?"

We got back to the trailhead and cut the hand holding and headed for downtown Coeur d'Alene. We bypassed the shops and galleries and headed straight for Hudson's, home of the best burgers in town. The place was packed and we were lucky to get two barstools right behind the guy flipping burgers. Mr. Idaho said he was a germaphobe and had to go wash his hands, which made my heart skip a beat. A kindred spirit! I wanted to go wash my hands, too, but people just kept pouring in to this little hole in the wall, and I was afraid if I wasn't there to guard our barstools, we'd lose our seats. I opted for the hand sanitizer in my purse.

We kept talking the entire time we ate. He told me to tell him something unusual about myself that most people didn't know about.

"I took a belly dancing class a few years back," I said. "I was in my mid-twenties and everyone else was significantly older. Probably trying to put a little spark back into their marriages. I don't have an outfit or anything, but I could still probably do a few of the moves."

I could still do ALL the moves, thank you very much, but I didn't want to come off as weird. It's not really a typical hobby. I told him about the BolderBOULDER, a 5k race held in Boulder, Colorado, every Memorial Day Weekend. I'd walked it with my friend Laurie once. (I do not run. Ever. My philosophy is you should only run if you're being chased . . . but really, if a bear was chasing me, I probably couldn't outrun it, so even then I'm not sure I would waste my last moments alive getting side cramps from running.) Anyway, the BolderBOULDER was crazy because as we were racing down the streets, locals were out on the corners, playing with their garage bands or spraying us with their garden hoses or belly dancing. A lot of the women who were belly dancing had bellies you really didn't want to see, so I figured it would be fitting to take up belly dancing again since I hadn't exercised regularly in months.

The waitress came by and asked if we wanted any pie. We declined. The big burgers were plenty. Mr. Idaho said his senior yearbook quote was, "I like two kinds of pies: apple pies and cutie pies." Groan . . . but still kind of cute. Oh, who am I kidding? He was really cute. I was smitten.

He had to go to work, so the date had to end. We stood on the sidewalk hugging for a long time. He smelled so good and his vest was so cushiony . . . I'm sure anyone who saw us thought we were a bit odd, but I wasn't going to be the first to pull away. He kissed my cheek and I melted a little more.

"I really hope I see you again," I said as he walked away. "You're dreamy."

Dreamy? Who tells someone they're dreamy? Marcia Brady? Ugh. I mentally kicked myself as I climbed into my car.

#38 – WASHINGTON

"When you said I should go on fifty dates in fifty states, did you actually think I'd do it?" I asked Molly. I was sitting at her kitchen table having dinner with her and Mark and their adorable baby boy. It had been a year since we'd sat eating in Colorado, the two of them preparing for Collin's arrival and me preparing to set out on an adventure.

"Um . . . no," she laughed.

"It was just too brilliant," I declared. "How could I not, after you'd given me the idea?"

It was true. There were days when I woke up and wondered what on earth I was doing, but the truth of the matter was that I was living a dream. How many people got to drive around the country and not work for nine months?

While I was living the dream in Washington, a friend on the other side of the country was living a nightmare. When checking my Facebook news feed one night, I saw another friend offering her condolences.

No! I thought. *Please let it be one of her grandparents who died.*

She had just gotten married in March. I knew her new husband was deployed, and I prayed that it wasn't him. I pored over her page but saw nothing else.

Please let it be a grandparent, I prayed again. *Maybe even one of her parents. I know that's an awful thing to pray for, God, but please don't let it be Aaron.*

The next day I got an email from another friend. Aaron was gone. On his ninth deployment to the Middle East, on his 30th birthday, my friend Brittany's husband had been killed. Before the honeymoon phase even had time to fade away, she was a widow at six months.

I wondered again about love and loss and whether the whole thing was worth it. I didn't know if I could bear that kind of pain. I cried for her and didn't know how she could possibly deal with that. I pictured myself curling up in a ball, crying my eyes out, and wondering how I could go on. I didn't know what to say to her. What could I say that would make her feel at all better? Her husband – a vibrant, Godly man who'd instantly won her heart – was gone.

And then, while thinking about Aaron and Brittany a few days later, I remembered the first time I'd heard about Aaron. I was sitting beside Brittany at a meeting, and she was glowing. She couldn't stop smiling. She'd never been happier. She already knew she was going to marry this guy.

I'd never felt that. I didn't know what it was like, to be so confident in the love you shared with someone that you just knew it was going to last forever.

I didn't make it to their wedding; I left Colorado a month before the ceremony. I saw her pictures on Facebook and heard from friends that there had never been a more beautiful, love-filled ceremony. Six months later, in that same church, Brittany somehow had the strength to speak at her husband's funeral, eulogizing the incredible man he'd been and giving thanks for the short time they'd had together.

I realized she wouldn't trade the monumental loss and pain, because that would mean never feeling the equally monumental love and happiness. Maybe that old expression, "It's better to have loved and lost than never to have loved at all," was true. It was time to stop being so scared. If I wanted love – love like Brittany and Aaron's – I had to open up my heart to the possibility of getting hurt.

Whenever I met new people and explained that I was dating a man in every state, one of the first questions I always heard was, "Is that safe?" People wondered if I got scared, meeting all those strangers for dates. I'd reply that it wasn't any different from dating when I was in one place. I still followed similar basic safety rules: meet dates in public places, don't share details like where I was staying, don't get into their cars, and don't leave drinks unattended for someone to slip something into. I also called my Chief Safety Officer before and after every date to let her know where I was going and when I'd made it home safely.

That said, I did make occasional exceptions to my own rules if the date had been recommended by a friend. I figured if a friend said this was a good guy to go out with, then he probably wasn't going to hurt me. That was how I came to be standing outside Mr. Washington's apartment door.

My friend Janis had recommended this guy. They'd gone to high school together, and although she hadn't seen him in years, she was pretty sure he'd avoided jail time since then. He was also a world traveler, which she thought would give us a lot to talk about. And he wanted to make me dinner. Sold!

I was lucky he'd sent me detailed directions to his place in Seattle, including a photo of the intersection where I needed to turn, because my poor GPS was utterly confused. He lived on the last bit of land before the only houses left were houseboats. It was a cool little area with a gorgeous view. We sat on his deck and talked . . . well . . . mostly he talked.

Sometimes, on past dates during the trip, I'd really had to carry the conversation. Not so with Mr. Washington. He started talking the minute I walked through the door, and after a while I realized, *Whew! I'm getting the night off!*

I looked across the little canal of water that connected Lake Union and Lake Washington and felt like I had been there before. Mr. Washington must have noticed me looking that direction.

"You can rent kayaks over there," he said.

"Is the kayak rental place by any chance connected to a Mexican restaurant?" I asked.

"Yeah, actually, it is," he verified, looking at me quizzically.

"I've been there! I kayaked here five years ago!" I smiled. How crazy is that? I'd been on a trip with my youth group teenagers and we'd eaten there, then rented kayaks for an hour. "I paddled by your house once and didn't even know it!"

"Well, I haven't lived here for five years," he clarified. Okay, fine. Never mind you. I'd been here before!

Mr. Washington's plan was to walk down to the famous Pike Place Market, buy everything we needed to make dinner, then come back and cook. I was already hungry. It sounded like a long process. Luckily he modified the plan and decided we'd take the bus part of the way there and back. It would cut off some time and some of the hike, too, thankfully; I was wearing $2 flip flops which aren't exactly made for trekking.

Before we entered the chaos of flying fish and whatnot inside the market, Mr. Washington said I had to go see the wall of gum. It sounded pretty gross. I said we didn't have to, but he insisted. It was just as gross as I expected. Basically, an entire wall is covered in gum. Why? No idea. I was perfectly content to view it from a distance and then quickly walk away, but a woman standing there with her daughter insisted with a twangy Southern accent that I participate.

"It's nostalgia!" she exclaimed. What? I couldn't recall any happy moments from my past where I'd stuck gum to anything. And the germs! I shuddered.

"Here ya go," she said, thrusting a pack of bubble gum at Mr. Washington. "We bought it just to come here and do this!"

I obliged and chewed the surprisingly yummy gum. Then it was time to do the deed.

"Y'all got a camera?" the excited stranger asked. I pulled mine out of my pocket and handed it to her. She excitedly snapped away as I took the gum out of my mouth. With one finger, very careful not to touch any other wads, I stuck it to the wall. I turned toward the camera and gave her a pained attempt at a smile, trying not to think about all the germs. Sensitive gag reflex! We left her and her daughter still happily hanging out at the great wall of gum.

We wandered around the market buying lots of veggies. I looked at his shopping list and let him know I would not be consuming his planned salad. The ingredients included tomato, avocado, and feta, none of which I was going to put in my mouth. Yuck. He bought two ears of sweet corn instead. Quick learner. I liked that.

We started back for his place and my tummy growled. I was starving. Every restaurant we passed made me a little more hungry. I'd eaten a granola bar around 10AM that day but it was long gone. I snuck raspberries out of the bag I was holding when he wasn't looking. My old roommate Sarah used to *need* food. We'd be out at a bar and she'd have to order some chicken strips and fries at midnight. She knew that if she didn't eat, she'd get cranky and not have any fun. I didn't understand at the time, but right then, I got it. If I didn't get some food in me soon, things were going to go downhill fast. I wanted a freaking hunk of meat.

We somehow started talking about my horrible drive-around-the-country diet of granola bars and fruit.

"Are you losing weight?" he asked. He was a doctor, and I'm sure my diet worried him.

"I don't know. I don't have a scale. My clothes still fit, so if I'm losing anything, it's probably muscle mass since I get no exercise."

"You must have lost a lot of weight when you were in Africa," he speculated.

"Fifteen pounds in three months," I verified. "I'd only brought drawstring-waist pants, though, so I didn't even realize how bad it was until I got home."

"Too much?" he asked.

"Yeah, you could see my eye sockets and cheekbones. It wasn't an attractive skinny; it was a sick-looking skinny."

We stopped talking about my weight loss and talked more about the full experience of being at the orphanage for three months. It struck me that out of the thirty-eight dates I'd been on so far, very few guys had asked about my time in Africa. It was easily one of the most formative experiences of my life, and I stated that on my website, but very few guys seemed to care. One had even cut me off when I'd started talking about the kids, saying, "What is it with chicks being so crazy about African kids?"

When we got back to his apartment, it was already after 7PM. We finally ate at 8:30. He was a good cook, but honestly, at that point, he could have microwaved me a bowl of Easy Mac and I would have declared him the next Iron Chef. I devoured his rice mixture that I had scoffed at when I'd seen the ingredient list. I shoveled in the salmon like it might swim upstream again if I didn't get it into my mouth right then. The corn on the cob disappeared like I was in some sort of county fair speed-eating contest. I even ate a bunch of thinly sliced grilled beets, telling myself they were kind of like potato chips. I was even more glad he was such a talker. I cleaned my plate instead of talking.

I grew to enjoy his company more and more as the night went on. I don't know if I got used to his excessive talking or if I was just in a much better mood once I got some food in me, but I decided he might make a good friend. I didn't have feelings beyond that, but I was kind of glad. I didn't know how I was going to reconnect with the five guys around the country that I already liked and was still thinking about. I wasn't sure I even wanted to meet any more that I clicked with.

"I've been trying to figure out what your 'thing' is," he said at the end of the meal. I furrowed my eyebrows to say, "What do you mean?" without having to open my mouth.

"Well, when you meet someone who's in their mid-thirties and not married yet, you wonder what their 'thing' is, you know?"

"Okay," I said. "I can take it. What's my 'thing'?"

He studied me for a bit, then unleashed it. "You're too picky."

I guffawed. Really? Of all the things you could have picked?

"I've heard that before," I said, "but I'd rather be alone forever than married to someone I'm only lukewarm about. I mean, you can't settle, right?"

"You might reach an age when you start to wonder why you passed on some of your earlier options," he said.

"Yes, Oh Wise One," I scowled. "I'm sure when I get to be as old as you – in two years – I will begin to look back on my love life with regrets."

"I've done a lot of thinking in the past two years," he explained.

I thought back over my past boyfriends. I still thought fondly of most of them, but there wasn't a single one I wished I'd married. I'm pretty decisive, I guess. Once it's over, it's over.

He offered me ice cream with raspberries (well, what was left of the raspberries after I'd pilfered some on the way home), but I declined. Shocking, I know, but I was stuffed. And I still had to drive two hours before I could sleep that night, so I headed out instead of eating dessert. Miracles happen.

It's hard to admit you're getting older and can't do all the things you used to do. When I'd spent a night with my old friends Matt and Wendi in Yakima, I met a guy named Richie who said he'd take me hiking later in the week when I got to Bellingham. Awesome! In retrospect, I probably should have asked for details about the hike, like how long it might be and whether or not it was uphill.

I met Richie and his two buddies Slim and Q-Tip (no, they weren't rappers — those were their YMCA camp counselor nicknames) on a drizzly morning and followed them to the trailhead. That was my first mistake. I should have left Cherry Cherry in a safe location and gotten into Richie's Jeep. I felt horrible bumping and jostling the poor girl down a gravel road. Then the gas light came on. Crap! Why didn't I ever check that before I got out in the middle of nowhere? I patted the wheel, apologized for the pot holes, and promised not to go on another road like this ever again if she'd stay with me. We ended up in a parking lot with an incredible view of the Washington coastline and the San Juan Islands. None of them brought water bottles, so I thought, *Hey, this must be an easy hike!*

We started down the trail, and by down, I literally mean down. I'm always a little concerned when a trail begins in descent, because that means eventually I'll have to haul myself back up and out of there. It seemed to be an easy hike, though, and I was easily chattering away as we walked, answering their questions about the adventure I was on. I started to get a little warm when the trail began climbing, but I took off my rain jacket and didn't worry too much. Pretty soon I ditched my wool hat, and not long after that I had to take a break to catch my breath. That was embarrassing. A little further down the trail, I took off my fleece jacket and wrapped that around me, too. I really didn't want to look like an old lady, but being thirteen years older than them, they definitely had the youthful advantage over me. I was guessing they were all in fairly decent shape; the only exercise I'd gotten lately was flexing my right calf muscle as I pushed the pedal to the metal. Honestly? I was hurting.

"You guys go on ahead without me," I urged. Richie had to get back to town to work later in the afternoon, so I didn't want to hold the whole group up. Slim had said that after the bat caves, the trail went straight up. I didn't know where the bat caves were, but if we weren't even to the hard part yet, I was definitely in trouble. I was feeling a little woozy. I waited for them to get out of sight and then I sat down and put my head between my knees for a minute.

I continued on after I no longer felt the need to fall down, and there they were, patiently waiting at the top of a steep hill. Oh, geez. Gentlemen. I didn't want to be dramatic, but seriously: *Save yourselves! I'm not gonna make it!*

At a big rock with a nice overlook, I finally persuaded them to go on without me. There was no way they'd make it at my pace if Richie was going to make it back to work on time. Plus, I wanted to start back without them; the older I got, the more cautious I got. That meant carefully placing my feet where they were least likely to fly out from under me. Washington was wet and slippery! I really didn't want to bite it on a slick rock and break a hip. I'd just paid big bucks for a ferry ticket to Alaska, and I'd be danged if that boat was leaving without me while I was in traction at the nearest hospital!

I made it to my car before they came back, so they didn't see me huffing and puffing. I consoled myself a bit by reasoning that even when I was 22, I probably couldn't have kept up with them. It wasn't that I was old, or even that I was out of shape; I ventured a guess that I was in better shape than half the women my age in this country. They were just abnormally fit and made me look bad. Given no time constraints, I could have made it to the top of that hill. I might have puked up a lung along the way, but I could have made it. Probably.

#39 – ALASKA

Thank God for Dramamine.

I'd been indecisive about Alaska, like I'd somehow magically find a way there for the budgeted $100 if I just held out long enough. I found a semi-cheap cruise for $899. I reasoned it was a deal because transportation, food, and lodging were all included. It was an inside room with no view, but I figured I could go stand out on the deck to see the scenery. I didn't need a window. And I'd had some problems before with seasickness, so maybe an inside room wouldn't rock as much. I bit the bullet and called to book the cruise. I was told, though, that they didn't sell to singles. Rooms were for two people, so if I were to go alone, I'd have to pay for double occupancy – $1,798 . . . plus tax. Yikes!

It seemed so unfair – not sexist or ageist, but something along that line. Why were they punishing me for being single? Was I the only person in the world who was traveling alone? Why did I have to bring someone along to get the normal rate? I felt like writing an angry letter to Holland America, but I didn't figure it would do much good. Discrimination!!

I checked into flights. My friend Nina had a friend in Anchorage who she thought would let me stay for a few days. I found a flight for $450 and asked her to check with him to see if those dates worked. Three days later when I went back online to book it, the price had jumped to $600. I didn't know whether to swear or cry.

My friend Matt clued me in to the Alaskan ferries. It seemed to be a cheap version of a cruise. Instead of a private room and all-you-can-eat buffets, though, you slept in a deck chair and brought your own food. At $652, it was a little more expensive than the flight, but it went through the Inside Passage, which I'd heard was incredibly beautiful. Plus I'd be on the boat the whole time, so I'd avoid the cost of the rental car I'd need in Anchorage. I booked it.

That's how I found myself desperately praying that the granola bar and juice I'd had for breakfast would not reappear.

Years ago, my sister and I had vacationed in Southern California. We'd taken a ferry to Catalina Island, and that was when I first discovered my aptitude for seasickness. In the middle of a game of Travel Scrabble, I'd leaned back in my seat, closed my eyes, and clutched the armrests.

"I need Ginger Ale," I'd said weakly. My sister looked at me for a second.

"Does that mean you forfeit?" she'd clarified. When I nodded wordlessly, she knew I was really sick. I don't forfeit in Scrabble. Ever. She came back with the requested beverage and a plastic bag, which I quickly filled.

"You're the quietest puker I've ever seen," she told me as I handed the bag over to some poor ship employee. Everybody's good at something, I guess.

Back on the Alaskan ferry, we were going through a rough patch. The boat was pitching from side to side. Looking out the window, you'd see nothing but sky, nothing but sea, nothing but sky, nothing but sea.

"Don't puke. Don't puke. Don't puke," I muttered to myself. I hate throwing up. It's so violent. I've hit my head on the toilet seat before because my body spasms out of control while I'm puking. And then I cry. And I hate crying.

"Have you taken the ferry before?" I asked a young woman in the ship's tiny bathroom. She was clutching the sink and looking ghostly pale.

"No," she murmured.

"Me neither," I said. "I didn't expect it to be quite so rough."

"Neither did I."

"I've got some Dramamine if you need it," I offered. I went for the door but the ship rolled and I stumbled back to the sink.

"Thanks. I'll let you know," she said as I lunged for the door in attempt #2.

The year before, I'd read a series of books about some shipbuilding Scandinavian immigrants. They'd made living on the open seas sound adventurous and beautiful, stopping at romantic-sounding ports like Ketchikan. I hated that author right now. And anyone who chose to work on a ship had to have a screw loose.

I thought maybe a nap would be helpful. Maybe the rolling of the ship would be comforting, like being rocked in a cradle. But the coin operated lockers behind me kept banging open and shut again and again. I tried to ignore them. I considered digging in the seats for quarters to lock 'em all shut. I finally drifted off, but was jolted awake by screaming children. I sat up, expecting to see people running for the lifeboats.

Nope. Just obnoxious children, banging on the windows and screaming every time the boat rolled toward the waves, like this was some amusement park ride. I wanted to go over and slap their parents and tell them to shut their children up.

I'll make a fabulous mother someday, won't I?

I wished I had my iPod. I'd purposely chosen not to bring anything of value. I figured if I were going to be sleeping out in the open, my stuff would be out in the open, too. If I went to the bathroom or the dining room or out on the deck, all of my stuff would be lying there, open to theft. Instead, I had locked it all in Cherry Cherry's trunk . . . and then I worried all week about someone breaking into my car while I was on the ferry. (I could have brought her along for the ride, but that would have cost an additional $431, which seemed a bit outrageous.) I also thought it might be a nice change of pace to be without electronics. I'd become downright addicted to my laptop, and I was also pretty dependent on the iPod as I drove.

These kids were driving me nuts, though. They seemed to have one volume level: loud. When they were mad, they screamed. When they were excited, they screamed. I silently prayed they'd be struck down with a major case of seasickness. If their little mouths were full of vomit, they'd be rendered unable to scream.

And I generally like kids. Really!

An announcement was made over the loudspeakers to stay seated if you didn't have to go anywhere and to please stay off the outer decks, which are slippery when wet. You didn't have to tell me twice. I'm not a strong swimmer in warm water. I'd have no chance in the hypothermia-inducing waters we were rocking through.

The next day we were given half an hour to stretch our legs in Ketchikan. I hightailed it to the grocery store across the street from the dock and bought milk and a banana. I didn't really need anything else. My backpack was already nearly too heavy to carry from all the instant foods I'd packed. When I saw the prices in the ferry's cafeteria, though ($13 for a turkey dinner?!), I was glad I'd brought my own food. I was definitely on the budget cruise.

I inwardly cheered when I got back on the boat and found that the family with the obnoxiously loud screaming children was gone. Hooray! I settled in to enjoy my milk in peace and quiet.

As we neared the next stop, I talked to a woman who appeared to be a bit younger than me. She'd moved to Wrangle just a year before, she said. As we approached her port, I asked if the ferry was the only way in and out.

"You can fly on a seaplane," she offered.

"But you can't drive?"

"It's an island," she said gently.

She'd moved up there to lead adventure expeditions for at-risk youth. It sounded awesome but kind of lonely, too. I thought about how far away I'd felt from my family when my grandparents had died. It had taken me a day to get home from Colorado for their funerals. Living here, you'd have to take the ferry south for two days just to get back to the mainland, then continue on from there. It was pristine and beautiful, but it was also remote. I couldn't imagine being so far away from everyone I loved.

"I'm going to Anchorage," another young woman told me when we struck up a conversation later on.

"How long are you staying?" I asked.

"A month."

"Wow." That sounded like a long, expensive vacation. I asked if she had friends there.

"No. I'm hoping to find a job."

"For a month?"

"Yeah."

"And then what?"

"I'm going to all fifty states," she said.

"Oh! I'm on a fifty states tour myself!" I said. "Are you just staying longer in Alaska because it takes so long to get to?"

"No, I'm going to spend a month in every state," she said. I did some quick math. Fifty months would be four years and two months.

"Wow. Do you know people to stay with all over the country?"

"Not really. That's the challenge: find a job and a place to live every time. I'm writing a book. It's research."

"Oh."

"How about you?"

"Um . . . I'm just taking some time off to explore the country," I said. I felt like I'd be stealing her thunder if I said I was writing a book, too.

She was young – possibly just out of college. Maybe she had more energy than I did, or more stamina or determination. I didn't want to bring her down by telling her I'd only been a vagabond for seven months and I was already anxious to land in one place again.

I'd heard people say that it's nice to go on vacation, but it's even nicer to come home. I never really agreed with that until this adventure, and now I didn't have a home to go home to. How do you tell someone who is so optimistic that there are days on the road when all you crave are the mundane things in life, like going home after work and making dinner, or lying in bed reading a few chapters of a good book before falling asleep?

That night, a pack of teenage girls flooded the lounge where I was camped out. They were a high school volleyball team and they'd been in Petersburg for two games. Now they were headed home, an overnight journey via the ferry. I felt bad for complaining in high school about riding a school bus for an hour to get to our games. Things were certainly different up here.

Remember back in North Dakota when I said I'd never looked worse on a date? Well, I definitely set a new record in Alaska.

The ferry arrived in Juneau at 3AM. As in three *in the morning*. Mr. Alaska, a friend of my friend Matt's friend, had said he'd pick me up, but I still felt bad when I called and woke him up. I stumbled off the ferry, half-awake, no make-up on, and clad in a completely non-figure flattering rain jacket. I dumped my big backpack in his truck bed and we headed out.

I do not advise going to any man's house at 3AM, but a) being the friend of a friend of a friend, I'd been assured he was not an ax murderer, and b) I didn't feel like I had any other options. The ferry docked twelve miles from the actual city of Juneau, and walking twelve miles in the rain at 3AM might taint my opinion of the state for the worse.

Crashing on Mr. Alaska's futon at approximately 3:15AM was definitely the oddest start to any of my dates thus far. Later on when we were both fully awake and semi-coherent, he made scrambled eggs and fried potatoes before we headed out for the day. Impressive.

Mr. Alaska had planned a uniquely Alaskan date. In borrowed overalls and my bulky rain jacket, we set out paddling kayaks around icebergs in Mendenhall Lake. It was amazing.

You'll never do this again, I thought, *so take it all in . . . the clean, crisp air; the perfect blue in the ice; the wispy fog filtering through the trees.* I felt that sense of grateful awe I'd felt so many times on this journey. *How did I get here? This is my life, experiencing all this! It's not a movie; it might feel like it, but it's real. I am so freaking blessed!!*

Lurking over us was the massive Mendenhall Glacier. Part of the Juneau Ice Fields, this massive block of ice meets the lake here. Giant chunks of it sometime "calve," breaking off into the lake and becoming these giant icebergs. We paddled over to the side of it, beached the kayaks, and started scrambling over the rocks, trying to ignore the drizzly rain.

Not too far in, we found the entrance to an ice cave. Mr. Alaska handed me a helmet, donned one himself, and easily slid in. I was a bit more hesitant. He put his hands up against the flat, steep rock to give me footholds so I wouldn't have to just slide haphazardly in. Very gentlemanly, I thought. The temporary fear was worth the payout. The cave was big enough to stand upright in and about a block long. The walls and roof were smoothed over by years of melting and freezing so that when you ran a finger over them, it was like touching glass. Inside the ice you could see rocks, dug up by the glacier who knows how many years before, varying in size from pebbles to bowling balls.

We exited the cave in a different spot and I had a much easier time getting out than I'd had getting in. We climbed higher, parallel to the glacier. You could see peaks and crevices in it like a mountain.

"Do you want to walk out on it?" Mr. Alaska asked.

"How can I not?" When in my life would I ever have the chance to walk on a glacier again?

He took off his backpack and pulled out crampons. They strapped onto our shoes like old-fashioned roller skates, but with spikes instead of wheels. He had to adjust mine quite a bit. The last person who'd used them was a man with much bigger feet than mine.

"My buddy has lived in Juneau his whole life and had never walked on this glacier," Mr. Alaska explained, "so one day I brought him out here."

I had a hard time imagining it, living here and seeing it all the time but never getting close enough to touch it. But then again, when I'd lived at the base of Pikes Peak in Colorado, I was surrounded by people who saw it outside their window every day but had never climbed to the top of it. I'd lived there for seven years before I'd climbed it. I believed Mr. Alaska when he said most people stand at the overlook by the Visitor's Center and just gaze at the glacier from the other side of the lake.

He handed me an ice ax and away we went. We weren't doing anything risky enough that we'd need to use them if we didn't want to fall to our deaths, but they looked good in the pictures we took. We didn't go too far out. I mean, I'm adventurous, but not a thrill-seeker. Looking at the crevices from a safe distance, I was amazed again at the pure blue color deep inside the ice. I didn't want to see it too closely, though. Mr. Alaska had all the ropes and carabiners and whatnot that he'd need to rescue me, but I wasn't all that interested in playing the victim.

We hiked back over to the rocks, took off the crampons, and scuttled our way back down to where we'd left the kayaks. We paddled between the glacier and its most recent break-off, and I was awed by the enormity of them. I was also silently praying, "Don't break off now! Please don't break off now!" It would be cool to see a glacier calve, but not when I was so close that I would likely get tossed into the lake in the tidal wave-like aftermath that would surely hit my kayak. Any water cold enough for icebergs not to melt in would probably be too cold to survive for long in. It was one of those moments that was a combination of cool and freaky. I paddled a little faster.

When we got close to a waterfall and I got my camera out to take a picture, I realized I was losing feeling in my fingers. I decided maybe it was best to be done now. We paddled back to where we'd put in, then loaded the kayaks back up on the truck.

It was an awesome date . . . but I still had nine hours 'til the ferry left. I felt bad, taking up Mr. Alaska's entire day, but he was really sweet about it and seemed happy to be my tour guide. We went and got some fish and chips (Alaskan Cod!) and sat talking for a while. He'd lived all over the West: California, Idaho, Colorado, Utah, and now Alaska. He loved living in Juneau, but it was expensive. A small house cost $350,000. Everything had to be flown in, so everything cost more here than it did on the mainland.

"And is it true that there are a lot more men than women here?" I asked.

"The joke around here is that you have to import your own woman like everything else," he laughed. It seemed like a good place to move if you were a lonely woman with a lot of money.

He gave me the drive-by tour of Juneau. With a population of 30,000, it's the third-largest city in Alaska. I had no idea a capital city could be so small. It had that small-town charm with quaint old houses that looked cozy and homey but probably cost an arm and a leg to heat in the winter. We drove by the governor's mansion and the state building and the city's only skyscraper, then went back to his apartment. It was like the never-ending date. I still felt bad but hoped the fact that it had rained all day meant I wasn't keeping him from mountain biking or something fun. We played a few rounds of Bananagrams (yes, I had it in my backpack . . . you never know when you might find a willing challenger!) and watched three episodes of Arrested Development. Then I repacked my backpack and we headed to the ferry terminal.

How do you say thank you to a guy who was not only your Alaska date, but also your 3AM taxi driver, your B&B provider, and your all-day tour guide? I wished him luck, advised him to join an online dating service to lure a lady to Juneau, and left him with a hug.

Then it was back on the boat for three more days.

I woke up to the sound of heaving. Not detecting a stench with it, I decided it was a better sound to wake up to than screaming children.

The first day heading south was pretty uneventful. I read an entire book.

Day two I got bored. I cajoled two young guys into playing Bananagrams with me. I beat them three games in a row while blushing every time I made eye contact with the one across the table. He was dreamy. I declared him "The Hottie." I sat next to the other one (whom I labeled "The Cutie") and tried not to giggle as he sang Coldplay's "Viva la Vida" while strategizing.

Then an announcement was made that we were stopping in Ketchikan for a few hours. Hooray!! I was ready for a long walk that didn't involve going in circles around the deck while fearing I might slip overboard and plummet into freezing water.

You know how, in movies, people standing on the sidewalk get drenched when a car driving by hits a puddle and douses them in water? I always thought that was one of those Hollywood tricks – like that doesn't actually happen. In Ketchikan, rainiest spot in Alaska, I found out that yes, yes, it does actually happen. It happened to me. About seventeen times. I was not in a happy mood by the time I got into the actual town, two miles down the road. The pants I'd spent a boatload of money on at REI in Seattle last week? Definitely not waterproof. I really needed to read labels before I bought things. And I could feel water sloshing around in my shoes. I hadn't been this wet since that day I'd walked on the beach in Cape Hatteras, North Carolina, and ended up looking like Chris Martin in Coldplay's "Yellow" video. It was only six months ago, but with all that had happened between, it felt like a lifetime ago.

I walked past a cruise ship, docked right beside the downtown shops and restaurants. I shook my fist at it. It was the boat I had tried to book a cruise on before finding out they hate single people. They got to dock in a prime location while we second-class citizens on the ferry had to hike two miles into town. I hid out in a restaurant for a while, then figured I might as well take the wet walk back. It wasn't like the boat was going to come and get me.

I changed out of my wet clothes and kicked myself for not bringing a second pair of shoes. Everything else was locked up in Cherry Cherry back in Bellingham, still two days away. I snuggled down into my sleeping bag to warm up. I looked around and didn't see the guys I'd played Bananagrams with. I hoped they didn't miss the boat or I'd have no one to flirt with for the next two days.

The next day was much the same. I read another book (being a life-long nerd, I was a pretty fast reader) with a break halfway through to play Bananagrams again. One of the two guys I'd played Bananagrams with the day before sought me out for a rematch. I was a little disappointed it wasn't the one I'd been making eyes at (My friend Matt, who'd told me about the ferry, also told me that one of his friends had met her husband on the ferry, so heck yeah, I was in flirt mode! It could happen!), but I was happy just to have someone challenge me.

I had some free time (okay, I had nothing but free time), so I made a list of differences between cruise ships and ferries, just in case anyone I knew might one day have to decide which route to go. It had been several years since I'd taken a Caribbean cruise, but I figured most cruises were pretty much the same. Here's what I came up with:

1. On an Alaskan cruise, you'd pay $899 for an inside room with no windows ($1798 if, God forbid, you're a social leper who travels alone). On an Alaskan ferry, you'd pay $652. There's no charge for traveling alone, but you don't get a bed, either, unless you fork out an additional $308.

2. On a cruise, there are midnight buffets, all you can eat pizza and ice cream 24/7, and four-course dinners with lobster, lamb, and steak as options. On the ferry, you microwave whatever you brought with you.

3. Onboard entertainment? Cruises have performers singing and dancing, casinos, bars, a spa, game shows, and in-room movies. The ferry has a nightly showing of a straight-to-DVD movie. (Example: Bruce Willis in *Surrogates*. You've never heard of it? Yeah, I hadn't either. And no, you're not missing anything.)

4. Plenty of water to entertain you on a cruise with multiple swimming pools and hot tubs. On the ferry? Well, you could

splash around in the water fountain . . .

5. On a cruise ship, you have a private room with your own shower. On the ferry, you share your room with fifty new friends, many of whom would benefit from a shower.

6. Finally, cruises organize off-shore excursions. On the ferry, they dump you out two miles from Ketchikan so you can take a hike in the rain to the downtown area . . . where you'll see the jerks on the cruise ship you wanted to be on waving at you from their luxurious deck rooms. But who's bitter?

I hung out with The Cutie again later that night in the dining hall. He microwaved some Rice-A-Roni while I zapped a can of soup. Neither one looked appetizing. We were obviously both on a budget. I asked what he was doing on the ferry. His name was Bjorn, and he and his friend Jeremy, the one I'd been drooling over, were on an around-the-world adventure. They'd started in South America and were ending in South Africa. It sounded awesome. And tiring.

We talked about my trip and he confided that he'd just been on a date. Both he and Jeremy had recently graduated from a Seventh Day Adventist college, and there was another Seventh Day Adventist college in Oregon. He'd searched the school directory for girls with a compatible Myers-Briggs test type, then contacted the one he liked best and gone out with her when they passed through her state. I laughed and said that was one method I hadn't yet tried. We talked for an hour and a half, 'til I could barely keep my eyes open anymore. I felt bad that I'd been disappointed earlier with only his company and not The Hottie's, too. He was fun.

The next morning the *Malaspina* docked back in Bellingham, seven days after I'd boarded. Despite some bouts of boredom on the ferry, I was a little sad to get off. It had forced me to slow down, and I was grateful. I'd gotten caught up on sleep, caught up on writing, and had even read two books. I hadn't felt that relaxed in ages.

I was heading through Seattle (The Cutie and The Hottie's next destination) on my way to Portland (my next destination), so I asked if they wanted a ride. I'd like to say I was being Good Samaritan-ish, saving them the train or bus fare, but it might have had something to do with wanting to enjoy their company for a little longer. Plus, I'd found out they'd both volunteered in Africa while in college. I figured if they'd done that, they were probably good guys who weren't dangerous. I just hoped they weren't tag team murderers posing as innocuous little Seventh Day Adventists.

Bjorn had told Jeremy about our conversation the night before, and now it was his turn to ask questions.

"It's too bad you've already had your Washington date, or I would have done it," he said. Oh, man. I would've needed eye drops. (No blinking? From staring into his gorgeous eyes? Never mind.)

"You probably wouldn't have met my age requirement," I said.

"Well, using the 'half your age plus seven' rule . . ." he countered. He must have asked Bjorn how old I was. ". . . that's 17 1/2 plus 7, which is 24 1/2. And I'm 24 1/2."

Melt. Melt. Melty-melt.

We stopped for breakfast and they both prayed before they ate. Such good boys. Maybe I'd have to dip down into a younger age bracket to find a good guy. They asked how I had come up with the *Fifty Dates in Fifty States* idea.

"It wasn't even my idea, really," I confessed. "My friend Molly said that lots of people had written about driving around the country, and I needed a hook."

"I need a hook," Bjorn said. He'd mentioned the night before that he might write about his trip.

Jeremy instantly started singing the chorus of "Hook." Oh my stars, The Hottie was a fellow human jukebox? He might just be my dream man.

"Weren't you in elementary school when that song was popular?" I teased.

"Blues Traveler is awesome," he declared.

Driving away from the restaurant, he pointed out an old car he liked.

"I guess I just like older things," he said. "Older music, older cars, older women . . ."

I shook my head and laughed.

"24 1/2," he reminded me. Melt, melt, melt. Puddle on the floor.

I considered advising him to stop flirting or I might not drop him off in Seattle as agreed, but I didn't want to scare him. But seriously, if he'd been ten years older . . .

I reluctantly dropped them off at their friend's house and wished them well on the rest of their journey. I envied the fact that they had each other for companionship, but thought about how it probably wouldn't go as well for me if I'd brought a friend along. Girls get catty. I don't know why we do, but we definitely do. And as much as I missed my friends, I didn't want to ruin any of those friendships in exchange for a few months of road trip companionship.

It was now my third time in Seattle (first with the youth group kids several years ago, then for my date with Mr. Washington last week, and now dropping off the guys) and I still hadn't seen Mount Rainier. The first time I'd been there, I'd been looking at postcards in an airport gift shop as we waited to board our flight home when I made a crazy discovery.

"There's a mountain here?" I asked as I stared at the picture of the Seattle skyline with Mount Rainier in the background. It had been foggy the entire week we'd been there.

On my return to Seattle, I'd had no luck seeing it, which was pretty much my one goal. Besides the date, of course.

So now, my third time there, I got out the map and chose a scenic route. It got me off the interstate (ding!) and significantly closer to Mount Rainier and Mount Saint Helens (ding! ding!). It turned out to be a fabulous choice. The mist vanished and the sun came out. Golden leaves fluttered off the late-September turning trees as I cruised the backroads.

When I was in high school, I'd painted a Washington mountainside panorama based on a photo I'd seen in a National Geographic magazine. My dad had reminded me of it when we'd seen a similar painting in a Montana coffee shop a few weeks before. I'd been surprised and touched that he remembered the one artistic accomplishment of my life. As I drove the backroads, I couldn't help but wish I could capture the views I was admiring. I knew my photos wouldn't be able to. I just had to drink it in and try to store it in my memory forever.

The only thing missing was that elusive Mount Rainier. I couldn't believe I wasn't going to see it. Again. Then I looked over my shoulder, to where it should be, and slammed on my brakes. Lo and behold, there it was. I pulled over on the narrow country road, ignored the rude logging truck driver who honked as he barreled past, and had a little photo shoot. Finally see Mount Rainier? Check.

Washington wasn't quite done awing me, though. I wound through the forest on a tiny two-lane road for the next two hours, seeing various views of Mount Saint Helens, the volcano that erupted when I was five. I'm sure it had scared the pants off people that day, but on this perfect fall day, it was beautiful. I was sorry I'd spent my first thirty-five years judging Washington on Seattle alone.

#40 – OREGON

I crossed the gorgeous Columbia River late in the afternoon. I was mad there was no "Welcome to Oregon" sign for me to take a picture in front of, but I forgave them since the view was so spectacular. I stopped at the postcard-perfect Multnomah Falls, then headed for Portland. I had a promise to keep. Back when I was working at the church, a fabulous young lady named Morgan was thinking about going to college in Portland.

"Oooh, I've always wanted to go to Oregon!" I enthused. "If you go there, I'll definitely come visit you."

She did, but I hadn't, and now she was about to graduate. Better late than never, right?

I got to her way-nicer-than-I'd-expect-a-college-apartment-to-be apartment and met her roommates. We were all hungry, so we went to a local fave, the Grilled Cheese Grill. From the looks of the long line, somebody was making a boatload of money from a very simple idea. You ordered at the window of a trailer, then ate either at an outdoor picnic table or inside the school bus parked nearby. One of Morgan's roommates split the Cheesus Burger with her boyfriend. It was made up of a hamburger patty between two grilled cheese triangles instead of a bun. Insanity.

Later that night, we went to another of their favorite local places, Voodoo Donuts. The decor was an eccentric mix of coffins and Kenny Rogers memorabilia. I do love me some Kenny, so I was an instant fan. They had all kinds of crazy toppings on donuts like

Froot Loops or grape Kool-Aid or bacon. While I'd love any of those toppings alone, I wasn't interested in combining them with a donut. I went with a comparatively boring maple-frosted donut and a quart of milk to wash it down. It was nearly 1AM when we got back to the apartment. I had forgotten how much later you stay up when you're in college. I could barely keep my eyes open.

At 5AM, they popped open real quick. I ran for the bathroom. The night before's crazy menu had done me in, I feared. Grilled cheese, chips, strawberry pop, a maple-frosted donut, and a quart of milk had me kneeling on Morgan's bathroom floor. *Stay down*, I willed the churning contents of my stomach. *I will do better tomorrow, I promise.*

It did. But I didn't.

Well, I started out alright. We all slept in and I had a bowl of Cheerios once I got up. That was good for me. But then Morgan's roommate Denise and I took the local train downtown for the Saturday Fair, this very cool big ol' market kind of thing that took up blocks and blocks, and I saw corndogs. They looked so good. I resisted temptation at first. We walked around all the booths and admired what everyone was selling, from framed photos to sweaters for puppies to jewelry made out of silverware. There were food stands selling foods from all over the world, but what did I eventually go back to? The corndog stand. They say the heart wants what it wants, and the taste buds do, too.

We sat and ate (Denise got Polish food, which looked slightly healthier but not nearly as tasty as my deep-fried goodness on a stick) and did some people watching. Some poor Ukrainian guy was trying to save people from hell (according to the sign in front of him, that's where everyone was headed) but people were distracted from his message by a homeless guy who'd parked himself two feet away with a message of his own. His sign said, "Jesus cheats at poker. Give me $3 and be saved from hell."

I'd heard that Portland's homeless have the most interesting signs. I saw one that said, "Ninjas killed my parents. Need money for karate lessons." Another made no attempt to fool you about where your money would be going. It simply read, "Spare some change for weed?"

Denise went home to do homework and I wandered up to Powell's bookstore. I'd heard about its massiveness and how easy it was to get lost in its multiple rooms and levels. I spent far too much time and far too much money, but I bought lots of good gifts for some little readers in my life. I was pretty sure I'd never been tempted by so many great children's books. I didn't actually buy anything for myself since I still had several books in my trunk. Before leaving Colorado back in February, I'd thought this trip would give me lots of time to sit and read. I'd packed a small box of books to entertain me while out on the road. Now it was October and I'd only finished four books in that time (two of which I'd read while on the Alaskan ferry). Most of my time was either spent writing or talking, so I didn't have time to read.

Once I finished up at Powell's and was trying to decide what to do next, I remembered the pictures of Haystack Rock I'd seen on display back at the Saturday Fair. I'd always wanted to go there. It's where they filmed the final scene of *The Goonies* as the pirate ship comes sailing out. I wondered if I could get there by sunset. I called Morgan and told her I'd be home late, then pointed Cherry Cherry toward the ocean. I thought the big rocks and the fading light would make for amazing photos.

It was pitch black by the time I got out there. I was steaming mad . . . and kicking myself for planning so poorly. It hadn't looked that far away on the map, but it had taken two hours to get there.

"Well, it is October," my sister said when I called her to complain. "It gets darker earlier . . ." This was a hard concept for me to grasp, and here's why: driving around the country, not really having any responsibilities, was kind of like being on eternal summer vacation. So the fact that it was now fall and the sun set earlier? Yeah, that hadn't even crossed my mind. Turning around and going home would mean driving four hours and not seeing anything, so I called Morgan and told her I was just going to camp there for the night.

Again, poor planning. As previously mentioned, it was no longer summer, so almost all campgrounds were closed for the season. The one that was still open wanted $35 for the night. $35? To sleep *on the ground?* In *my* sleeping bag? In *my* tent? How exactly did they think they deserved $35? I headed into town to check out my other options. I found a public restroom that was open, so that was a good thing. Every hotel and restaurant in town appeared to be high class. I hadn't eaten anything on the way out because I'd been hurrying, not wanting to miss the sunset. Now I was in a town with no fast food joints or grocery stores. I continued to drive around, hoping for the best. I found a Christian conference center and prayed they were generous, forgiving, and not very tight on security. I parked alongside the vehicles of their paying guests, then crawled into the backseat and tried to sleep.

I missed the ferry.

I'd promised my mom way back when I'd started the journey that I wouldn't sleep in my car. I'd made the mistake of mentioning, while car shopping, that I wanted a vehicle with a big trunk so I could fold the seats down and sleep back there. She pictured me in Walmart parking lots or interstate rest areas, alone, asleep, and completely vulnerable to the crazies of the world. So far I'd kept my promise, but I broke it that night. It seemed like the best option under the circumstances. Unfortunately, I found out Toyota Corolla backseats are not uber-comfy. Not even kinda comfy, to be honest. No matter which position I tried, I could not get to sleep. My late-in-the-day trip to the Oregon coast had been a very, very bad idea.

"Dancing Queen" rang through the car at 5:45AM. I'd set the cell phone alarm so I could wake up early and see Haystack Rock before hurrying back to Portland for church with Morgan. Little did I know I wouldn't need an alarm because I wouldn't sleep. I also didn't know it would still be pitch black at 5:45AM. Ugh! Stupid October!

I crawled into the front seat and headed out, trying to look at the bright side – I could find the beach and be there when the sun came up, right? First I spent forty-five minutes looking for a bathroom; the one I'd used the night before was now locked. I carried my knife into the second one I found, just in case some serial killer was an early riser, then found a spot to access the beach. It was getting lighter but still wasn't exactly bright out, so I pocketed my cell phone in one pocket and the knife in the other before hitting the beach. I needn't have worried, though – several people were already out walking their dogs or jogging along the beach. Haystack Rock rose out of the mist in the distance. All was quiet but the roar of the ocean, and I was glad I wasn't there in the bright afternoon sun with a thousand tourists. I liked having the beach nearly all to myself.

I spent half an hour roaming the beach, then had to get going back to Portland, so all in all, I'd spent about four hours driving for half an hour on the beach. I consoled myself with the fact that the drive had been pretty and I'd see more beaches in Southern Oregon and Northern California.

We made it to the church on time, and after finding seats, I asked the woman next to me the standard question you ask without expecting a real answer.

"How are you?"

"Oh my gosh," she started, and I could tell she'd just been waiting for someone to come sit next to her so she could tell this story. "I'm completely wiped out because I didn't get any sleep last night. At two in the morning we had to call the cops because the neighbors behind us had a flame thrower in a dumpster . . ."

Hmm. Alrighty then. I guess my night could have been worse.

I was almost dateless in Oregon. I'd been holding out hope that I would somehow be able to land a date with Donald Miller, an author who lived in Portland. While I realized having a crush on an author (when most women have crushes on athletes or actors) made me a total nerd, I didn't care. I'd read his book *A Million Miles in a Thousand Years* while making plans for my road trip, and his message about living a meaningful life felt like validation. I wanted to meet him and thank him . . . and persuade him to marry me and make some nerdy, book-loving babies. Famous people have people who keep away people like me, though, so I wasn't able to set anything up. Bummer. Luckily Bjorn from the Alaskan ferry had called his buddy in Portland while we were driving from Bellingham to Seattle. After a bit of waiting to hear whether or not he was willing, we were on!

We met at the Japanese Gardens in Washington Park. First impression? Cute! Blonde, thin, clean cut – my grandma would have approved. We wandered around the ikebana display, the waterfalls, and the pagodas. He thought before he spoke; I babbled freely, filling the silences. He confessed that he wasn't the most social guy. At parties, he said, he was generally off on the side talking to one person rather than working the crowd. I asked if he'd believe me if I said that was generally how I operated, too. He looked at me skeptically.

"So dating men all over the country has made you more outgoing?"

"I still have to force myself to strike up a conversation with a stranger," I said. "I'm kind of shy by nature. And even though I can keep a conversation going on these dates, I often feel like it's the same conversation, you know? Like, every guy asks the same questions, so I have the same answers. It kind of feels like cheating. It's harder to make small talk with people who don't know what I'm doing, because they ask different questions that I don't have practiced answers to."

We talked about the various places we'd lived and the jobs we'd worked. He'd taught math at one point and loved it.

"Ooh, I have a dating idea for you!" I exclaimed, remembering a guy I'd dated back in Colorado. "A math teacher once drew me a probability chart showing how likely it was that he'd ask me out on a second date. He said I had a 3 out of 4 shot."

He thought about it for a few seconds.

"I'm not sure I want to be defined by math . . ."

"Oh, it was definitely dorky," I admitted, "but notice that I still remember him."

The Japanese Garden was closing, so we headed downtown. We wandered around for a while, then got some frozen yogurt and sat talking in Pioneer Square. He was a Seventh Day Adventist, too, like his friends I'd met on the ferry, so I asked why he goes to church on Saturdays.

"Imagine you're invited to a big warehouse," he said, "and once you get there, your host invites you to come in and sit off to the side. He says, 'Watch this!' While you watch, he creates all kinds of beautiful things, and it's really awe-inspiring. But now imagine a second host inviting you over. When you arrive, he invites you to come and sit with him in the center of the room, in the midst of everything that's already been created and prepared for you.

"These two hosts have two different styles that say two different things. And if you replace the host with God and you with Adam, you see that God didn't create Adam first, then try to wow him with creation. He created everything, then just wanted to be in the midst of it all with Adam. So I go to worship to be with God, since what he wants is to be in relationship with us."

Cool. But I guess I should have phrased my question differently, because what I'd meant was, "Why do you go to church on Saturdays *instead of on Sundays, like Lutherans?*"

Oh well. It was the springboard for an hour of theological talk, and I love talking theology. I missed working in a church and sharing and questioning and debating things of God and faith. After an hour of hashing things out with Mr. Oregon, though, my toes were starting to turn blue as the daylight faded. I obviously hadn't yet grasped that October idea and was slightly shivering in my flip-flops. We headed back to our cars.

"You should really take more chances in those social gatherings," I said as we parted. "You should mingle with the cute girls and be brave and ask them out. You're a good date."

Back at Morgan's apartment, I headed for the laundry room. I hadn't had a chance to wash my clothes since the week before I'd gotten on the ferry. My laundry bag reeked. While the washer did its magic, we watched the Amazing Race. I was extremely jealous because a) I want to be on the Amazing Race and b) they were competing in Ghana that night, and I hadn't been to visit the kids at the orphanage in over a year. I missed them tons. I wished a magical money tree would appear overnight outside Morgan's window.

Later, while watching the local news, I almost started crying as they showed a local high school Homecoming Queen being crowned. She'd been in a wheelchair since being in a car accident the year before, and when they announced her name, she started crying and shaking. Her dad helped her to her feet, and her legs wobbled as they handed her a bouquet of roses.

People always asked me if I was scared, driving around the country by myself. I wasn't completely naive, or so overly optimistic and positive that I wasn't aware that there were definitely bad people out there who might like nothing better than to hurt me. I firmly believed, though, that for the most part, people were good. Most people were just trying to make a better life for themselves and their families. Most people were still willing to take time to help their neighbor. And some people were good-hearted enough to give a girl in a wheelchair an honor she'd never forget.

The next day I headed out for Crater Lake National Park. I'd heard that the water was the bluest blue you'd ever seen, and it was true. I had not heard, though, that it's extremely frickin' cold. I didn't even bother setting up my tent that night because I knew I'd freeze to death. Having tried out the backseat two days earlier and finding it stunk for sleeping, I reclined the driver's seat as far back as it would go, wriggled into my sleeping bag, then stargazed through the moonroof. It was beautiful. I fell asleep praying that the giant tree hovering over my car wouldn't fall and crush me to death in the night.

The verdict? The front seat wasn't as bad as the backseat, but it wasn't great either. I wasn't too cold, thanks to the sleeping bag I'd spent a boatload of money on, but I wasn't comfortable enough to get a good night's sleep either. I wriggled out of the sleeping bag at 6:30AM and pulled out of the campsite. The temperature? Twenty-three degrees. I saw a Eurovan a few sites down and had to bite back the jealousy. Oh, for a money tree.

Oregon was one of the most beautiful states I'd seen. I drove along the narrow, tree-lined roads, loving all the fall colors. In the middle of a shallow river, people were contentedly fly-fishing. Upon reaching the coast, I meandered my way down it, pulling Cherry Cherry over occasionally to take pictures of the rocky shoreline.

I didn't notice how low my gas tank had gotten until the signal light flicked on. Grr. I really needed to pay more attention. I came to a little town with a gas station, but the price seemed ridiculously high. I checked my map and decided to go on to the next town since it looked bigger and the gas would probably be cheaper . . . not realizing that, despite how close they looked on the map, the next town was actually thirty miles down the road. I swear that nagging little light glowed brighter and brighter as I begged Cherry Cherry to hang in there, apologized for my stupidity, and promised to never let it happen again. (She'd heard that before.)

I watched the signs and silently cheered as the miles to town got lower and lower. Walk eight miles for gas? That would be really bad. Six? Doable but not enjoyable. Four? I could handle that. Three, two, one, and the yellow Shell sign came into view. Hallelujah!

The cost of gas was less than it had been in the previous town, but some quick math showed me I'd saved a whopping one dollar by risking it. Dumb. Dumb, dumb, dumb. One dollar was not worth half an hour of stress.

A guy came out to pump my gas, which still threw me for a loop, despite it being my third fill-up in Oregon.

"Why can't I pump my own gas?" I asked as we stood there by the pump.

"It's against the law. $5000 fine."

"I would get fined or the gas station would get fined?"

"You," he said.

"Seriously? Why?"

"Some kid was smoking while he pumped his gas. Blew himself up and then the parents sued the state. So now nobody can pump their own gas. It was years and years ago, but it's still the law."

I quietly got back in my car and waited for him to hand me my receipt. If I'd thought the cost per gallon was bad, $5000 for ten gallons would hurt a whole lot worse.

#41 – CALIFORNIA

I woke up cold and achy. I was getting sick of camping. I thought of my big, comfy queen-sized bed piled high with blankets. I remembered taking a hot shower every morning. It seemed like paradise. I tried not to think about my cute little townhouse that I'd sold and couldn't go back to. Now my bedroom was my tent and my dining room was the driver's seat. My pants doubled as a napkin. I'd been wearing the same clothes for three days. I smelled.

I packed up the tent, annoyed that it was wet again, quickly making my fingers go numb. I climbed into Cherry Cherry and headed out for a drive around Lake Tahoe. The car in front of me passed the car in front of it, and suddenly my new view was of a hearse . . . and that was definitely a coffin in the back.

Camping's not so bad, I reminded myself. *Beats the alternative.*

I wondered if married people got sick of their spouses. I mean, if I, who used to love camping, was getting sick of camping, was it human nature to get tired of things, even things you loved? Was that why so many couples got divorced? Or why people were always remodeling their homes? Did parents get sick of their children?

It was a long day of driving, but I saw a lot of Northern California and was surprised by how beautiful it was. My first three visits to California had brought me to the not-so-scenic L.A. area, so I'd never thought of it as a pretty state. Even though I paid $3.99 per gallon for my next fill-up of gas, I tried not to hold it against them. Yosemite National Park was downright amazing. I was glad I'd made the detour.

I had planned my California date long before I found a guy to be my Mister there. I wanted to hear those three little words everyone dreams of hearing: COME ON DOWN!

I'm a bit of a game show fanatic. Before meeting Mr. California at *The Price is Right*, I'd already been there two previous times over the years. I didn't get called to "come on down" either time. I'd taken the online *Jeopardy* test twice but had never gotten on that game show either. (If only I could get on Kids Week! I was really good with those questions! Or Celebrity Week! Those questions were even easier!) I even auditioned for *Wheel of Fortune* when the Wheelmobile came to Colorado. I made the cut for a second audition, but got sent home before the third. That rejection, out of all my game show experiences, was the biggest bummer; I don't want to brag or anything, but I kick ass at *Wheel of Fortune*. I solve the puzzles faster than the contestants 99% of the time. The chances of a humiliating defeat are much smaller on that one than on *Jeopardy*. Anyway, I love game shows. Also, I didn't know how else I was going to afford Hawaii, so I was kind of hoping to win a trip to Honolulu on *The Price is Right*.

I found Mr. California on a dating website. I liked him for several reasons: a) He listed *The Goonies* as one of his favorite movies; b) I liked the personality and hobbies I saw showcased in his pictures: sporting a bow tie, playing guitar, hiking in Nepal, and wearing those nerdy-cute glasses; and c) He was in the biz there in L.A., which I thought might mean some flexibility in his work schedule, i.e., he might be available on a Tuesday to go to *The Price is Right* with me. I shot him an email, and he couldn't say no to such a crazy idea.

I'd stayed at my friend Stephanie's house the night before. We lived on the same floor during our first year of college and had only seen each other a couple of times since then, so it was odd to see her changed from the party girl to the working mom. She now had a three year old and a three month old. I was again struck by that inner debate: Am I behind in life, not having kids, or am I the sane one, living it up instead of being tied down? She knew how to cook now. She'd even made a cheesecake. A cheesecake! When did we become grown ups?

I left at 5:15AM to drive the two hours into L.A. Steph was already awake, having just fed her youngest. I swore off motherhood as I stumbled sleepily out the door. Mr. California had said to meet him at 8AM, and though my GPS said the drive would only take two hours, I wanted to give myself a little breathing room, just in case traffic was bad. Turned out I almost needed a ventilator, traffic was so out of control. I tried not to panic as I sat on the parking lot they called a freeway. Mr. California texted that he was there. I texted back that I wasn't even close. He went to the ticket booth to get our tickets and was told they were in my name, not his, so I needed to get down there ASAP before they gave them away to someone else. I drove like a maniac once I got off the freeway and onto a normal street. I ran three blocks from the parking garage, trying not to heave up a lung. I so, so, so hate running.

    I crossed the CBS gate like an Olympic finish line (but with a bit more huffing, puffing, and sweating than an Olympic athlete) and held up my wallet to show my ID to a security guard.

    "Cute kids," he said, pointing to the pictures of my nephews he assumed were my offspring on display alongside my driver's license.

    "Thanks," I replied, not taking time to correct him before continuing my power walk. It was now 8:43AM. The information I'd gotten had very clearly stated that all reserved tickets would be given away if not claimed by 8:30AM. I dialed Mr. California, not sure how else to find him in the swarm of people. Dang. Looked like everyone wanted to win a trip to Hawaii.

    "I'm on your left," he said instead of hello. After a few awkward moments of scanning the massive crush of humanity on my left, I spotted him. Cute! And he'd worn the glasses. Yay!

    "I'm so sorry," I started, fearing we'd lost the tickets and would have to come up with a Plan B.

    "No problem," he said, holding up two tickets. "I talked her into giving them to me. I said it was our first date and she seemed willing to help."

    "Oh good." I tried to sound enthusiastic, but seriously? I'd just run for nothing?

    "Relax," he said. "Breathe!" I must have been looking pretty awful. Have I mentioned I don't run?

    "I've got something for you," he said. "Now, if you hate them, we don't have to wear them . . ." He held up two matchy-matchy green t-shirts. The first said, *I'm writing a book: Fifty Dates in Fifty States.*

The second said, *I'm Date #41: California.* Fabulous!

We were in line forever, but it's amazing how time passes quickly when you have someone interesting to talk to. Mr. California was an assistant director on movie sets.

"Have you worked on anything I would have heard of?" I asked. He rattled off a bunch of movie titles. I was impressed.

"I'm currently working on *The Hangover 2*."

"Oh my gosh, that's awesome!" I gushed. I'd just assumed that everyone in Hollywood was the struggling actor type. You know, waiting tables while waiting for their big break? But this guy was actually making a living in the business.

"We're going to Thailand to shoot from Thanksgiving to Christmas," he said.

"What kind of plot line takes them to Thailand?"

"I can't say."

"Is it the same group of guys as the first one?"

"I can't tell you," he said again, but nodded his head up and down. "That's nothing you couldn't find on the internet, so it's not like it's a huge secret."

We had to fill out some forms with our legal names and Social Security numbers, just in case we won and had to pay taxes on prizes. A red-coated intern came around to write our names on the big yellow nametags. She read our shirts and said it was awesome.

"Have you, like, dated any women?" she asked.

"Um, no."

"You should," she said. Mr. California started laughing.

"I'm into guys," I explained.

"Yeah, but like, if they make your book into a movie, it would be, like, more interesting if you had at least one girl date in there. I mean, like, from the Hollywood aspect."

I was so not Hollywood.

"I think I'll, like, stick with men, but thanks," I said. She didn't notice my valley girl mock.

We were moved from one area to another, still staying in the order we were in before. I'd say it was like being part of a herd of cattle, but cattle don't stay in single file lines. And cattle can graze as they go. Man, I was hungry. We'd been in line for about two hours already, and that granola bar I'd eaten at 7AM as I sat on the freeway was long gone.

"So what have you learned about dating from doing this?" Mr. California asked.

I thought about it for a minute. "I think I'm less picky. No, that's not a good way of putting it. I'm more open to giving guys a chance than I used to be, I guess." I still didn't feel like I was making sense.

"There were guys I passed up in the past because there was something about them I didn't like. A friend wanted to set me up with a guy who had a good job, his own house, and a couple of cats, and I just cut her off right there because I prefer dogs to cats. Another time, I met this guy who was great but he was a math teacher, so I lost interest."

"So, hypothetically speaking," Mr. California began, "if one of your fifty dates happened to have been the captain of his high school math club, and even came up with the name 'Divide and Conquer' for said club, would that automatically disqualify him?"

I laughed. "No, that's what I'm saying. The clever name shows you're good with words, too, and not just numbers. And having spent a few hours with you, I can see there's much more to you than math. In the past I would have said, 'I hate math. I don't want to be with someone who loves math.' But now I realize that just because someone has one quality I don't like, it doesn't mean he's not someone I could be with."

"It's not like that's the only thing I did in high school," he said. "I played tennis. And I was on the Homecoming Court."

"Me, too!" I said. "I probably had less competition than you, though. I only had twenty-five people in my senior class."

He laughed. "So I'm not a nerd."

"It's not even that," I tried to explain. "I like smart guys. I was just really bad at math in high school. I think it's an issue of my own insecurity more than thinking the guy might be nerdy. Like, what if he thinks I'm not smart because I'm not good at math and he is?"

"Hmmm . . . deep," he mocked.

"Whatever. So has online dating worked well for you out here, or is this the only offer you've gotten lately?"

"It's alright. My brother met his wife online, so I figure there's always a chance."

"This might sound bad, but I picture all women out here as wannabe actresses and models. Are those the only women you meet?"

He laughed. "You know, I drive by schools and hospitals and realize there must be teachers and nurses in this city, but for the life of me, I can't find them. Honestly, though, I don't have much time for dating anyway. I mean, we generally put in fifteen hour days on the set."

I wrinkled up my forehead. Yikes. Who wants to date someone who works fifteen hour days? I mean, it's bad enough that he's never there, but when he does come around, he's probably exhausted and cranky and not really interested in doing much more than popping in a DVD and falling asleep halfway through it.

"I'll get out of the business once I get married and have a family," he assured me. "They'll come first. I won't be able to do both."

The line moved again. It was our turn to wow the producer. Being selected to "come on down" is not about luck. In groups of ten or so, you stand in front of a producer who quickly moves down the line, asking who you are and what you do. You've got about twenty seconds to make a better impression than the other 300 people you're in line with. "Church youth worker" had not impressed anyone the two previous times I'd tried to get on, so I was hoping "dating my way around the country" might be more impressive. Bonus: we had the cute t-shirts Mr. California had made.

"What do you do?" he asked a woman.

"I'm a cupcake maker," she said. My stomach growled. We'd been in line for over three hours. I wanted a cupcake. Or a cake of any kind. I could seriously have eaten an entire cake right then.

"How about you?" he asked the guy next to me.

"I'm a professional biker," he responded. I'd seen him writing his info on his little card, saying BMX had thousands of fans. I had considered re-writing my info; I mean, if we were going for numbers, millions of people *read*. I could consider them all fans, right?

The producer stepped in front of me. "What do you do?"

"I'm driving around the country, dating," I said. I may have stuttered a little bit. Or stammered. Or both. I was nervous, okay?

"This is Mr. California," I said, gesturing to my handsome date.

"So, how long have you known each other?" he asked.

"We just met here this morning," Mr. California said.

"Weird," the producer said, then called my date a gigolo. Dang it! Why did everyone in line think it was a cute idea, but the one person I needed to impress to win a fabulous Hawaiian vacation thought it was strange?

We were moved to yet another area to sit and wait for yet another length of time. All told, we finally moved into the studio about four hours after we got there. They were playing music, and Mr. California and I stood there dancing while everyone else sat taking in the bright lights and the smaller-than-you-think-it-would-be stage. When "You're The One That I Want" from *Grease* came blaring over the sound system, Mr. California tugged me out into the aisle and started swing dancing. Cute, smart, and a good dancer? Ding, ding, ding!!!

Sadly, a great date was my only prize that day. Was I bummed? Yeah. I mean, sitting there watching other people get called up to play Plinko and win cars and hug Drew Carey was like being given a toy horse to play with when the person next to you got a real pony. It was slightly torturous.

I returned to Steph's house dejected, but I quickly forgot about my disappointing day while kicking a soccer ball around with her three year old. He was stinkin' adorable, making a part of me want a cutie of my own. Her baby was screaming, though, so not all of me was jumpin' on the mama train.

I appreciated how honest she and her husband were. "The baby stage stinks," they admitted. Some people love babies. I tend to think I'd be a better parent if my kids arrived as well-mannered, toilet-trained four-year-olds.

Both Stephanie and Josh are teachers, so I left the house at the same time they did early the next day. I made it to the border of California and Arizona right around lunch time and pulled into a McDonald's. I'd done a pretty good job of avoiding fast food for the majority of the trip, but they had recently fired up their Monopoly game again, and I'm a sucker for winning free stuff. I'd taken to driving through their fast food windows just to order smoothies or orange juice; they were healthier choices, but you still got two game pieces on each medium-sized cup. I needed to use the bathroom, though, so I opted to go in instead of drive through.

A woman who appeared to be homeless was sitting near the entrance.

"Got a dollar?" she asked.

I used to be a good person, before I started this trek around the country. I helped out the homeless ministry at church and staffed the family room welcome desk at a local hospital a few times a month. I did the charity walks for hunger and cancer and the like. But while on the road, I hadn't done much of anything to help anyone. My charity work since February consisted of attending that one fundraiser in NYC and occasionally buying food for someone.

"Are you hungry?" I asked.

"Yeah," she responded in a tone that sounded like, "Are you stupid?"

"What would you like?"

"I want a McChicken sandwich, large fries, and a large tea," she shot back. Huh. Not even a little bit of hesitation. "Sweet tea."

I went in, placed her order, and got an eighty-nine cent hamburger for myself. I carried the food out to her but almost yanked it back when she reached to take it from me. She had a manicure – French tips with fancy black stripes on the little white ends. I had hangnails galore on my own hands, not thinking a manicure was a valid expense when you're trying to stick to a budget. She closed the distance, grabbed the bag, and muttered thanks. I went back inside to bitterly eat my crappy little burger.

#42 – ARIZONA

I got out of my car to fill up my gas tank in Arizona and thought I might melt. One hundred and two degrees. In the shade. In October. All I could think was, *Why would anyone want to live here?*

I felt kind of bad, sitting in my car applying an extra layer of deodorant and slapping on some mascara. I thought back to my first date of this adventure, back in New Mexico, and about how worried I'd been about how I looked. And now, for Mr. Arizona, I hadn't even showered. In my defense, a) I was tired from getting up early for *The Price is Right* the day before and couldn't bring myself to get up early two days in a row, and b) Mr. Arizona was taking me hiking. In Arizona. Where it was 102 degrees in the shade in October. So really, why bother? I had started sweating while pumping gas, a relatively sedentary activity. This was not going to be pretty.

It turned out I didn't have to worry about excessive sweating. Mr. Arizona didn't get out of work as early as he'd hoped, so we weren't going to have time to hike to the top of the mountain to watch the sun set. We'd have to drive up instead. Gosh, was I ever disappointed.

We met in the parking lot of the park, and getting there ten minutes before he did, I used the spare time to organize my car. It was getting rather messy. I guess it wasn't beyond reason to expect that – I mean, I was driving around the country and pretty much living in it – but still, it bothered me. I like organization. There was a certain order of things in my trunk: the clothing tubs on the left, the camping gear on the right, and the small tubs of socks and underwear snuggly tucked in on both sides. In my backseat, the food crate was in the middle (so I could easily reach back there and grab snacks while I drove). The tub with my jumper cables and the can of Fix-a-Flat was behind the driver's seat and my jackets and pillow were behind the passenger seat. I straightened it all up but tried not to overdo it; I didn't want to have a heat stroke just reorganizing my car.

Mr. Arizona arrived just as I finished; my face had a lovely wet sheen, but he was too nice to say anything. I was a little surprised by his appearance, though: he bore a striking resemblance to an old boyfriend.

I could tell you some really good things about that guy, but here's what I remember the most about him: he came *incredibly close* to doing the sweetest thing any guy had ever done for me. So close. If he would have just kept his mouth shut, it would have been awesome.

I had hinted a few times over the month and a half we'd been dating that I loved chocolate-covered strawberries. He had obviously paid attention, because after I'd had a particularly rough day at work, he called and said he wanted to bring me something; ten minutes later, he rang my doorbell with a plate of homemade chocolate-covered strawberries. I was speechless.

"I know you had a really long day and you're tired, so I won't stay. I just wanted to bring these over," he said. I melted and gushed over how sweet he was.

"And I'll be thinking about you every time I use butter for the next few months," he said. When I looked at him quizzically, he continued, "I wasn't sure what to do with them after I dipped them. I thought if I laid them on one side, it would mess up the chocolate, so I put toothpicks in the ends and then stuck the toothpicks into sticks of butter until the chocolate hardened."

"You're so sweet," I fawned. No guy had ever done anything so sweet for me. But then he ruined it.

"Yeah, well, I was going to buy you some, but they were $50 a dozen on the internet and I thought that was ridiculous, so I just made you some instead."

Ouch. I mean, yeah, that would be a ridiculous amount of money to spend on chocolate-covered strawberries, but now instead of thinking he was sweet and romantic, I thought he was kind of insulting. I'm not worth $50? Way to make me feel horrible about myself, dude.

Mr. Arizona and I, with no chocolate-covered strawberries, made our way up to the top of the mountain and took in the city. I'd never studied a map of Arizona, so I had no idea that so many cities kind of blobbed together to make one giant city. Phoenix, Tempe, Mesa, Chandler, Scottsdale, Gilbert – boom! There they all collided in one big mass. I thought of all that concrete down there and the heat rising off it. Summers had to be miserable.

"Why would anyone want to live here?" I muttered. I didn't really mean to say it out loud. It just kind of slipped out.

"It's great in the winter," Mr. Arizona said.

"But summers have to be awful."

"Well, we have air conditioning."

The sunset was beautiful. I'll give them that.

"What brought you out here?" I asked. I knew from his online dating profile that Mr. Arizona had relocated from the South.

"A girl," he said sheepishly. "One of my friends kept bugging me to do online dating. He'd met his wife that way. So I did it. I didn't really find anyone near me I was interested in, so I opened it up to a nationwide search. And I met this girl out here, and she seemed fabulous, so I thought, 'Why not?' And I moved out here."

"But now you're back on the online dating site, so it must not have worked out?"

"It was fine for a while. We even talked about getting married, but I got the feeling she was more interested in the *idea* of being married than in marrying *me*."

I could relate. I told Mr. Arizona how my last boyfriend had been like that, talking about wanting to marry me when I didn't feel like he even knew me. When I talked about things I was passionate about, he didn't seem to get how much they mattered to me or why; for example, when I talked about the kids at the orphanage in Africa, he told me that phase of my life was over and I'd need to focus on him and our kids now. There were a number of things wrong with that relationship, but he was furious when I broke it off. He was engaged to someone else within six months, though, which pretty much validated my belief that he wasn't as interested in marrying *me* as he was in marrying *someone*.

Once the spectacular sunset show was over, I followed Mr. Arizona to a cute little farmhouse-turned-restaurant for a bite to eat. I was relieved that he was a talker. He talked and talked and talked . . . which was great, because by date number 42, I was tired of talking about myself. It was nice to just ask a question and then sit back and chew and nod occasionally to show I was still listening. Living mostly on granola bars, when I got a chance to eat, and especially a chance to eat meat, I was in heaven.

Mr. Arizona brought up a dating issue that none of my previous dates had talked to me about: the opinions of others affecting how you feel about someone. He had recently introduced a girl he was dating to a couple of women he volunteered with.

"Do you believe in dating someone outside your status?" they asked him later.

"What do you mean?" he asked.

"Well, like, someone who's not as attractive as you are," they clarified.

Up to that point, he'd thought the girl *was* attractive . . . but then he started thinking maybe they were right . . . and then he became less attracted to her. Hmmm.

"So what's important to you?" I asked. "In a woman, I mean."

He considered it for a moment.

"I want to be with someone who has her own life. I'm amazed at how many women I've dated who were ready to give up whatever they currently had going on to latch onto me. I don't want some vapid empty shell. I want a woman who has her own goals and plans."

I'm pretty sure he could have talked all night, but I needed to get going. I was staying with an old friend I hadn't seen in years, and it was already almost 10PM. I waited for Mr. Arizona to take a breath, then jumped in and said I needed to get going. He walked me to my car, then stood there still talking. I finally just opened up my car door, said good-bye, and hoped he'd move when I started backing up. Okay, no, I didn't really. I was tired but not outright mean.

I stayed in Arizona for two nights with my old friend Ina Kay, one of my many "Colorado moms." I was 24 when I moved to Colorado, and a group of church ladies had almost instantly adopted me. They'd signed me up for a women's retreat I wouldn't have gone to if they hadn't, partly because it cost $80, which I didn't have (but they paid for), and partly because no one else my age was going. I quickly learned, though, that these older women were *fun*. They played games and made me laugh, and to my surprise I found I *wanted* to be around them. Over time, I came to discover that I also *needed* to be around them. They had been through things in life that I hadn't. They'd carried and borne children and lived to tell about it. They loved their husbands and sometimes wanted to kill their husbands. They'd lost people they loved, survived illnesses and accidents, and somehow managed to keep going, even when life was nothing but pain. They had a wisdom that came with age, and I realized over time that if I only had friends my own age, I'd never grow as a woman. I needed these mentors in my life.

Ina Kay and her husband had left Colorado a few years before I had, but the conversation was as easy as if we'd just had lunch the week before. She was still the same . . . and she was still teaching water aerobics.

I went to water aerobics a few times when I had a short-lived gym membership. I was younger and fitter than the majority of the class back then, so I figured I could handle Ina Kay's class when she asked if I wanted to go, even if I was miserably out of shape. The bigger issue was hair removal. I'm not even going to tell you how long it had been since I'd shaved. Let's just say I was in the shower for quite a while before I declared my legs ready to see the light of day. But then, when I put on my tankini and stepped in front of the mirror, I gasped.

"Is that cellulite?" I whispered to myself in horror. I poked at my flesh, right where the butt cheek and the top of the thigh kissed hello. Hoooolyyyycrap. Was it cellulite? Or had my butt cheek gotten so flabby that gravity no longer had any competition? I repositioned myself and looked again. A little better. The key, it seemed, was to not lock the knees. Keeping the knees slightly soft, everything didn't cram together right there. I wasn't sure how I was going to walk, though. I just had to hope all the other ladies at the pool would look worse than I did. I mean, come on, I was a good twenty years younger than most of the women who'd been in water aerobics back in Colorado. This would likely be the same, right?

Not so much. Ina Kay, I found out a short drive later, taught water aerobics at the hippest, most popular gym in Phoenix. Sure, I looked better than the seventy-year-old bathing beauties in water aerobics, but I was downright pudgy compared to some of the women in the locker room. I walked from the locker room to the pool as fast as I could. A pregnant woman climbed out of the pool, and I came to the horrific realization that the bump on her belly was the only thing big about her; even pregnant women were thinner than me, apart from that whole belly issue. I needed to lay off the junk food.

#43 – NEVADA

Vegas: the only date where I found a dead body. (Kind of.)

I wanted to do something exciting in Vegas. I had considered suggesting the Bellagio Fountains, like at the end of *Oceans Eleven*, but I wasn't sure that would be much of a date. I'd found a Mr. Nevada via the internet, and he said we could walk around the old part of Vegas and see all the flashing neon signs. That also didn't sound like it would take more than half an hour to see, though. I went internet fishing until I found something that looked cool: *Mystery Adventures Las Vegas*. I may or may not have been addicted to *CSI* at one point in my life (and may or may not have had to stop watching the series when I developed a pattern of freaky nightmares every Thursday night), so solving a mystery in Vegas sounded awesome. Mr. Nevada agreed, and we were all set.

My Chief Safety Officer Alicia had booked a flight to Vegas a few weeks before so we could hang out.

"And we ain't sleeping at no Super 8," she declared in her syrupy Southern twang. I said I didn't want to spend too much (well, couldn't spend much, in all honesty) and she said not to worry; she'd take care of it. A little while later I got an email from her saying she'd booked a room at the Venetian. I'd never been to Vegas, so I wasn't sure, but that sounded awfully ritzy. I went online and found it.

"I'm never leaving the room," I told her over the phone a few minutes later.

"I ain't goin' to Vegas to hang out in a hotel room," she said.

"Well then, you shouldn't have booked such a nice room. 'Sunken living room? Roman tub with separate glass-enclosed shower?' Seriously, I'm not leaving. I've never been anywhere like that before."

I drove from my friend Ina Kay's house near Phoenix straight to the airport in Vegas. Once Alicia's flight got in, we went to the lap of luxury and checked in. I'd like to say we were calm, cool, and collected, but once we got to our room, there may have been a bit of hooting and hollering and some belly flops onto our beds. We had big fluffy comforters and ten pillows each.

"Put on your sunglasses! Let's take a picture!" Alicia instructed. We took a senior picture-style shot on our beds (lying on our bellies, one hand tucked under our chins, feet up and crossed at the ankle) and another in the sunken living room. We used the remote control to open and close the curtains and lift and lower the shades. We looked down at the swimming pools below us and hotel after hotel on the strip. We admired the bathroom, bigger than our kitchens back home, then called the front desk to report that our promised fluffy robes were not there and we'd appreciate it if they'd please send some up right away. Then I had to take off for my date.

"I'll be gambling," she said.

"Get it out of your system now, 'cause I don't have money to sit around and gamble with you tomorrow," I instructed.

I got to Mystery Adventures Las Vegas a bit before Mr. Nevada and talked to the proprietress for a bit. They'd originally come up with the idea as a birthday gift for a relative. Moving from location to location and searching for clues to solve a mystery had gone over so well that someone had said, "You could make a living off of this." And so they were.

Mr. Nevada showed up, then a group of six friends, and finally another couple. All together there were ten of us, five women and five men. We were given a letter that said someone had been rushed to the hospital and foul play was suspected. We needed to figure out what was going on, and there was a briefcase of tools for us to use to solve the crime. We all stood around feeling a little silly, then boarded the bus and headed out for the first location.

At first glance, there didn't seem to be anything interesting to look at in the first office. We found some papers that might be something, and someone got on the computer and started rummaging through files and email messages. From what we could tell, the guy who had been poisoned moonlighted as a private investigator. It seemed logical that someone had seen him snooping around and tried to get rid of him. We collected everything that seemed like it might be important and some things that seemed random, too, just in case.

We headed out for the next location, and that's where things started to get weird. We found some clues that seemed to be connected to things in the first office, but grew confused when we found picks and shovels and brushes; a video journal on a computer showed a woman at an archeological dig, and while that made sense with the tools we'd just come across, we wondered what it had to do with the private investigator. Behind a framed picture of a little boy, we found the password for the email account, then read an email telling the woman it had been five years since the accident and she needed to move on; she just wasn't the same and it wasn't her fault. *Huh?* About that time, someone hollered for everyone to come and look – there was a secret passageway in the back of a closet. Awesome!! I had a feeling things were about to get good.

We crept through the little passageway, darting our flashlights around, just like on *CSI*. Another door opened into another room that appeared to be used for scientific experimentation, like where you dissected animals in high school science. Creepy. Someone found a light switch (Why, by the way, don't they ever seem to turn on the lights on *CSI*?? Always the flashlights! What's up with that?), and we found ourselves surrounded by doctor-y stuff and a large, stainless steel table. What the heck? There was another door, but it was locked. Everyone went back into the rooms we'd been in before and searched until a key was found. It fit in the door and opened up to a room with a huge stove . . . full of human bones. Yuck. I wasn't too grossed out, though, honestly. We were all taking pictures of ourselves with the skull, Hamlet style, and it was pretty theatrical. No need to freak out, right? Someone spotted an old video camera with a VHS tape inside. We found a VCR connected to a TV back in another office and popped it in. It showed a doctor injecting a cadaver with something that brought it back to life for a few seconds. Ew. We gathered everything up, boarded the bus again, and went on to a third building a few miles away.

This place was creepy. It was dim and our footsteps echoed off the tile floors and bare walls. Everyone spread out and started looking around. In one room, I found five child-themed birthday cards on a counter. Five birthdays . . . I remembered the email saying it had been five years since an accident . . .

"Hey guys," I called out. "I think maybe that accident – the one that the email was telling the woman she needed to get over – killed her little boy. There are a bunch of photos of the same kid whose picture was on her desk at the last place, and there are five birthday cards in here, too!"

Next to the counter was a refrigerator, and I opened it up, then screamed bloody murder. A little boy was inside. Well, in all fairness, it was a mannequin of a little boy, but that didn't stop me from slamming the door shut, jumping and flailing, and generally making my nine fellow investigators laugh. Why did I have to be the one to find the freaky thing? I should have called dibs on the computer files. Everyone came and took a look and we pieced everything together: the woman's son had been crushed in a landslide at her archeological dig, and rather than bury him, she'd kept him on ice, hoping her doctor friend could figure out the right combination of chemicals to bring him back to life. The private investigator had gotten too close to figuring it out, so they'd poisoned him in hopes of getting rid of him. Mystery solved. We rocked. I could almost hear someone say, "And I would have gotten away with it, too, if it weren't for you meddling kids!"

"There's still one thing you didn't see," our bus driver/host informed us. "It doesn't change anything, because you've already pieced it all together, but it's something everyone seems to like."

He gave us a hint, saying it was in the locked room. Since we couldn't find a key, he suggested we just look at the TV monitor that showed the locked room via a security camera inside. We huddled around the little TV, trying to read what was written on boxes and debating whether or not that was a reflection of a person in the window. No one could come up with anything new. Most everyone wandered off 'til only one other guy and I sat there, noses near the screen, occasionally pointing at something and asking each other a question. And then a little ghost boy ran across the screen.

Cue scream #2. I flailed and jumped backward, nearly knocking over my chair. Why did I have to be the one to find the freaky stuff?? I hate crap like that. Mr. Nevada came in and rubbed my back. I wanted to scream, "I don't like to be touched, either! You're not helping!" . . . but that seemed rude and I didn't want to embarrass him in front of all those people.

We got back on the bus, relishing our victory. Back where we started, Mr. Nevada said that had been fun but we hadn't really gotten to know each other. He suggested we go get a drink. It was already nearly 11PM – it had taken a lot longer to solve this mystery than I'd expected.

"Well, my friend Alicia flew in to hang out with me for the weekend, so I feel really bad that she's sitting back at the Venetian all alone."

"We could all have a drink together," he suggested. That sounded like a good compromise. He followed me back and I called Alicia to find out where she was.

"I'm in the bar, listening to this great band, and there was this couple that was like *Dancing With the Stars*," she slurred. "I wish you would have been here! There was this couple dancing and it was like they were on *Dancing With the Stars*! They were so good! You should have seen them! It was like watching *Dancing With the Stars*!"

I love happy drunk people.

We found her and joined her in the people-watching. The *Dancing with the Stars* couple had gone, but plenty of other people were dancing. Some better than others. One guy looked like he could be Steve Carell's blonde twin brother, and I desperately wanted a picture to document it.

"Pretend I'm taking your picture," I yelled at Mr. Nevada over the band, then zoomed right past his ear to the lookalike. I'd done this once before with Alicia, back in Colorado Springs a few years before. We'd been having lunch in a diner, and she'd nearly spit out the sip of Coke she'd just taken.

"Oh my gawd, Abraham Lincoln just walked in," she'd drawled. I turned around and gaped. Tarnation and reincarnation!

"Pretend you're taking my picture," I said, handing her my camera across the table. I scooted to the edge of the booth. She zoomed past my ear, focusing on Abe's twin. It was a perfect shot.

My shot in Vegas, unfortunately, was less successful. The guy was leaving the bar, and someone walked right in front of him just as I hit the button to take the photo. Fail. But I swear, he looked straight out of an episode of *The Office*, except with blonde hair, and he even had Michael Scott dance moves.

"Let's take a picture!" Alicia said. "Put on your sunglasses!"

"Why do we have to put on our sunglasses for every picture we take in Vegas?" I questioned.

"Just do it," she demanded, thrusting the camera at Mr. Nevada.

I'm afraid Mr. Nevada probably didn't get the get-to-know-you conversation he was hoping for at the bar, either. I mean, we chatted some, but it was hard to talk over the band. It was really loud in there. It was awkward, trying to have a conversation. And when it wasn't awkward, it was uncomfortable, just sitting there looking at each other. I started yawning a little after midnight, and as it neared one, I decided it was time to wrap this date up.

"I hate to be the party pooper, but I'm tired. Are you ready to go up to the room, Alicia?"

"Yeah, I can go up," she said.

We walked Mr. Nevada to the escalator that led to the parking garage. I thanked him for a fun night, hugged him, and waved goodbye as he disappeared into the crowd. We continued down the hall toward the elevators that went up to the rooms.

"I'm not really all that tired," I admitted. "Wanna go back to the bar?"

"That's my girl," Alicia responded, turning around.

The hotel alarm clock went off at 5AM. I swatted at it, hoping to hit some sort of snooze feature. It continued to play. Loudly. I peeled back a corner of my eye mask and tried swatting at it again. This time it flew back and hit a light switch, bathing Alicia's bed in fluorescent brightness. I kept hitting the alarm until it turned off.

"You okay, honey?" Alicia drawled groggily.

"Fine," I said, turning off the light and rolling over.

Ten minutes later the dang thing went off again. I repeated the process of hitting it until it stopped. I managed to not turn on any lights this time.

When it went off the third time, I got out of bed, wrestled the nightstand away from the wall, reached behind it, yanked the cord out of the plug, and collapsed back into bed. When I woke up again, my cell phone said it was 9:44AM. Alicia was stirring over in her bed.

"We're wasting our weekend in Vegas!" I lamented. "The morning's half over!"

She looked at the blank alarm clock in our nearly pitch-black room. We'd used the remote control to close the curtains before we went to sleep.

"Is the power out?" she muttered.

"No. It's almost ten."

"What happened to the clock?"

"The alarm kept going off, so I ripped it out of the wall."

"I didn't hear it."

"Alicia, I had earplugs in and I heard it."

"I may have had a bit more to drink last night than you did."

"It went off three times. You never heard it? I accidentally hit that light switch and the light came on over your bed, and you asked, 'You okay, honey?'"

"Nope. Don't recall. I probably thought you were Finley," she said, referring to her five-year-old.

"And you didn't hear me moving furniture?"

"Nope. Hey, I've got a message on my cell phone. From 2:45AM. Who the hell could that be from?" She listened, her smile getting bigger, then turning into a laugh.

"Girl, I got a booty call!" she exclaimed, then played it again on speaker phone so I could hear it.

"Who's that?"

"Well, when you left me for five hours last night, I met him in the bar. He seemed a bit young, but I could tell he was into me."

"Rrrawrrr." I made a clawing motion as I gave my best cougar roar. "Are you going to text him and tell him that you're an old lady who was already asleep by 2:45?"

"I'm not doin' nothin.' But it's nice to know I still got it!"

We got ready and headed out for the day. I got to wear the cute little sundress I'd hoped to impress Mr. Wisconsin with but hadn't had warm enough weather to wear since then. We had brunch, then took a taxi down to the Bellagio. We toured the conservatory, then went outside and waited for the fountains to start up. Music played for the tourists gathering around, and I giggled when a Culture Club song came on. Alicia laughed at me when I started singing, "I'll tumble for ya, I'll tumble for ya," along with Boy George.

"Don't laugh at my happy childhood memories."

"Were you hot for Boy George?" she asked.

"No. But I *was* in love with George Michael."

"A bit misguided," she observed.

"Yeah, but I didn't know it then. I was totally bummed when my mom took his tape away," I confessed.

"Was she punishing you for something?"

"Well, there was some parent night at the school where they told moms and dads about the evils of rock music. Mom came home and went through our tapes and confiscated all the ones that had long-haired men on the covers. Like Bon Jovi."

"Yeah, they were the epitome of evil. But George Michael didn't have long hair," she pointed out.

"No, but he did have a song called 'I Want Your Sex.' My brother got his Madonna tape taken away because it had 'Like a Virgin' on it. But later that week I found them in a kitchen cupboard and took them back. She couldn't bring herself to burn them since we'd paid for them and she wasn't one to waste money."

The music changed to a Celine Dion song and the fountains fired up (just like in *Ocean's Eleven*, but without my fantasy boyfriend George Clooney or any of the other hotties). It was quite beautiful, four minutes of peace and beauty in an otherwise crazy town. We made our way down the strip and wandered around Caesar's Palace. These casinos were amazing, but I honestly felt a little sad, thinking of all the good that could have been done with the money it had taken to build these buildings. Or the money that people threw away every day in the slot machines and on the poker tables. This place was just not my style.

That night we went back to the bar where Alicia had been so entertained the night before. The *Dancing With the Stars* couple was back, but I wasn't as fascinated with them as Alicia was. He looked to me like a dirty old man who'd ordered himself a bride from the Ukraine and then taken her to dance lessons. Alicia admitted they weren't that great, now that she was watching them sober. Eventually they left, which opened up the dance floor for everyone who'd been intimidated to dance near them. The party really got started, and I was itching to get out there and dance.

When the band started playing "Bust a Move," my second favorite song to dance to (after ABBA's "Dancing Queen," of course), I started to get up and gave Alicia the "let's go" motion.

"Hell, no," she asserted, not moving in her chair.

"This is my song," I said, shocked.

"Get on out there," she encouraged me.

"I'm not dancing by myself."

"I'm not dancin'," she declared. My eyes filled up with tears.

"You are seriously jeopardizing our friendship right now," I warned.

"There are all kinds of people out there. Go out and dance with them."

I crossed my arms and slumped back in my seat, pouting. I hate doing nothing but sitting and drinking. If I'm at a bar, I want to be dancing. Or kicking ass in bar trivia.

We didn't stay out as late, so we didn't sleep in as late. We wandered around old Vegas with the neon signs the next day, and Alicia played more slots. I'd lost $20 to various machines over the weekend, so I was done. I just watched.

I was seriously bummed when I dumped her at the airport. If she hadn't come into town, I probably wouldn't have even stopped in Vegas. Oh, I probably would have driven down The Strip, just to say I'd been there, but that's probably about it. Seeing things with friends was so much more fun that seeing things alone. Luckily I was only going to have to be alone for a couple of nights before seeing more friends in Utah. I left the bright lights and big city behind me, pointing Cherry Cherry toward the Grand Canyon.

#44 – UTAH

Yeah, yeah, yeah. I know I promised my mom I would not sleep in my car . . . but in this particular situation, I think she would have agreed that the car was the better option.

I'd had a long day. I'd spent the night before in a campground in the middle of nowhere Arizona, somewhere between Vegas and the Grand Canyon. When I'd deposited my money at the pay station long after darkness had fallen, I'd been happy just to be done driving for the day. I'd pitched my tent, then gone to the bathroom to wash my face. I turned off the water mid-wash when I heard a horrible noise. I hoped maybe the place had really noisy plumbing, but nope – it was a train rolling by, and it sounded very, very close. I finished washing my face, brushed my teeth, and checked my email while still inside the warm building. I shot off a few messages, then bit the bullet and bought a plane ticket to Hawaii. They weren't going to get any cheaper, and my hopes of winning a fabulous Hawaiian vacation had been dashed when I hadn't been called to "Come on down!" on *The Price is Right*. I'd considered having a Skype date with a Hawaiian for free, but every friend I ran that idea by said that wouldn't count. They, I countered, weren't the ones who had to pay for the trip.

I packed everything up after about fifteen minutes in the bathroom, then walked out to my tent. As I was putting everything back in my car, another freaking train thundered by. I could have thrown a rock at it, it was so close. What a crappy place for a campground! It was nearly 11PM by this point, so I hoped maybe the trains were done for the night.

No such luck. The trains continued to roll by about every

fifteen minutes. I didn't care if I wouldn't be able to hear coyotes, rapists, or Sasquatch himself approaching my tent; I dug my earplugs out of my backpack and jammed them in, then double checked to make sure my big knife and my can of Raid were within easy reach. I pulled my sleeping bag up over my head and lamented the fact that a rock was digging into my hip. The Venetian this was not. I was getting real tired of sleeping on the ground.

The next morning I woke up early (and "woke up" is a loose phrase, since I hadn't really slept much). I had some jelly beans for breakfast, which is one of those perks of being single and childless. (I first discovered this the day I had Thin Mint Girl Scout cookies for breakfast . . . you can't serve that to your children without Social Services getting a call.) I packed everything up and took off for the Grand Canyon. My original plan, when I'd begun my adventure, was to hike to the bottom, camp out for a night, then climb all the way back up and out the next day. Instead I stood at the top and took pictures like the majority of tourists who visit. Yes, I was sick of camping, but even worse, I wasn't sure I could have made it back out of the canyon without crying. I was in horrible shape. Possibly the worst shape of my life. I rarely got any exercise, just sitting behind the wheel and driving all day. I'd nearly puked and passed out while hiking in Washington, and I'd had weeks to get into even worse physical condition since then. I peered down at the Colorado River, far, far away, and decided that I'd have to get in shape and come back another time. Or rent a donkey to take me down . . . but even that seemed a bit unfair to the donkey.

I continued driving around the rim, then headed for Utah. I got to Zion National Park at the perfect time, just before sunset. This park had a road going down into its canyon, so I got to enjoy the monstrous rocks towering over me without having to make any sort of physical effort. The last beams of sunlight hit the red walls for picture-perfect shots, then disappeared as the moon rose over the rocks. Forget the Grand Canyon, so much more widely known and visited – this was where *I* wanted to come back and spend more time. I had somewhere to be the next day, though, so I kept driving. My hope was to find a campground somewhere between Zion and Salt Lake City.

Three hours later I saw a sign for a state park that had the little tent symbol underneath that indicated a campground. I pulled over, thankful to be done for the day. I was exhausted (surprise, surprise) after the sleepless train-after-train night and a long day of driving. The campground was completely deserted and I was glad. No noise meant lots of sleep. A bit of fog was starting to roll in off the adjacent lake as I pitched the tent. I grabbed my bathroom bag and my computer bag and headed for the shower house.

The bathrooms were quite fancy for a state park. The deadbolt on the door gave me a secure feeling as I used the toilet and sink. There was a shower to use in the morning, as well as a bench I sat on as I checked in with friends and family via email. It was really quite spacious. I clicked onto Facebook to see what was happening in the outside world, then clicked on a video Alicia had posted. It said, "Watch this beautiful little girl dancing." I watched as she twirled down the hallway, a scarf floating gracefully from her arms. Then she twirled through a doorway, disappearing from sight . . . and a giant, bloody screaming face jumped up from the bottom of the screen. I screamed and jumped and nearly dropped the laptop I'd paid big bucks for a year earlier.

"I hate you!!" I typed on her wall. My phone rang nearly immediately.

"Well, I didn't send it directly to you," she said. "It's not my fault you clicked on it."

"How am I supposed to sleep tonight when I've just had the crap scared out of me, Alicia?"

"Where are you?"

"I'm in a campground in the middle of freaking nowhere."

"I hate it when you camp. It worries me sick. Are there lots of people around you, I hope?"

"It's a Monday night in October! No one is camping! I'm the only tent set up in the whole place."

"Oh great. No one will be able to hear you scream if you get attacked."

"WHY WOULD YOU SAY THAT TO ME WHEN I'M ALREADY FREAKED OUT?" I yelled into the phone. I double checked to make sure the deadbolt was securely in place.

We talked a bit more and I assured her I'd call her in the morning to let her know I was alive. I couldn't bring myself to leave the bathroom yet, though. I had that bloody-faced image in my mind, and now I was also thinking that some crazy person was going to shank me the minute I stepped out of the safety of the shower house. I sat down again and watched an episode of *The Office* on Hulu, hoping I'd laugh and forget about the images I was trying to forget.

It didn't work.

I went on the internet and read celebrity gossip. Normally I hate reading about who just bought a billion dollar beach house or how much someone spent on a bedazzled onesie for their baby – it infuriates me, honestly – but I desperately needed to have something else on my mind so I could get out of this freaking bathroom. As midnight neared, I gave up. I thought about just driving away, but my tent was already up. To take it down would be to put myself out there unprotected for five minutes for a murderer to chop up, but it had cost me too much money to just drive away and leave. I decided the best compromise was to sleep in the car, doors locked. I collected my belongings, took a deep breath, then opened the door. My head snapped right and left, checking for any lurking crazies. I sprinted for Cherry Cherry, feeling foolish for being so scared when logically I knew there wasn't anyone around who was going to hurt me, but I jumped inside and locked the doors anyway. I wrestled my sleeping bag and pillow into the front seat, wriggled down inside the bag, checked the door again to make sure it was locked, and tried my best to picture George Clooney hosting me for the weekend at his Italian villa instead of a bloody-faced murderer.

It must have worked, because I woke up the next morning feeling fairly rested. It was only 6AM, but I was awake and ready to get out of there. A thick layer of fog blanketed the entire area, and I could see my tent was completely soaked in dew. It was cold. I mentally went through the upcoming states and realized this was probably the last time I'd have to deal with the tent on this trip. I'd have friends to stay with from here on out, and good thing, since it was getting too cold to camp anymore. I went out and shook off as much moisture as I could, then took it down. My hands were numb by the time I finished and jumped back in the car.

Cruising down the interstate, I kept an eye out for a Jiffy Lube. I needed an oil change, and that wasn't something I took lightly, relying on my car as much as I did. I found a place and sat in the musty waiting room waiting for the job to be done. As usual, the mechanic came in and named off several things that were wrong with the car and needed to be fixed. I'm always skeptical; I mean, do I really need a new air filter or are you just saying that because I'm a woman and you presume I don't know anything about air filters so you're just gonna try to see if you can make some money off me?

"I don't have a job right now, so I can't afford all that," I said.

"I noticed your car was pretty full," he said. "You livin' in there?"

"Kind of," I replied. I mean, I had slept in there last night, hadn't I?

"Well, I wouldn't go without a new air filter. This one's really dirty. It'll save you money in the long run, because your car will run better and take less fuel."

"Can you just blow it out?" I asked, trying to sound knowledgeable. I'd told Mr. Ohio my theory about mechanics always trying to make money off me with that air filter line, and he'd told me that often they just needed to have the dirt blown out of them.

"We can't do that, because if we accidentally blew a hole in it and caused damage to your car, then we'd be responsible."

"Fine," I said, not having the energy to argue, "but not all those other things you say I need. I can't afford anything else."

"Well, the chip repair on your windshield would be covered by your insurance company. They'd rather have us do it now than have to replace the whole windshield later when it cracks and spreads."

I okayed that one, too, since it was free. Another ten minutes or so and I was on my way. Well, after handing over my credit card, of course.

"Come over here," the mechanic said before I got into my car. He pointed out the door. "See that big building a block over? That's the Latter Day Saints Work Center. They can help you find something."

"I'm Lutheran," I said.

"Well, they might still be able to help you. What kind of work do you do?"

"Well, I worked at a Lutheran church for the last ten years," I replied. He frowned.

"Yeah, that might be hard to find around here. But I'm sure

they could help you out if you go down and see 'em. I came here with just the clothes on my back, and they helped me find a job and a place to live." I guess I hadn't clarified that I wasn't really homeless and I was out of work by choice, but it seemed too late now.

"I'm actually heading up to Park City to stay with an old friend for a few days," I said.

"Oh, well maybe he can help you find work. What's he do?"

"He works at a Lutheran church," I said sheepishly. He shrugged.

"Well, I tell ya, every day when I wake up, I think about where I was when I got here and where I am today, and I thank . . ." and I thought he was going to say, "God" or the more-favored-by-professional-athletes "my Lord and Savior Jesus Christ," but instead he said, "the Latter Day Saints."

Welcome to Utah.

I thanked him for his help and continued on my merry way. I pulled over for breakfast (Nutella and strawberries – I couldn't quite manage that while driving without either getting it all over me as I drove or swerving into oncoming traffic), then continued driving north. I got to Park City soon after my friend Russ picked up our other friend Julie at the airport. We were all excited for three days of catching up. We picked up sandwiches and went back to Russ's house so we could spend time with his wife Sarah and their year-and-a-half-year-old, too. I hadn't seen Christopher for over a year, and he was absolutely adorable. I declared him my favorite Christopher in the whole wide world.

We had a whirlwind of a time, strolling the streets where the rich and famous gather for the Sundance Film Festival, touring the location of the 2002 Olympics and trying to decide which sport we'd compete in (Julie and I first chose bobsledding, but then changed to curling since it doesn't involve spandex or high-speed crashes), and getting massages, Julie's treat, making her my new favorite person. We even went to a movie, which I hadn't done in months. It worried me a little, though, when I thought about the ending later.

"What if my story doesn't have a happy ending?" I asked Sarah the next day. "I mean, I'm having the time of my life, but what if none of these guys turns out to be the man of my dreams?"

"I thought you really clicked with some of them?"

"Well, yeah, but the guys in Texas and Virginia could be married by the time I get done with this. I mean, probably not, since it's only been seven or eight months since I met them, but I haven't talked to them since then. Mr. Wisconsin, either. I'm kind of keeping in touch with the guys from Michigan and Idaho, but that's it. I don't know how I'm supposed to form relationships with any of them while I'm still on this dating spree."

"Well, it'll be over eventually. Couldn't you get in touch with the ones you were really interested in once you're done?"

"Yeah, I guess I could. But the movie had a happy ending, you know? And isn't that what people pay money to see? What if people buy my book and I don't end up with any of these guys? Is everyone going to think it sucks?"

"Maybe some women reading it would find it refreshing to see that you're already happy on your own and you don't need a man to make you happy."

"That may be true, but I'm not sure that's what most people want to hear."

Sarah cooked up some fabulous food while we were there, and I ate more than I had in a long time. My stomach hurt. I wanted to stop, but I'd been eating granola bars and fruit for so long that I couldn't seem to put down my fork now that I had good food in front of me.

"When I was in Africa, it seemed like the kids at the orphanage would just eat and eat and eat when they got food. Like they weren't sure when they'd be eating again, so they wanted to eat as much as they could while they could," I told my friends. "I think I'm kind of like that on this trip. When I'm eating good food like this, I just shovel it in, because I don't know how long it will last before I'm back to granola bars and fruit."

"Or maybe you're like a dog that can't eat unless its owner is around," Julie suggested. "Maybe you don't enjoy eating unless you're with someone. Are you a social eater?"

"Um . . . maybe." Actually, it made a lot of sense. I just wasn't quite sure I liked the dog comparison.

I was bummed when Julie had to leave, but she had a job and a husband to get back to. I dropped her off at the airport, then went to meet my Mr. Utah. It had been nice to have a few days off from dating to just hang out with friends, but I wasn't dreading this date like I had dreaded some in the past. This date promised a new adventure, as I told my CSO on the drive over to his area.

"He knows a friend of Sarah's," I explained, "and when he sent me an email introducing himself, his picture was of him dirt biking. I said we should go dirt biking, since that was one of his hobbies."

"Have you ever been dirt biking?" Alicia asked.

"No. But I've ridden a regular bike plenty of times."

"It's not the same," Alicia sighed, sounding a bit weary from worrying about me so often. Whatever. How hard could it be?

Mr. Utah was out feeding his horses when I drove up. He gave me a carrot to feed one of them, and I tried to play it cool. The camp where I'd worked over the summer had horses, and I'd heard the safety spiel numerous times: *Keep your hands out of the horse stalls, because your fingers are kind of shaped like carrots, and you don't want one of the horses to think you're giving them a snack.* I made a fist, wiggled the carrot into the little hole, and held it out to the horse like a reporter holding a microphone out toward her interviewee. My fingers survived the feeding, and I gently petted the horse's nose. They were so beautiful. What a peaceful life, living out here with a bunch of horses to pet and ride every day. But he had a different plan for this day.

"I thought I'd have you try it out here first, before we go out on the trails," Mr. Utah said as we walked toward the house. He showed me a dirt bike his friend had lent him. It looked small but heavy. I got on it, ready to go. I looked around for a key to start it up, but there wasn't one.

"You have to kick down on this, fast and hard," he said, tapping a little pedal with his foot.

"Oh, okay," I said. That was different. I gave it a good kick and it revved to life underneath me. Awesome. I didn't even know what I was doing but I totally got that on my first try.

"Okay, now you need to get it from neutral to first," he said. Come again? I need to what? Crap. I knew nothing about shifting gears.

"You just have to use your foot over on this side," he explained. "Once for first, twice for second, etc. etc.," I followed instructions and got it into first.

"Now slowly let off the brake with your left hand and give it some gas with your right."

I did. It died.

And so began the most frustrating ten minutes of my journey thus far.

I hate not being able to do something. I don't need to be an expert, but I do like to be functional . . . and I was not functioning anything here. I'd kick it on, get it into gear, then kill it. Over and over and over and over. Mr. Utah was incredibly patient as I grew more and more frustrated. I was ready to take off. I wasn't interested in standing still. I finally got it to stay on and slowly made my way around the yard. I did a loop and came back, and he motioned for me to stop beside him. I pulled up, slowed down, came to a not-too-jerky stop, and the engine died.

I swore. Hopefully inwardly. I can't remember.

I kicked, clicked, and killed, over and over again. I mean, in retrospect, it's understandable that you don't want to take someone out in the woods if they're going to be stranded there, unable to start their bike, but it really just made me increasingly angry, failing again and again and again. When I finally got it going, I refused to stop, just doing circles around the yard. He declared me ready to go. He loaded up the bikes in the back of his truck and we took off.

It was the perfect fall day: golden leaves and rolling hills. We ended up in the middle of nowhere (technically it was a state park, but there wasn't much of anything around for miles and miles), and after several frustrating tries to get my bike going, we finally took off.

We started on a fairly wide gravel road, which was a nice confidence builder. I felt pretty comfortable, riding in a straight line over flat terrain at a low speed. I probably looked like a grandma, sitting perfectly straight and barely moving, but I wasn't going to take any risks. We got to a place where a stream ran over the road, and I slowed to a stop. The engine died. Grrr!! I was also a little worried about how deep it was. I'd had that "my shoes are soaked but I don't have any other shoes to wear" incident in Alaska, and I wasn't interested in repeating it.

"I'll go over first and see how deep it is," Mr. Utah said. He went over, and his feet weren't anywhere close to touching the water. There might be a bit of splashing, but it wouldn't be too bad . . .

unless I had to put my foot down to catch myself if I started to fall. Then my shoe would be full of water for sure. He turned around and crossed it again to get back to me.

"Do you want me to drive your bike over and you can find a place to jump it?"

"I think I can do this," I said. I probably didn't sound too confident, but he'd made it look so easy. I thought it was worth a try. It took me a while to get the bike moving again, but once I did, I headed for the water and held my breath. I made it! I beamed. Mr. Utah gave me the thumbs up and kept going. I followed him down more narrow trails and several more water crossings. Keeping the bike upright was getting harder, but I wasn't scared. We started heading up a steep, rocky, narrow path, and I was riding high on the confidence I'd built on those previous successes.

"I'm such a badass," I said to myself as the bike bucked beneath me. Mr. Utah kept turning around to make sure I was still upright. I felt awesome. Who knew I was so good at dirt biking?

And then I bit it.

Pride goes before the fall, right? I guess I got a little too big for my britches out there in the hills, because right about the time I was thinking I was awesome, I started falling over. I tipped to my right, put my leg down in an effort to catch myself, and discovered that it was too little too late. I was definitely going down. I put my arm out to break my fall and caught a sharp rock right on the ulna. Or radius. I couldn't really remember what was what from high school anatomy. The point? My arm met the rock and it hurt. Really, really bad.

"Are you okay?" Mr. Utah asked, pulling the heavy bike off me.

"I think so," I muttered. I wasn't crying, so that was a good thing, but man, did my arm hurt. I rubbed it a little. I felt a bump, but I hoped it was just swollen and not broken. I rotated my wrist. I clenched and unclenched my fingers in a fist. Everything seemed to work; it just hurt like crazy.

Mr. Utah took my good arm and pulled me up. Ow, ow, ow. My hip and knee on my right side had taken beatings of their own.

"How about you start it up for me?" I suggested. I had a hard time picturing myself using the pained side of my body to kickstart the bike. He did, and I climbed on. Miraculously, I didn't kill it when I shifted gears and got it going. We kept going up, up, up, every bounce sending a jolt through my arm. He turned around to see if I was okay, but I was right behind him, so I had to brake . . . and then, of course, the bike died. Uggggghhhhhhh! I tried really hard not to burst into tears from the pain-and-frustration combo.

"I'll ride up and see if we're almost to the end of this trail," he said. "I don't want you to have to keep riding over this rocky stuff."

"I'll just wait for you here," I agreed. I needed the rest. I was suddenly exhausted. The initial adrenaline rush of trying something new had gone, leaving me with nothing but pain shooting through my right limbs. I had a few good minutes to breathe before I heard the whine of his bike coming back.

"It's not much further to the top, and then we can get on a flat, wide road like the one we started out on," he said. Hallelujah.

We made it up to the top and enjoyed the scenic fall views. A young couple came by on a four-wheeler and asked us to take their picture. I willingly obliged, and Mr. Utah held back his laughter until they rode away.

"I saw him up here a few weeks ago with a different girl on the back of his ATV," he said.

"This must be his go-to woman wooing activity," I laughed.

I was really cautious on the way down. If I'd looked like a grandma on the dirt bike before, I must have looked even more grandma-ish now. I was a little afraid I might tip over just from going so slow, so I tried to speed it up a little. I was just so tired. Maybe it was the soreness from the fall, or maybe holding on to the handlebars of a constantly vibrating machine wears out your arms (and I definitely didn't have any muscles left after eight months of not working out). All I knew was that I was done.

We made it back to the truck and drove down into town. We went out to eat, and sitting across the table from Mr. Utah, I wondered how important shared interests are in a life-long match. I loved our conversation – he was funny and smart and a good, good man – and he was attractive, too. But I wasn't sure I had any desire to get back on a dirt bike again anytime soon. Did that matter? I think it's important that couples share some interests, because if you're both working and you don't have much free time, then you probably want to do some things together. But couldn't I go for a hike or read a book while my husband went dirt biking or hunting or some other activity I wasn't all that interested in?

I got back to Russ and Sarah's after dark.

"How did it go?" she asked.

"Give me an ice pack and some wine," I instructed, "and I'll tell you all about it."

#45 – WYOMING

Maybe you've already picked up on this, but I feel it's important, before you read about Mr. Wyoming, to remember that I'm a bit of a germaphobe. I'm a fastidious hand washer. I once heard that parents should teach their children to sing Happy Birthday or Yankee Doodle while washing their hands so they'll wash long enough. I wish adults would sing, too. It grosses me out when I'm in a public restroom and I see someone run their fingers under the water for a millisecond. That's disgusting. They haven't washed off jack squat. I, admittedly, might go too far. I once tried out a new product at Bath and Body Works with my friend Stephanie, and I must have been a bit more of an aggressive/obsessive scrubber than most people.

"You're not going into surgery," she'd chided, instructing me to rinse and be done.

I've heard from my parents that while some children carry around blankies, I carried around a washcloth, so I guess my aversion to germs is just some weird quirk I was born with. It's not like I'm OCD or anything; I mean, I still go out in society. I tell you this so you might understand later why I was so grossed out during what should have been a perfectly romantic moment on my date with Mr. Wyoming.

I was worried that Wyoming was going to be a repeat of Illinois. I had asked everyone I knew to set me up with someone, but no one had any single guy friends there. I scoured three different dating websites but hadn't found anyone willing to meet me, or, more accurately, anyone whom I was willing to meet. Only one man had emailed to declare his interest, and he did so by commenting on . . . my . . . um . . . *shapeliness*. (That's the PG version of his vulgar comment.) If he was my best option, I was going to be dateless in Wyoming.

His rudeness reminded me of one of the fifty dates (who shall remain unnamed to protect him from the ridicule his friends and family would surely give him if they knew what he'd said on our date) who I also thought was a bit inappropriate. Here's a tip for him and all men: talking about sex on the first date is crass. You're in the wine and dine stage, buddy. Try romance. Saying crap like "Winter's coming, and I need someone to warm up my bed," or "Yeah, I like camping, too, 'cause you know there's only one way to entertain yourselves in a tent" is just as bad. (P.S. I personally enjoy playing Travel Scrabble in a tent. Broaden your horizons, dude.)

My friend Krystal threw up a fourth quarter Hail Mary pass the night before I was to arrive, and thankfully a decent, willing man caught the ball. We made plans on Friday morning to meet up Friday night. Nothing like waiting 'til the last minute.

When I arrived to meet Mr. Wyoming, I found a pleasant surprise in his backseat: a Golden Retriever! Date #45 and this was a first. The three of us drove up to an overlook and Mr. Wyoming unpacked a little picnic: wine (with real wine glasses! nice!), crackers, and a cheese ball. I smiled at the dog but didn't pet her, because hey, I'm a bit of a germaphobe, remember? I mean, normally I would have shown her some love, but I was eating. After a while, Mr. Wyoming headed off to use the bathroom and suggested I give the dog a cracker while he was gone. I dropped one and she caught it midair. I made sure her lips never touched my fingers. (Um, hello? No running water? And my hand sanitizer safely tucked in my purse back in the car?) Once he got back, though, I felt kind of rude, ignoring his very sweet dog. I compromised. I petted her with my right hand and ate with my left. I put away a lot of those crackers. I'm kind of a lightweight when it comes to wine, so I thought I'd better get some food in my belly.

Mr. Wyoming multitasked, throwing a ball for his dog to fetch while talking to me. When she brought it back, all full of doggie drool, he'd pet her and then throw the ball again. And then spread cheese on another cracker. And then eat said cheesy cracker with the hands he'd just petted the dog and touched the drooly ball with. I tried to focus on the dog and how cute she was, but almost lost all my wine and crackers when he licked some stray cheese off his fingers. Sensitive gag reflex!

When it started to get dark, we headed down the mountain and back into town. He seemed like a decent guy, the kind you could take home to meet your parents and not hear any objections. We drove past a haunted house. Halloween was only a week away.

"Wanna go?" he asked.

"Nope," I replied decisively.

"Oh. Well, that was kind of my plan for the night."

"Yeah, well, when you're a single woman traveling the country alone, you don't want any scary things to think about when you're lying alone in your tent at night." (For example, that freaky internet thing that had forced me to sleep in my car earlier in the week.) Besides, he probably wouldn't have gotten the reaction he was hoping for. I once had a boyfriend who thought watching a scary movie together would leave me clinging to him. Instead, he ended up bruised. I'm not just a screamer – I'm a flailer, too. None of my friends who've gone to a scary movie with me will ever accompany me again because I've embarrassed them so much. I yell at the characters on the screen, instructing them to run. I stay in my seat but demonstrate with my feet what I want them to do. I cover not just my eyes but my entire head, cowering down in my seat like I'm about to get a beating. Previews alone at that movie in Utah two days before had left my friend Julie pleading, "Would you stop? You're scaring the old woman in the row behind us."

So no. Definitely no.

A haunted house might lead to medical bills: mine, or his, or whatever poor haunted house employee I punched, kicked, or clawed when they got too close.

We went to dinner instead, and although it shouldn't have been scary, I did get a Jekyll-and-Hyde kind of show. I don't know what happened, really. We pulled into the parking lot as a car was pulling out of a parking space. We waited, but when the car drove away, there was a truck behind it that obviously wanted the spot, too. Mr.

Wyoming let them have it. No big deal, right? But as we started to pull away, a lady got out of the truck and yelled, "Asshole!" What? I thought he'd done the polite thing?

Mr. Wyoming slammed on the brakes. My neck snapped forward and back, which would have been annoying on a normal day but was downright painful the day after my dirt biking spill. He glared at her in his rearview mirror, and when her husband got out, I worried we were going to have a rumble right there in the parking lot (but without the finger snapping and dancing that made rumbling so fun in *West Side Story*).

He peeled out and whipped through the parking lot to an open space. He got out and stomped into the restaurant. I meekly followed. The hostess said there was a twenty-minute wait, so he stomped into the bar. I followed again.

The female bartender asked what we'd like to drink. I ordered water; I'd had plenty of wine already. Mr. Wyoming ordered a beer, and the bartender asked what size he wanted. Whatever it was he asked for, she said it didn't come that way. He thrust the menu at me and theatrically asked, "What does it say right there?"

Passive-aggressive much? He barked at her to just give him a water. I sat there, stunned, wondering what had happened to the nice guy I'd met over cheese and crackers. After we ordered, he stomped off to the restroom. I tried to make eye contact with the bartender, hoping she'd come over so I could explain that this was a blind date and I hardly even knew this guy, but I was really, really sorry that he'd been so rude . . . but she didn't.

When Mr. Wyoming came back from the restroom, he was Mr. Nice Guy again. I didn't know what was going on, but I pretty much walked on eggshells after that. Dinner was perfectly normal: pleasant conversation, a few laughs, and absolutely no seething anger. Color me confused.

"Where to now?" he casually asked as we left the restaurant. I took a deep breath. I was done; I wasn't sure how to state that nicely.

"Well, I haven't seen my friend Kim in nine months, so I guess back to my car so I can drive over to her house and catch up with her," I said. I felt kind of bad, but not really. I tried to keep the mood light as we drove.

"I never even asked earlier if you've ever been married or if you have children."

"No to both," he responded.

"Do you want to get married at some point?"

"I'd marry a woman if she could support the lifestyle to which I have become accustomed."

I wrinkled up my forehead. "Meaning?"

"I wouldn't mind being taken care of. Not having to work."

I couldn't really tell if he was kidding or not. I thanked him when we got back to my car and then headed over to Kim's house. I wasn't sure whether to call that date good or bad. I liked the romantic beginning and had enjoyed dinner; there was just that weird episode in the middle that still had me wondering what the heck had happened.

It was good to catch up with Kim; she had been a youth worker for as long as I could remember. We saw each other at youth gatherings and conferences when I worked at the church in Colorado Springs. She'd started dating Jeff, another youth worker in Colorado, shortly before I left, and I was eager to get all the details on how it was going. When I arrived, Jeff was there in the living room via the magic of Skype, so I got to hear the story from both of them. They were so cute and so in love. Both were divorced and in their fifties, and both were absolutely glowing. I was amazed at how two people who had been friends for years suddenly realized they were perfect for each other. I racked my brain, trying to think of any guy friends I'd not yet thought of in that way, but I came up blank. The two of them must have just gotten lucky. Or maybe it was more than that. Maybe they were blessed.

#46 – HAWAII

Don't you love those old movies that show people all dressed up to get on an airplane? It reminds you that flying used to be a privilege. That people got excited about it. That it wasn't always such a pain in the ass.

The new full-body scanners had just come out, and I was worried about being forced into a little x-ray booth for some totally unnecessary radiation. I tried not to think about it and instead played one of my favorite airport games: can I get through the security line faster than the people in front of me? The lady in the zebra print shirt chose line three. The guy in front of her, sporting a t-shirt in a strange shade of coral, went for line number one. I moved into line two and started charting my progress. Line one had a baby in a stroller. That was definitely going to hold up Mr. Coral Tee. Zebra Lady was cruising along nicely, but I still thought I could possibly beat her . . . until I saw people ahead of me swerving around an old lady in a wheelchair. She was slowly pulling items out of her suitcase and handing them to a frazzled TSA agent. I hoped I could swerve around her, too, but nope. The TSA lady gave us the "stop" hand and pulled Grandma up out of her wheelchair to shuffle slowly toward the metal detector. Dang it! There went my chance of jumping ahead.

I'd like to ask this question: who the heck dumps their grandma at the airport without a little prepwork? I mean, could you have told her that liquids aren't allowed? Maybe helped her select a pair of slip-off shoes instead of sandals with three buckles per foot?

I got through the line (beat by Zebra Lady but ahead of Mr. Coral Tee – not a bad day at the races) and hopped on the train. I have to admit that I do love DIA. I mean, not every airport has a train. And I've never been to another airport that's housed under a circus tent. (What? Those are supposed to look like snowcapped mountain peaks? Huh.)

I noticed that unlike the old-timey movies, very few people were dressed up to fly. I myself had on a t-shirt, yoga pants, and flip flops. I was looking at about eight hours of plane time, so I wanted to be comfortable. And since I'd done very little (read: no) physical activity in the past few months, my jeans were no longer comfortable. Can you say "muffin top"??

TCBY seemed like a good choice for lunch. That's one of the perks of being single: if you want to eat crap for lunch, you can, because a) you're not responsible for anyone's nutritional needs, and b) no one's going to see you naked anytime soon. It was generous of the lady at the counter to give me extra raspberry topping on my chocolate and vanilla swirl waffle cone, but as soon as I turned to walk away, raspberry juice started spilling over the edges. I thrust it away from me, kind of like I would a baby with a full diaper. When you're going to be wearing the same clothes for the next eight hours, you don't want to get dirty and sticky before the flight even takes off.

I found my gate without problems, but ten minutes after I got there, they announced that the plane's engine wasn't working. I was thankful they had discovered that before we got up in the air, but got a little worried when they said those of us with tight connections might want to head down to the Customer Service counter. Thankfully I'm a fast walker. I was eighth in line. About fifty people filed in after me.

After five minutes of standing in line, the first person was called up to the next available agent. I did some quick math: at that rate, I'd be helped in forty minutes. Ugh. Luckily it didn't take that long; I was called up to the counter in fifteen. A lady came running in and cut in front of me as I approached the agent.

"I need to rebook my flight," she announced. The ticket agent looked at her. Then she looked at me. I turned around and looked at the fifty-some people behind me.

"You'll need to get in line, ma'am," the agent said (much more kindly that I would have).

"But I'm going to miss my connection," she said haughtily.

So are the rest of us, duh, I wanted to say. *Why do you think we're all standing in this line? Free pony rides?*

I got rebooked on a flight through San Francisco instead of Los Angeles, arriving in Honolulu around the same time. I was pretty excited, because I love flying into San Francisco. (Okay, I'd only done it once before, but it was awesome. You're going down, down, down, and it looks like you're about to make a Captain Sully-like water landing and you're kind of freaking out, and then all of the sudden, hey! We're on a runway! On solid ground! Shut up, it's more exciting than landing in Omaha.) I was not excited, however, to learn that my newly scheduled flight was already boarding. That meant running to catch the plane, and – just in case I haven't made this clear yet – I HATE RUNNING!

I made it onto the flight, panting though I was, and found myself in an emergency exit aisle. Score! Bonus leg room without even paying for it! It wasn't first class, but it was something. One plane change and several hours later, I was on Hawaiian soil. Even my bag made it. Things were looking up.

My friend Eli and his wife Carolyn met me at the airport with a lei. It was just like that episode of the Brady Bunch, and I was hoping for a very Brady-esque week, minus the run-in with creepy Vincent Price. The airport was cool in that it was kind of an outdoor airport. I mean, there were indoor waiting areas by the gates, but no hallways. You walked outside to go to baggage claim, and for November, the weather was beautiful. I almost thought about asking them to take me directly to a beach, but I realized that according to my body clock, it was about midnight.

Eli & Carolyn both worked, but they were nice enough to lend me a vehicle for traipsing around Oahu. The next morning I drove to Pearl Harbor, intending to visit the Arizona Memorial. I burn easily, so I slathered myself in SPF 50 sunscreen (100 SPF for my face) before heading for the gate. I got some white stuff on my black sundress (the one I'd wanted to wear on my date with Mr. Wisconsin but had kept in my trunk all fall since it was too cold to wear anywhere but in Vegas and now here) and scolded myself for looking a mess before 9AM. Soon I found out my plans and not just my dress were already messed up. All the boat tickets to go out to the memorial were sold out until 2:30 that afternoon. I'd already paid a hefty sum for a different afternoon activity, so I decided I'd have to come back to Pearl Harbor another day.

I pointed the Dodge Durango north, headed for the North Shore. It felt odd driving their big beast of a vehicle. It was twice the size of Cherry Cherry and it was impeccable. It just felt odd. I was afraid to touch anything for fear of dirtying it.

I got out at Hale'iwa Beach and wandered along the shoreline. There was a wall that created a calmer area closer to shore, but beyond that, the waves looked huge. I was kind of glad I was just looking that day and not getting into the water. I feared getting sucked out in the undertow and drowning. I'm not a strong swimmer, and I think we've clarified that I was miserably out of shape by state #46. With no lifeguards in sight, there wasn't a chance I was going for a swim that day. I continued to drive along the North Shore, my jaw dropping as I looked out at the ocean. Crowds of people were standing around, staring at the thirty-foot crests. Signs everywhere said to stay away from the water. You didn't have to tell me twice.

The next day was date day. Mr. Hawaii wouldn't tell me what we were doing on our date. He told me he'd pick me up at 8AM and I should bring a swimsuit. On an island, that could mean pretty much anything.

"I'm hoping for parasailing," I told Eli & Carolyn over breakfast. "I've always wanted to do that." You wore a swimsuit for parasailing, right? It looked fun. I thought maybe standup paddle boards were an option. That seemed to be the latest craze, and easier to do than surfing. I feared we might be taking surfing lessons, though. I mean, that would be a very Hawaiian experience, so that would be cool, but, as previously mentioned, I'm not the strongest swimmer in the world. And I fear being eaten by sharks.

He was right on time and still as elusive about his plan for the day. My friend Kevin, who had set us up, had described Mr. Hawaii as "a crazy-ass Asian kid," so I figured we'd have a good time, whatever it was he had planned. He pointed out the Waikiki highlights as we drove, but then we headed out of the city. Hmmm. We stopped at various places along the road to take in the scenery. It was raining a little, but what did I care? I was in Hawaii!!!

After driving for a while, we pulled into Sea Life Park. Mr. Hawaii said some scenes from the movie *Fifty First Dates* had been filmed here, which seemed kind of fitting, since I was kind of doing fifty first dates, but with fifty different guys instead of just Adam Sandler (and while he's funny in a juvenile way, I think my fifty different guys were probably more entertaining). I still didn't know for sure what we were doing. Mr. Hawaii told me to stay put and went to pay. I could see a sign with varying prices, but I wasn't sure if he was buying tickets for the basic entry fee, the stingray encounter (Isn't that how the Crocodile Hunter died? No, thank you!), playing with sea lions, or what.

We wandered around for a while, watching the sea lion show and petting turtles. We passed by some people swimming with dolphins, and Mr. Hawaii said we were going to be doing that soon. Cue the jumping up and down like I'd just won a new car on *The Price is Right*! WE WERE GOING SWIMMING WITH DOLPHINS!!! We sat and watched the dolphin show and I was so excited. I was going to be in the water with those beautiful creatures soon!

"My first plan was to take you shark diving," he casually mentioned while we sat and watched.

"Come again?" I responded.

"You get in a cage and they drop you in the water with some air tanks, and then they drop bloody bait in so the sharks will come right up to the cage."

"Huh," I mustered. I felt a little queasy just thinking about it. Cool? Definitely. Panic-inducing? Quite likely.

"I'm good with the dolphin plan," I assured him.

We got our life jackets on and went to the pool. It was a weekday and it was still a little drizzly, so the crowd was thin. We were two of three people in the Royal Dolphin Swim, which meant we got lots of time with the animals. We started out by petting them and they took pictures of us kissing them. So cute! Then the real fun began. First, we went out into the deep water and held our arms out. I went first. Two dolphins came up behind me, one on each side, and I grabbed hold of their dorsal fins. They dragged me back to the shallow area. Awesome! I watched Mr. Hawaii go next. So cool! (He didn't seem to get a mouth full of water like I did. Secret skill? Or just smart enough to keep his mouth shut instead of screaming like me?)

We swam back out to the deep end for the grand finale. Mr. Hawaii went first this time and I went second. The instructions were to float on your belly with feet flat, toes pointed to the bottom of the pool. The two dolphins came up from behind again, but this time they put their little noses on my feet and pushed me up out of the water. I think I may have attracted the attention of pretty much everyone in the park with my screaming. Good screaming. Well, maybe slightly freaked out screaming, but mostly just amazed/this is awesome screaming. When in my life was I ever going to get to do this again?

It was over far too quickly. Mr. Hawaii said not to bother changing out of my suit, though, because we were going to a beach. We headed for Bellows, a private beach just for military folks. (I didn't realize that people in the Army, Navy, Air Force, and Marines all call Oahu home. What an ideal place to be stationed!) We rented boogie boards and hit the beach.

I'd tried boogie boarding once before on a house-building trip in El Salvador. We had worked side by side with the locals every day, then rushed back to our rental house on the beach to throw on our suits and hit the ocean. Well, maybe it would be more fitting to say the ocean hit us. The waves down there were incredibly strong. My worst moment was when I couldn't get up off the beach. The waves had flattened me, and when I tried to stand up, my feet got sucked out from under me. The waves smacked me down into the sand again, and when I tried to get up this time, the waves sent me rolling down the beach. When I finally managed to get up, I was covered head to toe in sand. The people who were with me thought it was hilarious, but I was pretty happy to have made it out alive. A day later, when I flipped my head over while blow drying my hair, salty water came rushing out of the deep recesses of my sinuses. That ocean had gotten me good. It seemed that boogie boarding just wasn't my sport.

The Hawaiian waves, though, weren't as punishing. We had an exceptional time on the nearly-deserted beach; just like at Sea Life Park, very few people were out on this drizzly day. And even without a life jacket to hide certain parts of my physique that had gotten a little squishy over the past eight months, I wasn't self-conscious. Mr. Hawaii was one of those guys I knew wasn't judging me, so I could just relax.

After dinner (I ordered fish – points for trying local food!), Mr. Hawaii dropped me off back at Eli & Carolyn's house. We had already planned to meet up again before I left, so it was more of a "see-ya-later" than a "good-bye." It wasn't even 9PM, but I was exhausted. Mr. Hawaii had planned an all-out marathon date day, and definitely one of the most memorable days of my trip.

During the three and a half days I had remaining in my little Hawaiian paradise, I hit as many beaches as I could. I was kind of bummed to be alone (especially when I developed crazy sunburn patterns on my back from trying to put sunscreen on all by myself), but honestly a little relieved that no one was close enough to see my not-so-fit self. I spent time with Eli & Carolyn, visited the Pearl Harbor Memorial, hiked, snorkeled, admired waterfalls, and thanked my lucky stars every night as I fell into a deep sleep.

Oh, and that second date with Mr. Hawaii? Incredible. We watched fireworks on the beach in Waikiki, then took off for a karaoke bar. He, a natural-born entertainer, sang Sinatra's "New York, New York," but changed to the words to, "It's up to you, Hon-o-lu-luuuuuuu!" He insisted I sing something, too, so I got up there and belted out, "I Will Survive." A group of women appeared out of nowhere and started dancing around me. I was a bit confused, but kept on singing.

"Did you arrange for them to do that?" I asked Mr. Hawaii once I sat down.

"I have no idea where they came from," he replied. Looking around the bar, they had disappeared as mysteriously as they'd appeared. He did have a trick up his sleeve, though. The next time he sang, he made me sit up by the stage. He pulled a couple of guys from the audience to sing back-up, then serenaded me with "Brown Eyed Girl." I love that song. And at 35, it was high time someone serenaded me. Hawaii was magical in more ways than one.

#47 – COLORADO

Speeding along a mountain pass, Mr. Colorado pulled off the road and parked at a secluded spot, far from any streetlights. He lowered the convertible top, giving us unfiltered access to a sky full of stars. It was amazing. Romantic. The perfect make-out spot. And then . . . we played Scrabble.

I'd planned to have my Colorado date before I left for Hawaii, but the guy who I'd initially selected, a rancher, had gone from "I can't wait to meet you" to "MIA" when I tried to pin down a time to meet him for the promised horseback ride. He left a message on my voicemail the morning I'd boarded the plane for Honolulu. Too late, buddy. I no longer had the time or the interest in making it happen at that point. It kind of left me in a lurch, though, and I wasn't happy that I had to spend time I could have been on a Hawaiian beach emailing, texting, and calling friends back in Colorado for leads. Luckily one of my old friends agreed to be my Mr. Colorado.

My jaw dropped when I saw him drive up in a convertible. Wow. I'm not normally impressed by cars, but it was a sweet ride. I had obviously not seen him in a while. He opened my door for me (I LOVE when guys are gentlemanly and open doors for me!) and I slid onto the leather seat, oohing over the baseball glove-like stitching. I'd never seen anything like it. Maybe I was more easily swayed by nice things than I wanted to admit. We zipped down the highway to . . . a dinosaur museum. Yep. A dinosaur museum.

I'd driven by the place multiple times when I'd lived in

Colorado. I mean, dinosaurs and palm trees in a mountain town catch your eye, you know? And I always thought my little nephew Henrey, who loved dinosaurs, would love to go there. I guess big boys wanna go, too. It was outrageously expensive, but hey, it was his pick and he really wanted to see it, so I just shrugged my shoulders and strolled along beside him, checking out fossils and skeletons. He teased me about never having seen Jurassic Park.

"I saw where it was filmed," I offered. "I just drove by the place in Hawaii yesterday." Yesterday! I probably should have been sleeping off the jet lag instead of wandering around a museum trying to make intelligent conversation. Oh, let's be honest – I couldn't make intelligent conversation about dinosaurs if I tried. The only information I knew about dinosaurs was what I'd learned from watching *The Land Before Time* with my dinosaur-loving nephew. When a museum employee asked if we had any questions, I was tempted to ask, "Hey, remember that time when the little dinosaur's mom died and he and his buddies had to find their way to the Great Valley?" But I didn't.

Soon (thankfully, before I embarrassed myself) we were off.

"I was thinking we could go up to a ski town for dinner," Mr. Colorado said. The last time I'd seen him, we'd been at Copper Mountain with another friend. I missed skiing. I'd only gone two days last season before leaving Colorado. He said he was going to miss snowboarding this season since he was under doctor's orders not to take any risks. I'd heard about his car accident from another friend, but he told me about it firsthand.

"I shouldn't be alive. Everyone who saw the car said I should be dead," he admitted. "And it sounds awful, but God smashing my head into my windshield was exactly what I needed. My priorities are straightened out now. Lots of time in the hospital gives you clarity like that."

I hoped I'd never have to find out for myself.

I found myself alternately laughing uproariously and entrenched in deep conversation. Why hadn't we hung out more when I lived there? Calling Mr. Colorado "my old friend" was a bit of a stretch. We were kind of friends of friends. We'd seen each other occasionally within a group of similar acquaintances. We'd never actually hung out, just the two of us. I never really knew if there was substance behind the pretty face. I figured there probably was, but I'd never taken the time to find out. I was regretting that now. A lot.

We drove up to South Park and ate at The Only Bar in Alma. Alma is the highest town in the U.S., and I can't say I'd ever stopped in for a visit. It's on the way to Breckenridge or Keystone if you're coming up the back way from Colorado Springs, so I'd been through it several times on my way to ski. The town was notorious for making money by handing out speeding tickets to skiers who failed to slow down while zipping through on their way home from the slopes. Every small town has a bar, and Alma, Colorado, is one small town, having less than 200 people. I worried a little bit, leaving Mr. Colorado's flashy little convertible out there on the street, but he didn't seem too nervous about it.

The bar had a fairly extensive menu (for a bar), and we ate and watched Monday Night Football with the locals. You'd think the Broncos would be the only team people in Colorado cared about, but one man must have been imported. He proudly wore a Steelers jersey and screamed obscenities at the Bengals. The locals were friendly, although we did get some funny looks when we started playing Scrabble after dinner. And really, Scrabble in a bar? I can't blame them.

But man, I love Scrabble. And I'm insanely competitive. The last time I'd seen Mr. Colorado, he and I and our other friend had gone out to eat after skiing and then played Scrabble. I keep one of my Scrabble games in my car at all times. I have four versions of the game altogether: super mini Travel Scrabble (which entertained me while I lived in Africa), regular Travel Scrabble in a soft, padded case (the one I kept in my car), the original Scrabble (inherited from some family member, circa 1973), and Deluxe Scrabble (with a turntable! yeah, a turntable!). When the three of us had played in Breckenridge, the game had ended in controversy. I won, but just barely, and the guys challenged my winning word. We had to drive around town, trying to pick up an internet signal on one of their phones so we could look it up in an online dictionary. (Oh, and P.S., I was right. Do NOT challenge me, suckas!)

I trounced him. He was a good sport about it. I'd had one drink and I teased that he should have encouraged me to have another. Between my low tolerance and the altitude (Alma is over

10,000 feet high!), me being loopy could have benefited his game. We wrapped it up and started the hour and a half drive back.

Climbing Wilkerson Pass, Mr. Colorado drove off the road and onto a little overlook. He pressed the button to put the top down on the convertible, turned on the heated seats, and cranked the heater so we wouldn't freeze. The sky was unbelievable. I couldn't remember the last time I'd just sat and looked up at the stars. *This is the perfect make-out spot*, I thought. *Did he bring me here to make out? I doubt it. But maybe I could talk him into it.* I couldn't help it. The setting was just so perfect. But I was going out with three more guys in the next few days, including one I was really excited about. I probably shouldn't kiss this guy if my dream guy was right around the corner.

As I sat there wondering, he pulled out the Travel Scrabble for a rematch. Soon I was kicking his ass again.

"One of my friends told me once that I should let guys win so they wouldn't be intimidated by me," I admitted. This was after I'd met a blind date for dinner in summery heels and agreed to a game of mini golf afterward, despite my footwear. I'd beat him soundly and never heard from him again.

"Actually, I think it's really attractive, how smart you are," he said. Hmmm. Maybe I really could talk him into making out. But he was my friend. You're not supposed to make out with friends, right? But did I mention he was really good looking? And not the cocky, "I know I'm good looking" good looking, but the sweet-and-kind-of-shy-when-it-comes-to-girls good looking. I kept looking at his hands, since they were right in front of me on the Scrabble board. They looked strong. I don't know what my thing is with strong arms and hands. I like it when I can see veins and muscles. Maybe it makes me feel like they would be good protectors. Maybe I just hadn't touched a guy in a long time.

A shooting star shot through the sky as we ended the game, and I wondered if I was stupid to not stay in Colorado. It was so beautiful. I'd been sad to leave Hawaii, but the mountains were incredible, too. I'd have a harder time finding the beauty in the next state, Kansas. When I'd crossed the border into Colorado, though, I'd felt a sense of "This is where I used to live" instead of "I'm home." Maybe it was time to move on.

We headed back out onto the highway and down into

Woodland Park. Mr. Colorado couldn't believe I'd never driven a stick shift, so he insisted it was time for me to learn. I've always dreamed of being on the Amazing Race, and I've seen racers blow it when they can't drive a stick, so I figured this would be a good skill to acquire. I couldn't believe, though, that he was going to let me drive his convertible.

"It's just a car," he said. Man, that accident really must have made him rethink his priorities. I'd let two people drive Cherry Cherry since I'd bought her almost a year before, and she was a Corolla. If this car were mine, no one would be touching it, let alone grinding her gears.

I quickly found that driving a stick was easier than riding a dirt bike. I got the hang of it fairly quickly after killing it a couple of times, and although I wasn't brave enough to take it out on the highway, I did quite well in the Walmart parking lot . . . and I didn't hurt myself by falling off of it, either.

#48 – KANSAS

Here was a new problem: two dates in one state.

The day before, I had no one lined up. A farmer I'd met online had given me a maybe, but I'd learned back in Illinois that a maybe wasn't a yes. One of my friends texted her sister, a KU grad, and she sent out a desperate all-points bulletin to her old college friends. They came up with a man for me, and we made a date for dinner the next night.

An hour later the farmer called and said he was available for lunch. Crap. I hated to say no. And I couldn't break the date with the guy I'd just made plans for dinner with since I'd been begging everyone I knew to find me someone. Soooo . . . I decided to have two dates, one for lunch and one for dinner. Two dates in Kansas would make up for the not-really-a-date date in Illinois with the tattoo guy in the coffee shop.

First up was the farmer who lived about an hour south of the interstate that bisects Kansas. It wasn't exactly on my way, but he seemed like a good guy. And really, how many single women can there be in the middle of nowhere? Probably not a lot. I didn't want to ditch him when this might be his only date the entire month of November. I called my CSO and let her know where I'd be as I drove through the tiny town. He'd told me I'd find him in his shop, working on a tractor, and I thought about asking him to teach me how to drive it, but it was already 1PM and he'd been waiting for me to go to lunch. It seemed cruel to starve him any longer.

Fifty Dates in Fifty States

I'd spent the night in a cheap hotel. I was exhausted and coming down with something. I had a cough and those all-over aches, so I really just wanted to go to bed early instead of having to talk to someone that night. Plus, couch surfing seemed to be much more popular on the East Coast than it was in rural Kansas. My options were slim. The good news? I was well-rested. The bad news? I still wasn't feeling great.

Mr. Kansas #1 had originally planned to spend his morning at the sale barn, and I had wanted to jump on that for our date. If you're not familiar with what a sale barn is, picture farm animals being paraded around a small arena and farmers and ranchers bidding on them. I was thinking maybe I could sneak over to the auctioneer booth and get a lesson on how to talk fast like that: fivefivefive gimmefivefivegimmefivehunerdollarsSOLDtothefarmerinthebigblack hat. I wondered if circular breathing was involved.

But alas, Mr. Kansas #1 hadn't gone to the sale barn after all, so instead of any farm-related activities, we just had lunch. The little pizza place in town was packed, and I wondered what the heck was going on.

"Hunters," the girl behind the counter said unenthusiastically. Apparently pheasant hunting season began the next day; lots of people had come early to scout out locations and find a place to sleep before getting up at the crack of dawn. I'd had fun shooting clay pigeons with Mr. North Dakota, but a) I don't get up before the sun and b) I have no interest in freezing my extremities off while hiking through wet, grassy fields to shoot birds. Therefore hunting was not in my future. I didn't understand the allure.

"Is it hard to find dates around here?" I asked Mr. Kansas #1.

"Well, there are about three of us from my high school class who still live here. Everyone else moved away. That's how it is with every class, so there aren't a lot of options."

"And I don't suppose single women are flocking here," I guessed. He laughed.

"Nope. That's why I got on the internet, but that's a problem, too. Everyone you meet is from far away."

"Well, I guess if you really want to get married, then you should be willing to look outside this area."

"Yeah, but the last girl I dated lived in Iowa. She came down here to visit me and I went up there to visit her, but in the long run, I wanted to stay close to my family and she wanted to stay close to hers. Neither of us was willing to move to make it work."

"I understand," I said. I'd started this crazy road trip thinking I could stay anywhere if I met a guy who was amazing. I'd found, though, that I didn't really want the man of my dreams to be in Mississippi or Nevada or Rhode Island or Idaho or any other place without a single person who already knew me and loved me.

We had a good time chatting over lunch, but he got three calls in the hour and fifteen minutes we were together. He may not have had many options for dating, but he was definitely busy with work. He asked if I wanted to stick around, but I declined. I felt pretty crummy and needed a nap. Plus I still had another date that night.

I continued on to the big city nearby with a population of 20,000. Wikipedia said it was the cultural center of the area. Hmmm. I guess if you live in a town of a thousand or two, you take what you can get. I didn't have time to sleep, but a couple of Tylenol knocked out my symptoms long enough to have dinner. I didn't want to smell like cough drops, so I bought a bag of starlight mints and tried to keep my throat coated.

Mr. Kansas #2 was a cutie, but he was confused about what exactly I was doing. All he'd been told was that some chick was desperate for a date, and despite living in the cultural center of his region, women weren't any more plentiful there than in the small town I'd been in earlier, so he'd said yes.

Mr. Kansas #2 had lived a very different life than Mr. Kansas #1. While Mr. Kansas #1 wanted nothing more than to stay close to home and farm with his dad, Mr. Kansas #2 had gone off to a big school, played ball, and even made it to the minors. After playing in the minor leagues for a while, he'd finished out his athletic career in European and Australian leagues. He was back in Kansas temporarily, working on a Masters degree. He wasn't planning to stay there forever, but since he was stuck there for a while, it would be nice to have someone to date, he said.

"How about her? She's cute," I said, angling my head toward our waitress after she'd delivered our food.

"Yeah, but she's about 21," he lamented. It had to be rough – don't date at all or date women ten years younger than you? I wondered aloud if he ever thought he should have found someone back when he was living in bigger cities.

"Well, I did, but she wanted a commitment of some sort and I was off in Australia," he said. "It didn't feel right."

"Is she still available?" I asked. "Maybe you could reconnect with her."

"I don't know," he shrugged. I wondered when I'd stopped trying to find the man of my dreams and had started trying to help guys connect with other women.

It was a short date, but I had three hours to drive before I could get some rest for my ever-worsening body that night. I drove away thinking again that a dating service should be my next career move. I wanted to find good women for all the good guys I was meeting. There really were good ones left out there – they were just in places most women weren't looking.

#49 – NEBRASKA

Oh, those crazy Cornhusker fans. I had heard before that the largest population centers of Nebraska are, in order, Omaha, Lincoln, and Memorial Stadium on game days. No other cities can compete with the 81,067 screaming fans who pour into the stands decked out in red. Seeing it with my own eyes, I had no doubt that this was indeed the third largest gathering of people in the state. And honestly, I was a little bit frightened.

I'd gone through the same old panic of being dateless in Nebraska. I'd sent emails to old college friends asking if they knew any single men. I'd contacted two guys through internet dating websites who seemed to have potential, but both had plans to go hunting on Saturday (I thought they should change the signs at the borders from "Nebraska . . . the good life" to "Nebraska . . . we like to shoot stuff"). Then I remembered that someone from Nebraska had sent me a message via Match.com a few weeks before. I had only skimmed it at the time because I was about to leave for Hawaii. I dug around until I found him again, thankful that the message hadn't been deleted (a dreamy guy from Wyoming had written me over the summer, wanting to be my Wyoming date, but his message had been automatically deleted by the time I got to his state . . . I really needed to read the fine print on those stupid dating websites). I emailed the guy in Nebraska back, asked if he was available on Saturday night, and voila, the date was set. And, since it was a Saturday night and the Huskers were playing, he said there was really no other option. We were going to the game.

Mr. Nebraska, I quickly realized upon meeting him, was the touchy-feely type. Have you gathered, by state 49, that I am not? That was a problem. I mean, I don't have an issue with hugging the people I love. (Well, most days . . . okay, that's kind of a stretch . . . fine, I'm not a hugger, okay? Geesh.) But a guy I met half an hour ago putting his arm around me? Uh, no. And seriously? Can you not tell by the way I keep my hands shoved in my pockets that I'm uncomfortable with your touchy-feely-ness?? STOP TOUCHING ME!

It was cold, being November, but not as bad as I thought it might be. I had two layers on my legs, three up top, plus a hat and mittens. I was doing pretty well, body temperature-wise, standing around the tailgate party (which, again, showed the craziness of these Husker fans — a giant, flat-screen television in the back of your truck to watch the pregame show? for real?). The people of Nebraska, even with their intense enthusiasm for the Huskers, were so darn nice and welcoming. I just love Midwesterners. I know people on the East and West Coasts think Midwesterners are a little slow, but by golly, the people are good.

Mr. Nebraska and I, along with his friends, joined the crush of people going into the stadium and wound our way up, up, up, to the upper deck. I had been to a couple of college football games before, but they weren't like this. I didn't know if it's because Nebraska has no pro teams or if there just isn't much else to do, but I swear there must be some rule that you have to be a Cornhusker fan to live in the state. They held the NCAA record for the most consecutive stadium sellouts, having a to-capacity crowd at every single game since 1962. That's just crazy. And it's not like the stadium is small. It's huge! And the marching band covered the entire field. It takes a lot of horn tooters to cover that much space. The team came roaring out of the tunnel and the game began. The crowd hooted and hollered and I started to relax. I was afraid everyone would be able to tell I wasn't a fan since I wasn't wearing red, but no one seemed to care. I even found myself screaming along with the throng of fans when they released tens of thousands of balloons after the Huskers scored their first touchdown. (But why the marketing campaign to call them Huskers instead of Cornhuskers? Is that really an improvement? I mean, at least with "corn" up front you know what exactly it is they're husking . . . what's a Husker on it's own? How is that better?)

"Ooh, he's so cute," I said, pointing to the mascot.

"That's Lil' Red," Mr. Nebraska's friend Paula said.

"*Lil'* Red?" I clarified.

"Yeah, like Lil Wayne," she said.

"Except Lil' Red hasn't been to prison lately," Mr. Nebraska added.

You would have had to walk all the way back down the ramp to get food, so they brought the food to you instead. It was mostly teenagers lugging sodas, candy, pizza and Runza's up and down the stadium stairs.

"You've gotta try a Runza," Mr. Nebraska said.

"I don't think so."

"Have you ever had one before?"

"No, but I had friends from Nebraska in college, so I heard about them. Aren't they, like, made of meat and onions and sauerkraut stuffed inside of bread somehow?"

"You can barely taste the cabbage," he countered.

"My mom is 100% German. There was a lot of sauerkraut at family gatherings in my childhood. The smell alone about makes me gag."

He wisely got one instead of two the next time one of the kids came around selling them. I leaned toward Paula and tried to breathe through my mouth. Ugh! I wasn't really hungry anyway, and my throat was getting worse; it kind of hurt to swallow.

I was happy the Huskers were winning. I wasn't sure how it would feel to have over 80,000 people booing their own team, but I guessed it wouldn't be pretty. But like I said, they were nice Midwesterners. I even saw a few people walk by in Kansas Jayhawks apparel (the opponent that night), and no one screamed obscenities or threw things at them. Good people.

"Paula grew up near a couple that has two sons in the NFL," her husband Matt said. "Their third son is in prison, so the dad jokes that they have two pros and one con."

Paula and Matt walked back to the tailgate party area at halftime. Besides the giant flat screen TV, they also had one of those big heaters you see on restaurant patios. They were going to go warm up and then come back. Mr. Nebraska was happy for the chance to get a word in. (Sorry, but if two women sit together during a football game, they're going to chat. Paula was like an old friend and we chattered away.) So my actual date and I had an actual conversation during halftime. We talked about life and love and growing experiences and hopes for the future.

"I bet you haven't had a conversation this deep during your trip," he said.

"What do you mean?"

"Well, it seems like on most first dates you don't talk about marriage and kids and serious stuff like that."

"You'd be surprised. Most of my dates on this trip have," I told him. I thought about it for a moment or two. "I guess I was probably a safe person to talk to. I mean, there was no need to impress me, you know? I was going to be driving away in an hour or two, so guys probably felt like they could tell me anything without worrying whether they'd get a second date."

It hadn't seemed unusual at the time, but maybe it was. During the cross-country dating adventure, I'd heard guys talk about getting their hearts broken, losing their jobs, hoping for twin sons someday, and more. Maybe it was because they didn't have to impress me, or maybe it was because deep down we all just really want to be heard, and I was willing to listen.

I waited for the majority of the red sea to find their seats after the halftime break and then headed for the bathroom. I'm not a big fan of crowds, and I didn't want to have to push through 80,000 people to pee. I walked down, down, down the ramp I'd come up, up, up. I wished I hadn't held it for so long. Man, it was a long way down. I felt like one of those women in commercials for frequent urination, desperate to get to the bathroom. Oh, and then I had to struggle to take off my mittens and two layers plus underwear. I made it, though. On the way back up, I saw a woman walk slowly up one ramp, then pause and catch her breath before turning and walking up the next one. At this rate, I estimated she might make it back to her seat in time for the fourth quarter. I wondered why she didn't buy more expensive seats somewhere lower . . . or invest in a gym membership so she'd be ready for game day.

Matt and Paula weren't back yet when I returned to my seat, but I wasn't really worried about them. I did wonder, though, where

Roger was. Poor Roger. Roger was originally going to sit in my seat next to Mr. Nebraska until I told Mr. Nebraska I was coming to town. The original hope was that all five of us could squeeze into the four-seat area on our bench, but it became quickly apparent that we couldn't fit. Roger moved to an empty spot one row below us, but when the ticket holders for those seats showed up, he had to move. That was at the beginning of the game. Now, with the third quarter ending, I felt really bad that I had displaced the poor guy. He had to be watching the game somewhere in the stadium all alone. Well, I mean, technically he was with eighty-some thousand people, but you know what I mean.

Things were fine until the fourth quarter; then, I choked. Not in a "I didn't know what to say" sense (come on, I could have had a conversation with a tree by state forty-nine), but in an I can't catch my breath/my eyes are watering/my nose is running/I might pass out if I don't get some air in my lungs soon sense. And not on food. No, no. That might be normal. No, my body just decided to make it clear that I was coming down with something awesome. I was coughing up a lung but had nowhere to go. The Huskers had a big lead, so the majority of the state of Nebraska was heading for the exit. If I tried to go to the bathroom, it would take fifteen minutes just to get down the ramp, and the chances of ever finding my group again to walk back to the tailgating area would be slim. All I could do was lean back (the people behind us had already left, thankfully) so I wouldn't be coughing in Mr. Nebraska and Paula's faces. I coughed and coughed and coughed, which is scary at my age. I've seen those commercials for Poise pads where women say they have little "accidents" sometimes when they sneeze or cough. I'm betting it has something to do with the fact that most women have pushed the equivalent of a watermelon through a drinking straw and therefore have weaker muscles in that region, but I fear it might just come with age, having given birth or not. I've dodged the bullet so far, but I can't help but fear that someday it will happen to me.

"Are you okay?" my date asked. I kind of nodded . . . and continued to cough violently.

"Need something to drink?" Matt offered. We had nothing. The concession kids had stopped coming around early in the third quarter. I shook my head. I couldn't even get enough breath to reassure them I'd be okay in a minute.

"Maybe she'd just like us to stop looking at her," Paula said. Thank you, thank you, for a woman being present and understanding. I gave a weak thumbs up, then wiped away some tears. Mr. Nebraska put his hand on my knee in what I'm guessing he thought was a comforting gesture, but hello? Personal space issues?! If I could have gotten enough air in my lungs to make it happen, I would have screamed, "Get your freaking hand off my knee!" Instead I folded up, still alternately coughing and gasping for air, and tried to pull my knee away.

I recovered eventually, but it kind of put a damper on the festivities. The game ended and we were carried along with the crowd, down, down, down the ramp and out into the street. Amazingly Roger reappeared beside Mr. Nebraska and we all headed back over to the tailgating area. The friends with the giant flat screen TV were still there, having watched the game in the parking lot. I personally would have watched the game from my warm living room, but I guess I just don't understand the Superfan concept. They were all so nice that I hated to be the first to leave, but I was pretty much feeling like crap at that point. Mr. Nebraska took me back to my car, and I thanked him and apologized for nearly dying.

"Would've made a great story," he suggested.

But not the ending I was hoping for.

#50 – IOWA

Iowa. I hadn't planned on my home state being my final date state when I'd started, but when I got about 3/5ths of the way through the dates, I realized it might be a fitting ending, having my last date back in the state where I first began my dating career twenty years before. I'd come a long way since I'd stepped on a cat attempting my first kiss on my first date at age fifteen.

I'd been looking forward to dating Mr. Iowa since the very beginning of the journey. When I'd sent out a Facebook message to all my friends, telling them what I was doing and asking them to set me up with great single guys they knew, two friends I knew from two different circles both recommended the same guy. They'd both gone to college with him and said he now worked with international students; knowing my Iowa roots and knowing how much I love to travel, they thought we'd have a lot in common. I'd been through a few states and dates when he sent me an email through my website that made me smile:

"Very intriguing. Mutual friends who know of my desire to be written about (apart from the police section of the town paper) alerted me to your quest. Let me know if Iowa is already taken and when the Midwest leg of your schedule is planned. I think I might make the cut according to the criteria listed on your web page. I are extremely smart and even more humble. Probably the most humble guy I know. You should be able to find a picture of me on Facebook and find that we may have other mutual friends (who probably won't vouch for me). As for showing off my state, I will have to ponder that one for a while since there are just too many superior options, especially when compared to the date venues of your previous states. I live in both the extreme sport capital and primary romantic hot spot of . . . well . . . the entire county! I'll think more on how I could make your visit unforgettable (in a good way) but thought I would send off this email to establish contact. Don't be lured by the charms of those sly Southern guys you are hanging around with now. Midwest is best but do be careful with the Norwegian bachelor farmers contending to be Mr. Minnesota. Take care."

I'd friended him on Facebook, liked what I saw, then worried the entire trip that he'd meet someone in the meantime and not be available to be my Mr. Iowa. He was funny. He was attractive. He was well-traveled. He was Lutheran. What more could a girl ask for?

We'd sent a few messages back and forth throughout my journey. Each one made me smile and look forward to the fiftieth date. When it had gotten close enough to actually make plans, I'd emailed him from the San Francisco airport on my way to Hawaii.

"Have you gotten hitched to one of the exotic international students you work with and forgotten about me, or can you still be my Mr. Iowa?"

"I'll pencil you in and tell the French-Polynesian supermodel student I advise that we need a break," he replied.

After my week in paradise, I sent him another message.

"I saw your French-Polynesian supermodel girlfriend dancing here on the island at the Polynesian Cultural Center and she said she's totally cool with you going out with me next week because she's got a little side thing going with the guy who demonstrates how to scale the big trees to get coconuts. Yay for sharing!"

I didn't have many ideas for a date in Iowa. It was now mid-November and too cold to do anything outside. The two guys who'd recommended him had suggested canoeing on the Upper Iowa River, but that would be miserable this time of year. Mr. Iowa, trying to keep up with the antics of others who had planned crazy dates, recommended base jumping off a grain elevator. That sounded like a death wish to me. I searched the internet for things happening the weekend I was going to be there and found the most non-Iowan event out there: a Haitian Vodou Drum Circle. His response the next day made me smile and pretty much solidified my belief that I'd definitely chosen the right Mr. Iowa.

"With the info you gave me, I think my relationship with the supermodel is headed toward termination. I always wondered why she had such an ample supply of coconuts and your intel only confirmed my suspicions. I think the only thing capable of exorcising her from my mind is a good cleansing Haitian Vodou Drum Session. I would have wanted to follow this up with a meal at the Bourbon Street Grill and then a drink at the Voodoo Lounge, but alas, they are closed on Sunday nights. If I meet you with a little doll which I occasionally stab with pins, please don't be alarmed: my licensed psychological counselor (and voodoo priestess) says it would be therapeutic for me. Send me a quick confirmation that this will work for you so I can get tickets. I look forward to our foray into the spirit world on our very Iowan 'Pagan Night Out.'"

Dorky. And I love dorky.

I drove into Iowa on a blustery day. It started snowing about an hour from my destination, and I was thankful the journey was almost over. I'd had to tolerate some rain and cold through the South when I'd started back in the spring, but for the most part I'd had good weather for traveling. That's important when you're driving a Corolla. It's not exactly known for being a beast on snow and ice.

I stopped by a gas station, filled the tank, and used what had to be the dirtiest bathroom in Iowa. I shopped around and took my selections up to the counter: orange juice, DayQuil, cough drops, and tissues. I'm pretty sure the cashier went hunting for some hand sanitizer as soon as I walked away.

As I drove the last hour, I thought about all the dates I'd been on in the last nine months. It had been amazing, but I was glad it was coming to an end. I was tired of dating. Cynically, I thought about how, from this point on, I could just cut to the chase with men and ask the important questions before bothering to shower and actually meet them. Do you have a job? What medications are you on? And you have *how many* ex-wives?

As I neared the meeting spot with Mr. Iowa, though, I felt something I hadn't felt in a long time. Seriously? Nervousness? Me?

Fifty Dates in Fifty States

I'd stopped getting nervous about thirty states and dates ago. Maybe this one, my last date of the fifty, was someone special.

"Don't have such high expectations," my Chief Safety Officer advised me when I called her to let her know where I'd be. "You're bound to be disappointed if you go into it expecting too much . . . although how perfect would that be, if the man of your dreams grew up just down the road from you but you had to travel all fifty states before you found him? That would be such a perfect ending."

"Yeah, thanks, Alicia. That really helps lower my expectations."

I pulled over in a church parking lot and brushed my teeth. I'd been sucking on cough drops for an hour straight, and I didn't want to meet the man of my dreams (you never know!) with cough drop-breath. I hoped no one saw me as I rinsed and spit. I pardoned myself with a "you worked at a church for ten years; it's totally okay."

I met Mr. Iowa at a Panera Bread. I parked along a wall of windows, and peering inside, I recognized him from his Facebook photos. I sat there spying on him as he passed through, probably looking for me. He was tall. Really tall. Much taller than I had expected him to be. He was handsome, too. This could work. This could be really, really fabulous.

Deep breath. Deep breath, Tiffany. Don't do that thing where you build him up to be someone he's not and then feel all disappointed later.

I opened the car door, nervously walked inside, and introduced myself. He seemed a little nervous, too, which was pretty cute in a big, strong man. We ordered hot chocolates and sat chitchatting for a few minutes. He had incredible eyes, blue as the sky. I'd always been more attracted to brown eyes, but I had a feeling I could get lost in his (cue the Debbie Gibson song!). We needed to get going to the Haitian Vodou Drumming, though, so we took our hot chocolates and headed out. It was just a mile or so down the road, but we had an issue walking from the parking lot to the event center. Remember my little choking incident at the Husker game? Yeah. Repeat it in Iowa.

I still had half of my hot chocolate left, so when I started coughing, I took a sip, hoping it would help. No such luck. I could sense it was just going to get worse. I flailed at Mr. Iowa, trying to get him to take my cup, but he was giving me some space (wise choice). I hit him to get his attention, handed it off, and then doubled over. Super attractive. At least this guy kept his hands off me. Soon I was crying and my nose was running, still choking. I felt like an idiot. And I really wanted to impress this guy! It started to subside, and I motioned for the hot chocolate back . . . and immediately sloshed it on myself. Could this get worse?

Once inside, Mr. Iowa pointed me in the direction of the bathroom where I tried to clean myself up. I was sure his first impression of me was icky. I prayed I wouldn't have another coughing fit in the auditorium and that we were in aisle seats, just in case. When I came out, he had the tickets.

"I was just faking the coughing," I croaked, trying to be cute. "That was my little ploy to get you to buy the tickets."

I'm pretty sure he didn't find me cute. I croaked out a few more coughs. Hot. I had the puffy, baboon-faced look I get when I cry, so when we found our seats and settled in, I was thankful the lights went down and he was sitting beside me, not across a table from me. I was not in "look at me" condition. I dug a cough drop out of my purse, figuring cough drop-smelling breath was better than another embarrassing choking spell.

I loved the Vodou drums. Three men drummed and sang, and one woman alternated between singing back-up vocals and dancing. The lead guy would talk between songs about Haiti, both its rich history and the struggle to rebuild after the devastating earthquakes. I tried not to giggle, thinking how uncomfortable my parents would be.

"I can't understand a word he's saying," my dad would complain. My mom would be more bothered by the dancer's skin-tight tank top.

"Can't they afford bras in Haiti?" she'd ask. She'd probably rally the church ladies to donate their castoffs to ship down there.

(My parents aren't exposed to other cultures very often. My sister told me they watched *Dora the Explorer* with Mom's daycare kids for months before one turned to the other and said, "I think she might be Mexican.")

The drumming didn't last nearly long enough. I didn't want the date to be over yet, especially since all we'd done so far was make small talk for a few minutes, then sit beside each other not talking (and that whole gasping-for-air/hacking up a lung bit that I was sure he hadn't yet forgotten).

Mr. Iowa suggested dinner, so off we went . . . but then that went too fast, too. I wanted to keep staring at him. He looked solid and hot, like a Viking who'd traded in his ship and horned helmet for a chance at life in the 21st century. And those eyes!

"*Megamind?*" he suggested. He said he loved animated flicks, and that one was playing in the local theater. Me? Not so much.

"Do you like wine?" he tried. Oh yeah. Way more than kiddie movies.

Mr. Iowa then revealed that he enjoyed winemaking and home brewing, and since he was a friend of my friends and likely not a murderer, we went to his place. Upon arrival, I giggled at his stereotypical bachelor pad. He needed to do the dishes. Badly. He could stand to tidy up the rest of the place, too, but there were books everywhere and I was a fan of that.

We drank some wine and he played the guitar and we talked and laughed. Have I mentioned that guys who play guitar are way more attractive than other guys? He was dreamy. And it was comfortable, just hanging out with him. I could get used to it. I took the guitar and strummed "Leavin' on a Jet Plane," but I didn't have much of a voice left after two choking dates in a row. I croaked unattractively, then gave up and handed back the guitar.

I sat on the couch, leaning toward him. He was on a chair, leaning over his guitar toward me. Mutual leaning. Good sign, right? Body language experts say that shows interest. It would have been easy to just lean a little more until my lips touched his, but a) I was sick, obviously, and therefore felt kind of unattractive, b) I might have been a little tipsy from the wine/Dayquil combo, so I wasn't sure it would be a good idea to start kissing this guy I'd just met, and c) I thought, *This might really be something good, so I don't want him to think I just want to make out and hurt my chances of something more.*

How long did we stay there? An hour? Two? Time flew. He gave me two bottles of his homemade wine to share with my family for Thanksgiving, then drove me back to my car.

I thought about an email I'd sent him a few months before, telling him I was saving the best for last; unfortunately, he was now getting me at my worst: sick and rundown with deep, dark circles under my eyes. Maybe I'd wooed him with my DayQuil & wine-induced blabbering and didn't even know it . . . but probably not.

Saying good-bye, I tried to think of something clever or cute to say to let him know I'd had a wonderful time and I wanted to see him again. Something that revealed I'd been looking forward to this night since he'd first emailed me six months before, and that I hadn't been disappointed.

"Thanks," I said. "It was fun."

So much for eloquence.

I sighed, slipping behind the wheel of my reliable Cherry Cherry for the last time. I felt like banging my head against the steering wheel, but I realized that wouldn't help anything. Even if I didn't end the evening saying something brilliant, it still felt like a perfect ending. Even if I didn't see him again, he was the kind of guy who gave me hope for the future. There were still good guys out there, guys I was attracted to and could see a future with. And after I'd recovered from my exhausting cross-country dating journey, maybe I'd find a nice one to spend more time with. Maybe.

And then, just like that, it was over. I couldn't believe it. Although I had never run a marathon, I felt like I imagined a marathon runner would feel if he crossed the finish line but no one was there to see it happen. I'd visited all fifty states, put 24,931 miles on Cherry Cherry, and now it was over with zero pomp and circumstance.

I was tired.

More than that, though, I was thankful. The journey had been amazing.

I'd seen places I'd probably never see again. I thought about Acadia National Park in Maine and looking down at the clear, blue water from the peak I'd climbed; driving past the red bud trees in Virginia, thinking it must be a beautiful place to live; huffing and puffing my way through the misty forest in Washington State, realizing I wasn't young enough to keep up with college kids anymore but still awed by the scenery. I'd purposely avoided interstates on much of the journey, wanting to see the back roads of America instead. It had been beautiful.

I'd met people who made me laugh and made me think. The couch surfing hosts had welcomed me like family. The dates had been brave and entertaining. I'd reconnected with old friends and relatives around the country. People I hadn't met nine months before

I now considered friends.

I'd done crazy things I'd never dreamed of doing. I knew I wasn't likely to skydive again, or kayak past a glacier in Alaska. I hoped to someday repeat my walk down an avenue of oaks near Savannah or maybe go see another Broadway show in New York City. But even if I did get to revisit some of the places I'd been, they would not be the same. *I* would not be the same. Circumstances would be different. I'd be older. I'd be at a different stage in life with different responsibilities and new worries. I might be traveling with different people. I would see everything through a changed lens. They had all been once-in-a-lifetime experiences.

I couldn't believe I hadn't had a single issue with my car, other than that minor running-over-a-dead-deer incident in Montana. I had avoided fender benders, despite close encounters with many horrible drivers who really needed to redo high school driver's ed. I hadn't been pulled over for speeding once, and was never even issued a parking ticket. Cherry Cherry was my girl. I wasn't sure how to thank an inanimate object for an exhilarating nine months, so I hugged the steering wheel, amazed at how reliable she'd been.

I might have been a little freaked out a night or two in the tent, but I'd never faced any threat or danger. Sure, there were some crazy people in America, but I still believed that ultimately, people were good and could be trusted. No one had tried to hurt me. Yes, I'd been smart and careful and cautious, but it's a two-way street. I was thankful that the world was full of so many good people.

And despite treating it like crap, my body had held up pretty well. I mean, sure, I was out of shape and my muscles had lost their tautness and it was going to hurt when I hit the gym again, but my body had been good to me. Until the last three days, I hadn't even gotten sick in the nine months I'd been out adventuring.

But the big question: was there going to be a happy ending? I didn't know yet. I was tired. There were a handful of guys I thought were great, but I needed some sleep and some time to think. I'd have a clearer idea of what I wanted and how to make something happen once I'd recovered.

It was amazing. It was daunting. It was over. I was relieved, but sad. Ready to be done, but not ready for it to be over.

I couldn't imagine a better nine months of my life.

EPILOGUE

I've never been very good at the traditional kind of praying. I'd fold my hands, close my eyes, bow my head, and start out strong . . . but soon I'd be visualizing how I thought God should solve the problems I was praying about, or composing a mental to-do list, or thinking about that TV show I'd just watched . . . which just made me feel guilty about being bad at praying.

Then one of my close college friends gave me a prayer journal. I'd been keeping a diary off and on since elementary school, and she knew I loved to write. She said a prayer journal was just like a regular diary-type journal, but you write out your prayers to God. Knowing my focusing-during-prayer issues, she thought it would help me stay on track.

I found a side benefit to the prayer journal she didn't tell me about: I could go back later and look at all those prayers and see how they were answered. Sure, there were some hard things that weren't fun to reread, but a lot of the prayers were prayers of thankfulness, and reliving those moments of contentment and joy brought more thankfulness and contentment and joy.

There was one subject area, though, that rarely brought those good feelings: dating. Reading through fifteen years of prayer journals, the dating entries are sometimes awkwardly comical but often just sad. When I began keeping the prayer journals, I asked God to show me which of my college classmates was "the one." I was annoyed when I'd graduated without a boyfriend, let alone a husband. I hardly dated at all in my twenties, and the entries were often borderline bitter. My thirties brought around some serious relationships, and with them confused, pleading prayers asking God to make it clear if this guy was right for me. Here and there, especially after I discovered traveling, I questioned whether I even wanted to be married. Sometimes being single seemed so much easier. I asked God to take those desires from my heart: if I wasn't meant to be a wife and a mother, then take away those desires and let me lead a content, solitary life.

It didn't happen though. I still wanted to share my life with someone who would stick with me, for better or for worse. When I held kids in my arms, my heart screamed that I was meant to mother. Someone asked if my trip around the country, dating fifty men, was a final act of desperation – if I didn't find someone, would I give up dating forever? I saw it as a final act of freedom; I felt in my heart that I'd be settling down soon, and I craved one last epic adventure.

And after all those years of praying, I finally met someone who loved me, flaws and all. Oh, it wasn't storybook; sunshine didn't part the clouds and butterflies didn't start flitting around our faces every time we looked at each other. We were two people in our late thirties who'd gotten accustomed to making decisions based on our own wants and needs without thinking of others. We had to work to make it work, choosing our steps carefully. But we each saw something in the other and each respected the other, and slowly, through lots of long conversations and laughter, we fell in love.

I admit that I fell faster than he did. It didn't take me long to see the diamond in the rough. He had those three qualities I always said I was looking for: he made me laugh with his dorky sense of humor, he was smart and easy to talk to, and his deep Christian faith easily made its way into our daily conversations.

Most of those conversations were on the phone. I hated it. I wanted so much to look into his eyes while we talked. I wanted to see his facial expressions, which often say more than words alone. Face-to-face time was limited to the weekends, though, when he would drive to see me or I would drive to see him. A long-distance relationship is never what I would have chosen, but I figured it was better than the alternative, which was not seeing him at all.

His friends often joked about how we'd met. Most were

fascinated by the process and wanted to know how he'd beaten out forty-nine other men. They alternately ribbed him, saying the other guys must not have been much to look at if I'd picked him, or praised him, declaring him the winner and asking who was going to play him in the movie version. (He's pulling for Brad Pitt.)

And then, fifteen months after our first date, he got down on one knee and asked me to marry him. All those years – all those questioning, complaining entries in the prayer journals – and here he finally was, the man I'd been nagging God about for years: Mr. Iowa, the answer to my many, many prayers.

He's not perfect, but he's pretty perfect for me. And to find someone who loves you, despite your imperfections, is something that amazes us both. We feel pretty blessed.

In retrospect, I'm glad I didn't meet him during college. It could have happened; we've figured out that at least twice we were in the same place at the same time with mutual friends, so potentially we could have bumped into each other. I don't think we would have felt the same attraction back then though. We both experienced so many things over that fifteen-year gap that shaped who we are and attracted us to each other when we finally did meet.

It's strange how things work out, though. I traveled all over the country, having the adventure of a lifetime, and who am I setting out on the new adventure of marriage with? A man who was literally down the road from me for the first half of our lives. He grew up in a little town intersected by the same highway that marks the northern border of the farm where I grew up, two and a half hours away.

For a long time, I thought the answer to my prayers was "no." Turns out God was chuckling, "Oh, Tiffany, just wait and see."

THANK YOU

First off, thanks to the fifty men brave enough to be my fifty dates! Some of you were proud of it and some of you were totally embarrassed, so hopefully I can make everyone happy by putting your name in print, but in alphabetical instead of chronological order to protect your anonymity. Thank you Aaron, Andy, Austen, Brian, Bryan, Caleb, Charlie, Chris, Clay, Cliff, Cristian, Dave, Doug, Edwin, Eli, Eli, Ely, Erik, Evan, Gregg, Harry, Herman, Jake, Jared, Jason, Jayson, Jim, Jimmie, Jonathan, Josh, Justin, Kai, Kerry, Kevin, Kevin, Kris, Lawrence, Mark, Matt, Mike, Nick, Rob, Shea, Shon, Steve, Tim, Todd, Tom, Tommy, and Tyler. I wish you great dates and much happiness in life! Thanks, too, to the many friends who recommended these guys and/or helped set up the dates – you picked some great ones for me!

Secondly, a big shout out to everyone, friend or stranger, who let me sleep on their couch or in their guest bedroom. You are amazing! I seriously couldn't have done this trip without your help, and I still can't believe how many of you welcomed me in without having a clue who I was. I wish I could have written about each and every interaction, but the book is too long as it is. Just know that I'm eternally grateful to you and I'll never forget your kindness. Lanz, Jeff, Rebecca, Amanda, Ron, Carol, Sam, Jana, Katherine, Ashley, Joe, Daphne, Lawson, Anita, David, Ron, Laurie, Haley, Megan, Abbey, Naveen, Ken, Linda, Ashley, Ken, Sue, Alan, Jay, Brenda, Andrew, Sheri, Micah, Nathan, Richard, Mary Ann, Sally, Chuck, Nora, Steve, Shon, Deborah, Steve, Laura, Sara, Clark, Erika, Kristen,

Chrissy, Gabe, Peyton, Sam, Kellie Mae, Marcy, Paula, Nick, Jennie, Fred, Abby, Dave, Sue, Bart, Sandy, Chickie, Kristen, Kevin, Zachary, Jill, Mike, Emma, Hannah, Ty, Jenni, Henrey, Riley, Shannon, Jean, Emmalea, Lucy, Monica, Greg, Teri, Erin, Kyle, Trisha, Matt, Wendi, Denali, Kai, Kian, Mark, Molly, Collin, Morgan, Denise, Casey, Bette, Stephanie, Josh, Ty, Sammy, Ina Kay, Tom, Russ, Sarah, Christopher, Kim, Kirsten, Elyse, Ryan, Evan, Alicia, Finley, Eli, Carolyn, Keith, Eileen, Julie, Scott, Brianne, Chris, Walter, Stacey, Tara, Noah, Mom & Dad (and anyone I forgot – please, please forgive me!) – my guest room is open and I'm ready to host you whenever you come to my neck of the woods.

Thank you, Alicia, for being my Chief Safety Officer and keeper of all my earthly possessions . . . and for resisting the urge to throw everything I own on the lawn whenever you got mad at me for doing something stupid or risky.

Thanks to every friend who acted as a cheerleader, calling to encourage me as I drove around. The only thing better would have been you sitting beside me in the passenger seat. Ginger & Krystal, Mom & Dad, and Alicia, thanks for joining me out on the road, giving me some company along the way, and paying for hotel rooms so I got a break from my tent. You're the bestest!

Good people of Ascension, bless you. I seriously would have starved had it not been for your gift card shower send-off. You are my Colorado family, and leaving you was the hardest thing I've ever done. Thanks for loving me and supporting me and always welcoming me back.

To the teachers who encouraged a much younger version of me and gave me confidence as a writer – especially Mrs. Peterson & Mrs. Brown – I am forever grateful.

Alicia, Julie, Mel, & Wendy – thanks for being my first readers and giving much-needed feedback. Mom & Tara, thanks for helping me find the mistakes before I let the whole world see it.

Thanks to the local businesses who hosted a date (visit www.fiftydatesinfiftystates.jigsy.com for extended thank you's), and thanks to friends and blog readers for all your suggestions.

Mom & Dad, thanks for enduring months of worry as I gallivanted around the country on yet another of my crazy adventures. I didn't come home from Africa in a box, and nobody murdered me as I drove around the United States. See? I totally know what I'm doing.

Molly, thanks for the idea that changed my life.

Ken, Matt, & Wendi, thanks for recommending the best mister of the bunch. Kudos on your matchmaking skills.

And finally, Kevin, thanks for being awkward with women so you were still single and relatively undamaged when I found you late in the game. You make me laugh every day, and every day I thank God for bringing us together. I'm looking forward to a lifetime of adventure with you!

ABOUT THE AUTHOR

Tiffany Malcom loves a good adventure; before setting off on her exploration of America, she hiked the Inca Trail to Machu Picchu in Peru, spent time volunteering at an orphanage in Ghana, helped build houses for families in El Salvador and Mexico, and climbed Mount Kilimanjaro in Tanzania. Generally her days are action-packed in a different way, having spent the past fifteen years working with teenagers. She often slaps her knee when she laughs, makes faces as she dances, and dreams of competing on *Wheel of Fortune* . . . all of which probably help explain why she was still single at thirty-five. In 2012, a wedding ring from her favorite of the fifty dates changed that. This is her first book.

Printed in Great Britain
by Amazon